Temple of Heaven & Earth

Temple of Heaven & Earth

Guide to Earth-Energy & Inspiration at Sacred Sites

Science and Wisdom of the Golden Age

Thomas Karl Dietrich

Our cover is a map of Jerusalem was made by Olfert Dapper, printed 1677 in Amsterdam by Jacob van Meus. This chart so beautifully illustrates the Kidron Valley energy rift-channel leading up to the Temple Mount. *This map is used by kind permission of:*
The Jewish National & University Library, Shapell Family Digitization Project, Eran Laor Cartographic Collection and The Hebrew University of Jerusalem, Dept. of Geography, Historic Cities Project.

Temple of Heaven & Earth
Printed by Create Space

Printed and bound in the United States of America. No part of this book may be reproduced in any form or by any electronic or mechanical means including information storage and retrieval systems without permission in writing from the copyright holder, except by a reviewer, who may quote brief passages in review.

Library of Congress Control Number: 2016908386
CreateSpace Independent Publishing Platform
North Charleston, South Carolina
ISBN-13: 9781533271068
ISBN-10: 1533271062
Copyright© 2016 Thomas Karl Dietrich. All rights reserved

Save Our Sacred Sites Society
San Bruno, California

TABLE OF CONTENTS

    Foreword vii
1. Energy at Ancient Sites 1
2. Cosmic Energy & Famous Energy Sites 40
3. Energy Art & Symbols 53
4. Astronomy is the Mother of all Science 70
5. Cycles of Change & The Four Seasons 97
6. Creation of Numbers & Geometry 117
7. Cosmic Man & The Great Pyramid 146
8. Monad & The Golden Ratio 163
9. Temple & Cosmic Religion 178
10. Cosmic Mind 208
11. Dowsing the Energy Grid 232
12. Wonders of the World 258

    Conclusion to the Temple of Heaven & Earth 287
    Bibliography 291
    About the Author 305

FOREWORD

Temple of Heaven & Earth

The Temple of Heaven & Earth is a wonderful focus around which we may weft and woof a tapestry of numerous subjects. In this way one thing sheds light on many, while each is illuminated by the other, until the whole is explained by its parts –and every part has been amplified by the whole. If only this unattainable goal were achieved *even* in part!

In the small community college in San Mateo, California, around the year 1968, Professor Rodney Smith came from England to introduce us to the early Greek philosophers such as Thales, Pythagoras, and Empedocles. I was absolutely smitten –here was 'real knowledge' at last! But what is knowledge –knowledge of what, and where did it come from? Knowledge is power; and powerful rulers are going to keep every bit of it for themselves. Where then, is truth and knowledge; if it is so carefully guarded? It resides in your heart, mind and being if you wish to unfold its creases and reveal it.

I was lucky to be able to live in Ireland for 13 years, and be exposed to one of the great ancient cultures of music, language, history, and megalithic holy sites. Here knowledge was executed in stone and dug into the landscape in giant henges, mounds, and escarpments to serve as the meeting place of people, law courts, rituals, fairs and festivals. Finally, here was the true material beginning of human knowledge, wit, and wisdom –not in one discipline; but in the full panorama of all that it means to be human in all endeavors from science to religion, government, morals, laws, and culture. The primeval holy site is not magic, but rather a fountain of energy producing subtle, sometimes powerful healing, inspiration, health, and joy. This Temple of Heaven and Earth combined ethereal and telluric forces as a gateway of communication with the future, the present, and the past. Our presentation will discuss astronomical phenomena which direct and modulate cosmic energy, pyramids used for seed and agricultural enhancement, geopathic stress lines that cause sleep-deprivation and cancer cells, and finally; the scientific foundation of many tenets of the ancient worldview from the Golden Age. The holy site as a confluence of earth and cosmic energies will give us many paths to explore the entire universe. In pastimes it was the entrance to the magic-mountain cave of our ancestors, the psychedelic rabbit hole to the underworld, the shaman smoke rising up the chimney as a vehicle to the upper-world, and the portal of the wise to all mystery and knowledge around us and deep within us.

Thomas Karl Dietrich –May 13, 2016

CHAPTER 1

ENERGY AT ANCIENT SITES

Understanding of the true nature of Machu Picchu is almost impossible because of its remote and ethereal location far from Cuzco and Ollantaytambo. The site is one of the great and powerful energy precincts on the planet –fascinating, calming, and beneficial. Yet, one is so enraptured in the adventure of the journey and the beauty of the place that one does not appreciate that these magical feelings are produced because of the proximity of powerful energy fonts. One mistakenly assumes that the euphoria is the product of the position of Machu Picchu within the amazing context of the far-reaching scenery of this real 'Shangri-La.'

A factual physical assessment of Machu Picchu shows that it is crossed by two faultlines which over time have torn the site to pieces producing a mountain that is literally falling apart. The site is also crossed by numerous fissures, caves, and cavities conducting energy flows to the sacred areas above. Modern clearing and excavation shows that the entire mountain has been continually restored, restructured, and fortified through expert terracing over millennia allowing gentle water dispersion and structural integrity. Reckoned in labor, costs, and time the question must be asked –why would anyone spend such resources rehabilitating this old mountain? The answer is that Machu Picchu is a phenomenal energy accumulator because of its 'Swiss cheese-like' composition. The energy factor is heightened by electro-magnetic 'island or peninsula effect' where a site is surrounded by water on three or more sides. Machu Picchu is a mountain peninsula within a loop of the Urubamba River at its base where also hot springs are generated. Anciently, the river was called *Willkamayu*, 'the sacred river' in Quechua; and *Willkanuta*, 'house of the Sun' in Aymara. The systems of terraces that support the mountain make the property too easily accessible to be a real fortress. It is without a doubt one of the great holy energy sites on our planet. In structure it resembles a natural energy pyramid.

Ancient Worldview

In order to understand the sacred energy of ancient holy sites and precincts it is necessary to understand some of the worldview of ancient people which is a dualistic system of knowledge concerning both the material nature and the spiritual nature of the cosmos and the world. Ancient people discovered many levels and layers of reality within three worlds of the past, present, and the future. Aboriginals, Shamans, alchemists, Hermetic philosophers, and masters of intuitive perception and projection employed the microcosmic structure of the human mind to explore the Cosmic Mind –which unfolded itself to create the universe. These seekers and voyagers explored the heavenly regions of the cosmos, and the theater of life under the orb of the Moon to the surface crust of the Earth, as well as the Underworld, realm of ancestors and events from the past reaches of time. These three regions represented the future, the present, and the past; which were accessible through communication with the Cosmic Mind. Ancients used intuition and reason; as well as a deep comprehension of science, astronomy, cycles, numbers, geometry, and proportions. The ancient worldview believed that everything was interrelated and holistic. We are children of the cosmos. Our minds are part of the cosmos and can ask anything, and understand anything. Our bodies are homeopathic –in that they are part of nature and can heal themselves.

The duality of the universe is an ancient worldview from the Golden Age which was shared by all of humanity around the world.

Alfred Huang in *The Complete I Ching –The Definitive Translation* tells us that two thousand years before Confucius, the ancient Chinese offered sacrifices to Heaven and Earth, and their ancestors. Heaven is *Qian*, the Creative Principle, which is the rising Sun radiating its light and energy, called *chi*. Earth is called *Kun*, Earth Mother. After Heaven and Earth have come into existence, myriad beings are produced. They also realized that to obtain the future they had to look to the past.

All life on Earth relies upon energy. The life of honeybees focuses upon energy management in their food supply to maintain their core hive-temperature to survive the winter, to give bee-scouts the extra food to discover new hive sites for the upcoming queen-bee swarm, and to sustain new worker-bees and drones. The queens are feed with high-energy royal jelly. Bee-scouts seek out new locations for hives above natural earth-energy portals. These scouts compare the quality and strength of various energy sites through their 'zigzag energy dances' that they perform in front of their fellows.

Ever since I traveled to Ireland about 40 plus years ago visiting ancient sites, I have become sensitive to the radiations of energy, wisdom, and health located at these special places. Through long experience and study I have become convinced of subtle but increasing benefits of visiting these holy sites. The terms 'holy' and 'sacred' are justified because the energies come from the heavens and are absorbed through the channels of sacred Mother Earth. After visiting the magnificent temple site of Tikal in Guatemala, my wife and I were talking to the other visitors who attested that they too had truly experienced something magical. We likewise had felt a lessening of the troubles of the world upon our shoulders. I was an early disciple of water and energy dowsing having read the classical work on the matter by Guy Underwood in his *The Patterns of the Past*. These studies helped me garner experience testing ancient places around the world –where I also received the benefit of absorbing cosmic energy. These energies have been documented and verified by scientists in various fields especially astronomy and geology. These energies are a fact of physics. Of course, modern corporate science does not comment upon beneficial or harmful radiations at energy sites that are open *free of charge to the public,* and which corporations do not own or control. We hope to define and refine this subject matter in the simplest of terms because it is one of the oldest and most useful of the sciences that we have inherited from our ancestors.

The Asian *I Ching* tradition of 'change' is symbolized in the dynamic dichotomy of Yin Yang. These opposite but complimentary natures are intertwined and spinning demonstrating the fundamental physics of the cosmos which promotes motion, change, and energy such as: day and night, summer and winter, hot and cold, good and evil, peace and war, order and chaos, spirit and matter, and heaven and earth. Of course, the duality of yin yang is in cyclical motion; and therefore wars eventually bring peace and extensive peace must again give way to war.

Many ancient cosmologies like the Mexica-Maya-Andean culture present a tradition of 'divine twins' to account for the duality of God allowing the existence of both good and evil in the universe. In the city of Hermes and Heliopolis in Egypt the heavens were regulated by four male frog-headed and four female snake-headed counterparts making the divine Ogdoad of eight principles. This divine-eight springs from the cardinal directions established by astronomy and is a world-wide cultural concept resembling the eight opposed trigrams of the Asian duality of yin-yang; as well as the different qualities of the eight winds from the Temple of the Winds in Athens, Greece. Life arose on a mound in a swamp. The Sun, which separated the darkness of chaos from the radiant light of order, was created from a lotus blossom, an egg laid by an ibis, or the Egyptian 'Great Cackler goose' that laid the golden egg from which the Sun was born. This cosmology devolved into religion, then myth, and eventually into folklore and fairy tale.

The Role of Astronomy in Energy
Astronomers recognize that the motion of the galaxies and stars create enormous amounts of energy radiating throughout the universe. Cosmic energy is absorbed in the channels and faultlines of the crust of the Earth where it takes on the negative polarity of our planet and becomes earth-energy. Earth-energy finally reaches the sources of fountain heads in the crust of the Earth where it can bubble-up and become united again with the positive cosmic-energy from the sky. Such unions of alternating double and triple spirals are depicted in ancient energy art. This creates the sacred union of heaven and earth, which is the physics behind all Hermetic wisdom –namely that Earth mirrors everything that exists in the heavens –"On Earth as it is in heaven; and in heaven as it is on Earth."

Energy can be transmitted to many places, and transformed into many things. There is energy in light, in all life forms, in rocks, and slow or fast moving weather systems. It is one of the most important principles in the universe. But to even begin to understand energy we must know a little bit about astronomy which is the prime vehicle for energy. Because astronomical bodies conduct energy; all ancient holy sites are orientated to the cardinal directions here on Earth, and therefore aligned to the current cycles of the Sun, Moon, and stars; as seen from our perspective at different latitudes.

The temple of Tikal is aligned to the cardinal directions so that the spring and autumn equinox-Sun rises over the staircase of the central temple. At the winter solstice the Sun rises over the right-hand, southern temple. On the summer solstice the Sun rises over the left-hand, northern temple.

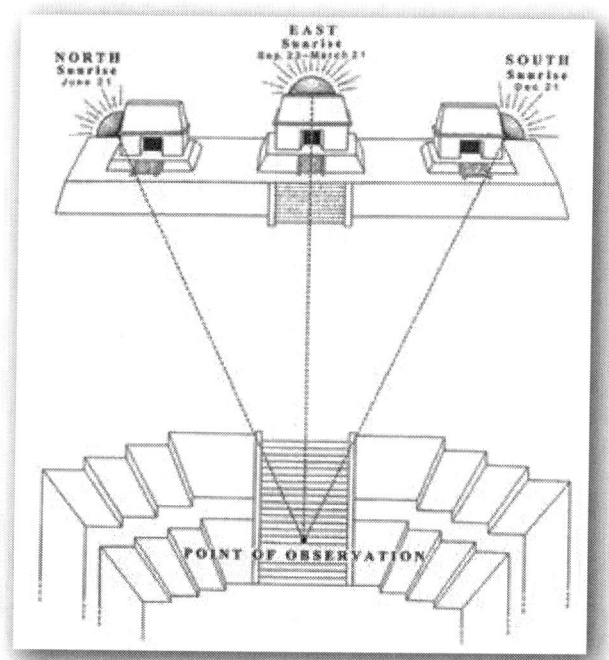

Tikal alignments (Diagram from ninebelize.com)

The position of the Sun, Moon, and stars in their cycles determine the strength of the force of the energy at the holy site. At rising and at mid-heaven the strength of a heavenly body is most powerful; while it abates as that body is setting. A planet's force is stronger if it is in conjunction, opposition, or in geometric relationship with Sun, Moon, other planets, and other heavenly bodies. No matter what

Galileo says, our perspective on the universe will always be; and can only be geocentric –unless we had colonies on Mars, where our perspective would be from Mars.

Astronomical bodies are powerful at their rising; most powerful at zenith; and less powerful at their setting. Energy readings from scientific instruments at the Lost World pyramid at Tikal were reported *as averages* by John A. Burke in *Seed of Knowledge, Stone of Plenty* (2005). The readings varied from day to day, and hour to hour because astronomy is always in motion and changing position. The cycles of night and day, phases of the Moon, seasons of the year, and the positions of the planets, and all astronomical phenomena modify the intensity of the flow of energy.

In very many instances the energy channels in the Earth were naturally (coincidentally) *geologically* aligned to astrological phenomena such as the winter solstice setting of the Sun. This natural alignment at undeveloped sites functioned for Druids as perfectly as the wondrous embellished temples and expertly built pyramids of Egypt. Guy Underwood's research that underground energy pathways below Holy Sites are closely aligned to astronomical phenomena has also been confirmed by Master Dowsers, Dennis and Maria Wheatley. Of course, it is well documented that the Temple of Jerusalem, El Castillo pyramid at Chichen Itza in the Yucatan, and the subterranean courtyard by the Kalasasya at Tiwanaku are aligned to the equinoxes. Stonehenge, on the other hand, is aligned to the avenue of the summer solstice, while *Bru na Boinne* at Newgrange, Ireland is aligned to the winter solstice. In my personal experience, the energy channel at Newgrange comes from some appreciable distance and finally assumes a perfect alignment toward the winter solstice within the rounded sanctuary of the megalithic stones. This fact was noticed previously by John Michell.

Most temples, churches, and cities are generally aligned to the four cardinal directions of north-south-east-west to insure the optimal benefits of health and warmth from Sun and Moon light, and the exposure to the eight winds. Such alignment is not only practical but symbolic of order, planning, forethought, and the formal union of Heaven and Earth.

Cosmic, Earth & Subtle Energies

Cosmic energy originates in the changing motion of galaxies and the universe. This energy force is captured by our own Milky Way galaxy which transfers some of the energy to our Sun and its solar system of planets. The solar system itself is wrapped in a blanket of energy called the *heliosphere*; which is an immense magnetic bubble containing all the planets, solar wind, and the entire solar magnetic field. Cosmic energy is gently absorbed through the Earth's electro-magnetic shield originating from both poles and protecting our planet from dangerous and deadly energy surges from the Sun, galaxy, and other components of the universe. The cosmic energy finds paths of least-resistance in the natural channels in the crust of the Earth.

The author of *Pyramid Power* (1973), G. Pat Flanagan writes, "Man is living in a sea of energy of which he is not usually aware." He says that we have become inured to this energy environment in which we operate. If we were to constantly tune into this sea of energy, it would be a nightmare of resonances, vibrations, and sensations. Once cosmic energy unites with our planet it becomes *Earth-energy* which is variegated like a vine-stock that adapts and adjusts to diverse minerals, soils, and geological formations to create a unique kind of energy at every location.

Many people call earth-energy at a holy site by the name of *Subtle Energy* implying that it is not easily recognized without some tutelage. Namely, that this energy needs to be explained and defined before it is readily seen and felt. Not all people who step on to an energy site are moved or inspired; because beneficial and healthful energy is subject to an individual's powers of perception, appreciation, and willingness to participate in its physics. As well, there is a mental aspect to appreciating a holy sanctuary through the belief that our mind is a microcosm of the Universal Mind, and in communication with the Cosmic Mind. In another sense, we have said that the ancient understanding of 'spiritual' equates with our modern understanding of 'energy' –and I now think that this is too simplistic and not accurate enough. The old meaning of *spiritual* implies design, logic, and purpose –and therefore our equation should be: *spiritual = intelligent and creative energy.*

Bernard Roger the alchemist, says that in Freemasonry ritual, in order to become a master; the *journey man* must travel into the *subtle* world, "from the square to the compass," according to the ritual. Again, we see that the square represents the material nature and the Earth; while the circle (drawn by the compass) has always represented the heavens above Earth.

However *subtle* the energy may seem, it has been continually recognized through all the ages. One of the great clues to this investigation is the fact that most of these powerful sites are very old and were taken over and adopted by different peoples, cultures, and religions. The Sedona energy vortexes are famous and attract visitors and energy-hunters worldwide. These vortexes were sacred to Native American peoples who explained and revealed them to early European pioneers who used them for their own special ceremonies such as weddings. The conclusion to be drawn from this fact is that these holy places are formed by a universal physics and energy which appeals to all nations, and is recognized by all of humanity. Guy Underwood in *The Pattern of the Past* cites the directives of the early Church of Rome that Christian missionaries were charged by Pope-Saint Gregory the Great (540-604 AD) to take over pagan sites and build churches directly upon them –keeping the location, and only destroying their idols.

Benefits of Cosmic Energy

Many years ago a group of youngsters and I visited the famous High Crosses of Ossory in Kilkenny, Ireland. We practiced and played with some forked-hazel sticks, and everyone was able to detect a mysterious force at this site as their diving rods twisted and turned. Young children naturally recognize earth-energy. Today, we live in the shadow of cancers, processed food of questionable nutritional value, polluted water, overcrowding, and overpopulation –all of which cause stress to our body and soul. It is recorded in ancient traditions that these ancient energy sites promote power, strength, health, mental acumen, inspiration, and above all, happiness. Why is modern society not protecting, investigating, and enjoying these wonderful places?

Brad Olsen in his *Sacred Places* series reports that the 'sacred valley of longevity' near Vilcabamba, Peru was noted for the health and longevity of its inhabitants who typically eclipsed 100 years of age, and generally lived to be from 120 to 134 years of age. The local mountain water contains valuable minerals and nutrients that benefit people, their agricultural soils and products. Cosmic energy is conducted by subterranean streams and channels where it accumulates many valuable mineral assets to become a specialized form of earth-energy.

Tibetan legends of the Potala Palace speak of a former glorious age when all people enjoyed telepathic abilities. This advanced race of humans could travel in the astral realm, see by clairvoyance and levitate gigantic stones into place. The people had the ability to utilize their 'light bodies' at will. Man degenerated and lost these wonderful gifts when they employed them for self-interest instead of the common good. The Tibetan Lamas retained these ancient human abilities. It is also apparent at many of these holy sites that ancient engineers modified and super-charged these natural energy fountain-heads through vast hewn chambers, caves, and passages that acted as energy condensers and accumulators. Such artificial energy chambers were incorporated into the underground vaults of great medieval cathedrals. Beneath the Potala Palace is an ancient volcano which formed a labyrinth of hidden caves, chambers, and halls said to contain a Temple of Secret Wisdom and the bodies of giants that formerly inhabited the earth.

Olsen further discusses the fact that some spiritual seekers have seen a discernible aura encompassing the holy River Ganges in spite of the pollution and garbage flowing along –which the modern Hindu say is just an indication of the polluted state of our entire Mother Earth. Even with all the filth in the river, scientific tests of water purity are wondrously high around the many Ganges' bathing centers testifying to another benefit of energy sites which promote health and purity. Olsen writes about a food-preservation larder at the all-quartz stone circle at Duloe in Cornwall. Olsen also mentions the healing powers of the stone rows at Carnac in Brittany, and the 5,000 spontaneous-healing events at Lourdes.

The citizens of the Golden Age believed that their world was the product of the will to create order out of chaos. They founded their homes, fields, and villages within an ordered context. The location of their human space in which they lived, worked, and socialized was not random but arranged around a sanctuary of sacred energy –the central Omphalos of their world. In the Golden Age, people had no need of a temple as they lived their lives within the precincts of a Holy Place. Ancient people marked special locations of energy with standing stones, henges, and later with more elaborate temple structures. These energy portals supported health, spiritual wellbeing, bodily strength, focus, truth, right-judgment, wisdom, clarity of speech, cures of maladies and disease, prophecy, communication with the divine, unity of purpose, and especially exhilaration and joy. People did not need artificial toys and mechanisms because life itself completed all their needs and expectations. As time went by, these sacred sites accommodated palaces and monasteries around which villages grew up and expanded into towns and cities. As one archaeologist remarked, "First came the temple, then the city."

The energy at these sites is real and demonstrable by scientific means such as ground electrodes, expensive fluxgate magnetometers (priced $30,000) for measuring the geomagnetic field, and electrostatic voltmeters for measuring electric charges in the air. There is also a large community of natural dowsers who use primitive dowsing tools including 'Y' shaped branches of hazel, willow, and a variety of water-loving woods, as well as crystal pendulums. Dowsers have a direct intuitive child-like recognition of energy which they are able to sense through their body and mind. They also use extensions of their body and mind such as water-witching rods, metallic 'L' rods, and extremely thin copper wires to tune into the elementary electromagnetic spectrum. Their paraphernalia and tools are merely an extension of their ability to 'sense' answers, diagnose sickness, and find locations of minerals, missing people, and lost articles. A natural dowser uses their own mind, body, and its reflexes as a scientific instrument to feel, sense, and know emanations and vibrations of energy from the ground and sky.

The field of energy science is associated with the names Thoth, Hermes, Mercury, and other mythical 'Masters of all Arts' throughout human culture. The famous pyramid complex of Saqqara was designed and built by the polymath and demi-god Imhotep, noted architect, savant, royal advisor, astronomer, and physician to the king. The Greeks identified him with their Hermes, hermetic traditions, and their demi-god Asclepius, the doctor. The ancient wing-less, single-serpent caduceus of Hermes is the recognized emblem of the medical profession as a symbol of healing through energy and knowledge. The serpent is the totem animal of both energy and knowledge.

Our world is all about energy. It is the seed in procreation, the nourishment in food, the gas in your car, the electricity in our cellphone and computer. It is the 'Giddy up' which overcomes inertia. Even stones have energy locked into their crystalline structure. Governments fight wars over it, and corporations try to dominate the energy marketplace. It is such an integral part of life, that we overuse the word and assume that our understanding of it is correct. We enjoy the exhilaration of energy in terms of adrenaline in sport and contests. We revel in the transmission of energy, whether in intellectual discourse or sexual intercourse. There are masters of martial arts who can project their energy-force like a projectile shot from out of their bodies. There are adepts who are said to be able to transcend space and time using energy encapsulation and teleportation. There are scholars who have mastered remote viewing. There are people who can heal at a distance, and can find lost persons. The understanding and use of energy is the key to all these miracles and mysteries. The super-creative powers of the Earth are not self-generated –but are a testament to cosmic energy transported along astronomical cycles of time and the ages to produce every variety of form and matter within the universe. Our world is the true sacred garden of Paradise, a holy chalice and cornucopia of delectable foods and all manner and variety of life.

Crop Circles & Super-Energy from Holy Food

Crop circles demonstrate that when cosmic-energy comes into contact with the Earth it exhibits its geometric nature and structure as 'intelligent and creative' energy. The transcendence of water becoming frozen into snowflakes reveals the infinite variety of geometric patterns in water.

Brad Olsen in *Sacred Places Europe* (2007) writes that over 10,000 crop circle formations have been reported worldwide, some as early as the 17th century. These appear quite regularly in fields near geoglyphs and ancient sacred sites, such as Stonehenge, and especially near Silbury Hill at the intersection of two powerful dragon lines. Eyewitness accounts describe the crop formations appearing within seconds, accompanied by strange lights, crackling and humming sounds, and small metallic-like balls of bright white light quickly maneuvering in and around the crop fields. Compasses placed in the center of the crop circle formations shortly after their creation spin wildly and randomly around.

Energy provides health and beneficial sustenance which the ancients called a divine elixir, manna, and a heavenly milk and food from our Mother in Heaven. In return for these blessings, ancient people brought seed and food offerings to energy temples. After a few days they would retrieve these gifts which had acquired a sweeter taste, while the seeds were more fertile, stronger, and developed faster. G. Pat Flanagan in *Pyramid Power* (1973) says, "Plants whose seeds are sprouted in a high intensity field of this type, sprout some four days earlier and grow three times as fast as plants in a low energy electrostatic field…In all cases the pyramid treated plant grew 2 to 3 times as fast as the controls, were more healthy and lasted longer after harvest…Not only did the foods taste good, they tasted better…"

The Michigan biophysicist, W.C. Levengood had the idea of experimenting with seed taken from crop circles. He found that these specimens were heartier, grew faster and larger than ordinary seeds taken from unaffected areas of the fields. John A. Burke in *Seed of Knowledge, Stone of Plenty* (2005) confirmed Flanagan's findings that seeds exposed to ancient energy sites grew faster and stronger. Burke used only modern scientific magnetometers and electro-magnetic apparatus to evaluate ancient energy sites all over the world. These findings seem to affirm that ancient people cultivated a range of holy food to extend and elevate human life. Maya temples are notably surrounded by overgrown medicinal trees and pharmaceutical shrubs. The ancients also appreciated and used the supernatural qualities of water found in holy wells located above energy fonts where water changes its structure and frequency.

W. C. Levengood disclosed the difference between man-made crop circles and the genuine natural crop circles created by energy where the apical nodes below the seed heads, as well as the second and third nodes were bent and elongated by a surge of super-hot energy. Other researchers have shown that some crop circles reappear the following year in the same place, as a less-defined shadow called 'a residual' of the original circle. During spells of dry weather in our own locality in Ireland countless ancient circles and dew ponds of various sizes boldly appear upon the agricultural fields during dry periods manifesting the presence of permanent underground forces. There are seventy documented eyewitness reports of the formation of crop circles by a fast moving ball of light accompanied by a crackling sound made by the node elongation of the plants. Hamish Miller and Paul Broadhurst in *The Sun and the Serpent – An Investigation into Earth Energies* describe their dowsing experiences near the *Druid Cheesewring* along the *Michael and Mary Lines* crossing southern Britain where geometric patterns of energy have been divined, documented, and permanently engraved into the rocks above by the dowsers who discovered them.

Brad Olsen informs us that, "One common feature of the Nazca Lines is that a single uninterrupted line outlines them all." Also some Nazca lines deviate only a few feet over several miles which would be an astonishing feat of surveying if they were designed by man. Most curiously, the spider image shows its distinctive reproductive organ attached to one of its legs, which can only be seen through a microscope in a laboratory. Again, observers have witnessed a ball of lightening following the Nazca Lines in much the same manner as observed in other places when creating a crop circle.

Ancient people trusted in the intuition of animals, birds, and insects to find healthy places to live and rear their young. They followed swarms of bees and found that these intelligent and highly organized creatures built their hives in caves, rock clefts and trees situated over energy fonts and spirals. The food of these wild bees, especially Royal Jelly, has amazing curative and nutritional properties which people of the Golden Age called 'the food of the gods.' This Golden Age came before the Age of Wine and the wine-god Dionysus, when honey-mead was the beverage of choice among gods and men. The town of Clonmel in the Golden Vale of Ireland, is anciently called 'the honey meadows' near the bee-hive shaped cap-stones of the Ossory holy sites. Ordinary button mushrooms in nature also grow over energy portals; and these have been found to be amazingly rich in 'super-energy;' while some of their cousins are noted hallucinogens used by Shamans to explore the secret levels of the universe. Finally, the famous wild Maya mountain corn was said to have been discovered at the entrance of a holy mountain energy-cave. So, honey, mushrooms, and mountain corn are traditionally divine energy foods of extraordinary value –presented to humanity by the gods.

Someone may say that honey in general is good for you! But, not all honey comes from wild hives located over energy fonts, nor is it raw and unfiltered, or lovingly produced by a kind farmer who loves his bees. A person must study and practice energy appreciation. Processed and manipulated food increases in weight and mass while it loses energy. Ingesting this type of food does not shape and sculpt the body; but only adds shapeless mass. The body must be healthy, and the mind prepared. Just because you visit a holy site – you will not necessarily be inspired. The modern world should try to understand how important personal health and holy food really is. A nation that cultivates sacred food and practices good health enjoys good society, respect, justice, and intelligent citizens.

In conclusion, it seems that the most harsh and inhospitable island of Skellig Michael off the coast of Ireland, located in the teeth of Atlantic gales must have produced 'holy food' of exceptional nutritional value to support the vibrant community of monks that sought isolation and refuge there. Common bird's eggs, herbs, and vegetables seem inadequate to have supported the construction work of unique paths, walls, and beehive cells. The geological make-up of Skellig Michael resembles the shattered, but energy-rich structure of Machu Picchu. This island is the northernmost point of the famous Michael Dragon-line that extends across Europe to the Holy Land.

Above, is a curious root extension from a redwood tree in San Bruno Park, California. This 'snake-head' like feature is directly above a positive spiral adjoining a negative spiral. This combination has twisted the tree's root into an unusual form. The negative and positive swirls are easily divined with a crystal or moon-stone pendulum. Twisted trees and growths of mistletoe are sure signs of energy activity beneath the ground.

Nearby the place of my birth in the Frankish town of Fritzlar was the famous site of the felling of the Dona Oak (Jupiter Oak) by Saint Boniface ending German paganism. The saint cleaved a small felling-notch in the tree to the cries of the cursing inhabitants –but suddenly and miraculously a blast of wind and thunder from heaven downed the extraordinary arboreal giant into four neat trunks of equal length which propitiously served as the pillar-posts for the first Christian church. It is a well-known fact that acorns thrive over energy spirals, and the renowned longevity of oaks is supported by being over an energy font; which unfortunately also attracts lightning. Below our cottage in Ireland we witnessed a lightning strike of an ancient oak tree which slaughtered six heavy-weight bullocks that sheltered underneath its bows during a tremendous thunder storm. The name 'Druid' is a Celtic word for 'oak.' And of course everyone knows that Druids held their assemblies and rituals in sacred oak groves where the holy mistletoe was ritually garnered from their branches. Streams of energized-water filled with medicinal properties spring forth at the foot of some venerable oaks —and the old oak and the stream became one of the prominent icons of medieval alchemy.

Folk traditions persist in tales of the dangers of accepting 'fairy food' upon entering the magical underground caverns and castles of the fairy folk. Nicholas R. Mann in *Energy Secrets of Glastonbury Tor* tells us that Gwynn ap Nudd, the Faery King, held court within the caves under the Tor at Glastonbury where musicians played and beautiful children of noble aspect danced in red and white livery; the colors of fire and water. Having eaten the fairy food a person might think that had spent but a day and a night in the castle; but would not return back to life for many years. Such is the story of Rip van Winkle on the Hudson River, the Seven Sleepers of Ephesus, and a certain Greek philosopher in a cave in Crete. These sleepers could not have transcended time without the presence of earth-energy. Again, the fairy food is described as the 'elixir of eternal Life' or the 'heavenly dew.' Sometimes a person had to eat fairy mushrooms to enter these Underworld castles (shown in children's books as red and white-speckled toadstools with a little green-clad fairy man seated atop). A group of our acquaintances once ingested some of these very-poisonous and protein-rich mushrooms on the top of Mount Slievenamon; and *did indeed* see leprechauns; in addition to experiencing the horror that their own flesh appeared to be melting from off their bones.

Nicholas Mann tells us that the ancient Order of Avalon of the Golden Age regarded Glastonbury Tor as an *axis mundi*, a Gateway between the Worlds –a place of many colored jewels, divine music, and guarded by a dragon. Robert Graves in *The White Goddess* tells of the *Caer Sidi* and *Caer Arianrhod*, the spinning crystal palace which is the axis of the northern polar stars circling the heavens, and the jeweled lights of the Corona Borealis. The master dowser Guy Underwood describes the Primary Spirals ay Holy Sites as both right-handed and left-handed; producing spirals of seven coils, and multiples of seven, but never any other number. The stone in front of Newgrange has mystic spirals inside-out and outside-in informing the visitor of the presence of massive convolutions of energy within.

The Human Aura & The Earth's Halo
According to *Pyramid Power*, cloud-like haloes of energy, spirit, aura, and quintessence appearing around the human body have been called by many names by many cultures: Ga-Llama (Egyptian), Prana and Kundalini (Hindu), Tumo (Tibetan), Chi or Qi (Chinese), Manna (Hebrew), Charisma (American), and Mana Loa (Hawaiian). The Soviet electrician S.D. Kirlian using a high frequency oscillator was able to photograph the human body and other living things to show that they radiated powerful and colorful flames of energy around themselves. Sacred images of Our Lady of Guadalupe are depicted with a flame-like halo around her entire body. The ancient hill behind her holy site outside Mexico City has also been credited with the sounds of celestial music. The Russians called these halos *bioplasmic energy* (just another new name for ancient cosmic energy) –which creates magnetism, electricity, heat, and luminous radiations –that every ancient shaman and priest have known about for millions of years. G. Pat Flanagan says that his studies convinced him that the human body is a complex integrated electronic system incorporating a magnetic field (like that of the Earth)

which responds to radiation and stress. The field changes with conditions and can be affected by the mind. The shape of the human energy field is the same as that described by mystics and can be measured by modern electronic electroscopes.

The ancients had a curious expression termed the 'Sub-Lunar sphere' which extends from the crust of the Earth to the limits of Earth's atmosphere just below the protective electro-magnetic shield of our planet. This is the bio-sphere where life flourishes in the realm of plants, animals, humans, birds, winds, hurricanes, and cosmic and earth energy. The ancients even measured this Halo of the Earth in which all life existed to 1080 miles above the surface of the planet. The current Space Station is orbiting well within its confines at a mere 200 miles high.

There are innumerable forms of energy manifestations. They may be a gentle dove-like fluttering aura descending from above; or a fierce, dragon-like exploding ball of energy from earth or sky. Traditions are rich in tales of St. George and St. Michael as dragon-slayers; whose meaning is that they now control and have power over these energy sites in the name of the New Savior. Adam, Eve, and the Tree of Knowledge; or the tree of the Golden Apples in the Garden of the Hesperides –are both guarded by dangerous, powerful energy serpents and dragons. The Tree of Knowledge symbolizes the World Tree as the axis of the Earth, and the Golden Apples are the planets circling the Sun which illuminates their surfaces in golden light. Energy manifests itself in incredible shapes and forms from the peaceful dove, to fabulous dragons, and intricate geometric forms carved by energy-balls in crop circles, or the geometric shapes of the Nazca images replicated on the southern deserts of Peru.

Rifts, Caves, Faultlines, Discontinuities & Volcanic Tubes

Energy from the sky penetrates into the subterranean mantel of the Earth where it travels through caves, channels, volcanic flow tubes, faultlines, rifts, and geological conductivity discontinuities marking the boundary between different geological layers in the crust of the earth. These geological conductivity discontinuities also disturb the velocity of earthquake waves. All of these phenomena provide the pathways for energy from the sky to fructify the Earth and arrive at holy sites.

In *Sacred Places Around the World* Brad Olsen tells us that Lake Baikal is the *center of the universe* for the Tungus Shaman for healing, spiritual renewal, and vision quest. Like Machu Picchu, Lake Baikal holy site is situated between two fault lines in the massive Baikal Rift System. This lake is the deepest lake in the world. The second deepest lake is Tanganyika along the East African Rift which brings energy up the Jordan River to Jerusalem and the Holy Temple Mount.

In *Twelve-Tribe Nations*, John Michell confirms that Earth-energy is connected to fault-lines when he says (p.101), "Megalithic monuments and the more elaborate temples that succeeded them.....are generally situated above or near geological fault lines, over subterranean springs and watercourses, or at nodal points in the earth's energy field. These places are centers of geomagnetic and other measurable energies..."

Every ancient holy site such as Machu Picchu, the Oracle of Delphi, and the Temple Mount at Jerusalem is seated directly upon an energy portal at the culmination of subterranean channels, fissures, and faultlines. Physics explains that electric and magnetic forces go hand in hand –namely that where there are electric forces, there will be magnetic forces; and conversely –where there are magnetic forces there are electric forces. These terms are joined together and understood as electromagnetic energy –which is the definition of the energy at these special holy sites.

Holy Volcanoes

Volcanic activity occurs at mid-ocean ridges, coastal subduction zones like the Pacific Ring of Fire, and weak zones in the Earth's crust called hot-spots like Yellowstone and Hawaii. After eruptions, lava-flow tubes drain rapidly of their super-heated magma, allowing the upper tube to cool off becoming the roof of channels and caves as the hot lava stream recedes beneath. Volcanoes create numerous side vents, tubes, caves and channels for earth and cosmic energy beneath their hardened plugs of dried magma. Brad Olsen discusses the 13-story Potala Palace of the Dalai Lama in Tibet, which is constructed directly above a pre-historic volcanic plug mound 420 feet tall. The present palace is constructed above earlier palaces and fortifications which also utilized the earth-energy flowing through the old volcanic channels present at this super-holy site. Olsen further mentions three volcanoes sacred to the Maori in New Zealand; and the volcanic Mount Kilimanjaro in Tanzania, 'House of God' and a sacred promised land to the Masai.

Potala Palace, Edinburgh Castle; and Borobudur temple in Central Java, Indonesia are all founded upon a volcanic plug over an energy font. Borobudur Stupa consists of six square terraces that are surmounted by three circular terraces bearing 72 latticed *dagoba*. Each lower façade has 108 Buddha statues and 1300 relief panels depicting the life of the Buddha (All these numbers are related to astronomical cycles: $36 + 72 = 108$, while $36.0555 \times 36.0555 = 1300$). The sacred mountain landscape of Mount Fuji in Japan also derives its energy from the currently inactive volcano. For Shintoists, the mountain of cherry and plum blossoms and snow is the virtual incarnation of Gaia Earth spirit. A major dragon line intersects Mount Fuji and is the source of great seismic activity. The scenery and powerful ambience curiously make this one of the most frequented for suicide.

The Haleakala (House of the Sun) volcanic crater was a very sacred place for the ancient Hawaiians. Dowsers and geomancers detect enormous energy coming up through the volcano, saying that there must have been a massive crystal formation pushed up from underneath. Mount Shasta in Northern California is a towering volcano above incredible energy which Native peoples regarded as the sacred center of the universe, their place of origin, and most important pilgrimage site. Their Great Spirit is said to dwell on the mountain. Numerous apparitions including Big Foot and ancient Lemurians have been reported upon the volcano who are said to inhabit vast caves in its interior.

Geological Boundaries & Faultlines

There is a notable mountain in every tradition and culture. Mount Kailash (aka Mount Meru Parvat and Sumeru) is almost three miles above sea level. It has never been climbed as it has four sheer walls that align almost perfectly to the four cardinal points of the compass. Mount Kailash is revered as being holy by millions of Asian people, and thought to be the seat of Lord Shiva. The mountain is shaped like a phallus and is the source of the Ganges, the Indus, the Sutlej, and the Brahmaputra rivers. It is a popular pilgrimage site. The geological structure of the mountain is subject to wide-scale faulting through intrusion of igneous granite upon limestone making it a broken boundary easily accessible to cosmic and earth energy flows.

John Michell in *The Dimensions of Paradise* tells us that, "Temples were sited at nodes and centers of the earth spirit, above fissures and underground caverns where it accumulates." He also says that rites and mysteries of the chthonic deities were celebrated in these caves and catacombs where life-giving streams arose.

Martin Gray on *sacredsites.com* (2/13/15) tells us in his article on the sacred oracular site at Delphi, Greece, "During the late 1990's however, a geologist, an archaeologist, a chemist and a toxicologist teamed up to produce a wealth of evidence suggesting that the ancient legends had in fact been accurate. The region's underlying rocks turn out to be composed of oily bituminous limestone fractured by two hidden faults that cross exactly under the ruined temple. Tectonic movements along the faults created friction that heated the limestone to a temperature at which the petrochemicals methane, ethane and ethylene vaporized. The two faults also created cracks through which underground spring water and the fumes could rise to the surface and help induce visions. In particular, the scientists found that the women communing with the oracle probably came under the influence of ethylene –a sweet-smelling but psychoactive potent gas once used as an anesthetic. In mild doses, ethylene produces feelings of disembodied euphoria and visionary insight. Concerning the effects of ethylene, some years ago an American anesthesiologist Isabella Herb discovered that a 20 percent mixture of ethylene produced unconsciousness but that lower concentrations induced trance states in which the patients remained conscious, were able to sit upright and respond to questions, and experienced out-of-body states and euphoria.

Earlier archaeologists studying the Temple of Apollo and its oracle chamber had noted several anomalous features of the temple's architecture. The *adyton*, the inner sanctum where the oracular priestesses had sat, was set two to four meters below the level of the surrounding floor; it was asymmetrical with a break in the internal colonnade having once accommodated a now vanished structure; and built into the foundations next to the recessed area were subterranean passages and a drain for spring water. Each of these features seems to indicate that the Temple of Apollo had been specifically designed to enclose a particular area of terrain where issued the oracular waters and vapors, rather than the temple having been created to house an image of a deity, such as was the primary purpose of other Greek temples," so says Martin Gray.

The major holy sites on the planet are proximate to geological faultlines, namely: Holy Jerusalem, Carnac in Brittany (home of the Veneti sea kings, and surrounded by 32 seismic fault-lines), and mystical Machu Picchu crossed by dual fault-lines. In Bolivia, the great temple compounds of Tiwanaku and Puma Punku are flanked by seismically active fault lines which ultimately generated earthquakes and a tsunami that destroyed this fabulous energy site. The Island of the Sun on Lake Titicaca, claimed to be the beginning of the culture of the Andes, is an electromagnetic center crossed by a major seismic fault. The cradle of technology and the internet in the Silicon Valley south of San Francisco is located upon the San Andreas Fault line and its branches as well as gravitational and geological anomalies. It is also strange that the San Francisco Bay Area is home to the universities of Stanford and Berkeley which have produced more medal winners in the modern Olympics than most countries in the world. The San Francisco Bay Area has also produced the largest number of Nobel laureates in the world, as well as eight Super Bowl football trophies. My own personal researches in dowsing find this fault to be a powerful energy conductor. Microsoft has also established itself in Seattle at the meeting place of three major fault lines along the American Continental, the Pacific, and the Juan de Fuca plates. Most of these locations are known for their dramatic scenery sculpted by geological upheavals over time; but the true attraction of these places is their boundless supply of stimulating energy for the body and minds of its residents.

All subterranean passages and caves have the facility to convey and transfer bursts of energy. The *Book of Revelation* was composed in an imposing cave high up on the Island of Patmos. Edinburgh Castle is built upon an ancient volcanic plug running along the Royal Mile leading up from another powerful energy vortex at Holy Rood Castle.

Every ancient city sprang up around a holy site that sat upon a high acropolis built upon a rocky outcropping above caverns, caves, and natural ducts that convey energy. The Acropolis at Athens has many ancient caves in the bedrock underneath several layers of ancient construction from early Pelasgian times. A vast system of caves and chambers was discovered in the 1970's at the heart of the Pyramid of the Sun at Teotihuacan outside Mexico City. In 1817 explorer Henry Salt wrote that he and Italian explorer Giovanni Caviglia had investigated cave 'catacombs' at Giza for a distance of several hundred yards before coming across a spacious chamber. This chamber linked to three others of equal size, from which went various labyrinthine passages. In 2008 a large system of caves has been officially acknowledged and is being explored and investigated. In 2009 Andrew Collins wrote *Beneath the Pyramids* documenting numerous underground natural caves and precision crafted passage ways; as well as reviewing folk traditions of a pre-historical subterranean holy complex over which the present pyramids were built. Brad Olsen also tells us that new ground-penetrating radar has revealed a labyrinth of underground tunnels under the Maya pyramid complex at Tikal. The complex system has been mapped and reaches far into the distant countryside. Olsen also relates the tradition of the Coricancha Temple in Cuzco containing subterranean vaults and a tunnel complex that extended for miles. There is now enough evidence to suggest that most temples and pyramids were founded over natural caves which were often extended and amplified by man: Pyramids of Giza, Teotihuana, Tikal, Coricancha Temple of the Sun, Potala Palace, Edinburgh Castle, Jerusalem's Temple Mount, and Chavin de Huantar.

Photo by Blueskylimit of the extensive subterranean passages of Chavin de Huantar north of Lima

A drawing of a sculpture at Chavin de Huantar seems to suggest bursts of energy emanating from the head of the local guardian deity spirit. This site was visited for over 2,400 years by pilgrims from far and wide for its transformative holy energy, powers of alteration of consciousness, and renowned oracle. Chavin de Huantar in the northern Peruvian highlands at about 10,300 feet above sea level is built of monumental stone blocks covering labyrinthine passageways, sunken courtyards and electrically active rushing water channels underneath the site. The complex is honeycombed with passages, stairways, air vents, and large rooms covered with stone roofs, and no fenestration. At the intersection of the vertical and horizontal axis stands the 13 foot tall *Lanzon Slab* depicting a part human, part serpent, and part caiman deity –perhaps an esoteric symbol of the energy from the Milky Way galaxy which was highly regarded and celebrated in Andean astronomy.

The Aztec & Maya built pyramids over sacred and fertile caves filled with the bones of their ancestors –believing that the energy might enliven the bones which could then communicate with their descendants to advise, help, and cure. Bones also represent the cycle of life, death, and rebirth. This is why mandibles are displayed at Chichen Itza and Teotihuacan in Mexico City as symbols of regeneration and rebirth from out of the Underworld. We have seen ancestral family skulls proudly displayed upon the mantelpiece to bless the homes in Ollantaytambo in Peru. Energy sites have seven dimensions like the Maya complex at Tikal. These are the four cardinal directions of east-west-north-south which align the astronomical influences of the Sun, Moon, and planets to the precinct and its temple. In addition there are the three levels of the different worlds of the Shaman: the Underworld (of ancestors and the past), the Middle World (of the present), and the Upper World (of Heaven and the stars).

The world's greatest cities have been placed upon active and inactive faultlines which transfer energy to their location. Jerusalem is connected to the Dead Sea Rift which is an adjunct of the Great

African Rift Fault. Babylon is on the Persian Gulf Fault. The city Charleston, South Carolina and San Francisco, California are founded upon powerful earthquake fault lines. Many cities like Seattle are founded directly upon the geologic plate boundaries. Energy is stimulating and people are drawn to these dangerous but exciting centers.

Geological Conductivity Discontinuity

The St. Michael's and St. Mary's Dragon Lines are founded upon the unique boundary line (geological conductivity discontinuity) of the Cretaceous and Jurassic formations of southern England which apparently conduct an impressive flow of energy. The famous Glastonbury Tor upon the Michael's Line is an extinct volcanic mound full of caves and caverns. Its 13th century church was demolished by an earthquake along an ancient fault line which simultaneously destroyed the edifice at St. Michael's Mount on the very same day –a distance of 150 miles. Miller and Broadhurst analyze the Mary and Michael Lines and present their conclusions, "The way the currents operate and their association with rocky out-crops had also led us to believe that, on a purely physical level, they were connected with geological fault lines."

The energy pathway of the Michael and Mary line sits upon the Cretaceous chalk formation between the Chiltern Hills and the Jurassic formations. Indeed, the geologic formations of Ireland, England, and Scotland exhibit this diagonal north-east to south-west thrust. Also, the south-east part of the Michael-Mary is in the middle of a lengthy peninsula where energy is concentrated by 'the peninsula or island effect.' In general, one may notice the Highland Boundary Fault and the Great Glen Fault through Inverness, Scotland which also follow thrust direction and numerous abutting geologies as an abundant source of *geological conductivity discontinuity*.

Most ancient cultures use the general name 'Dragon lines' to indicate rift lines, faultlines, channels, lay lines, and all subterranean

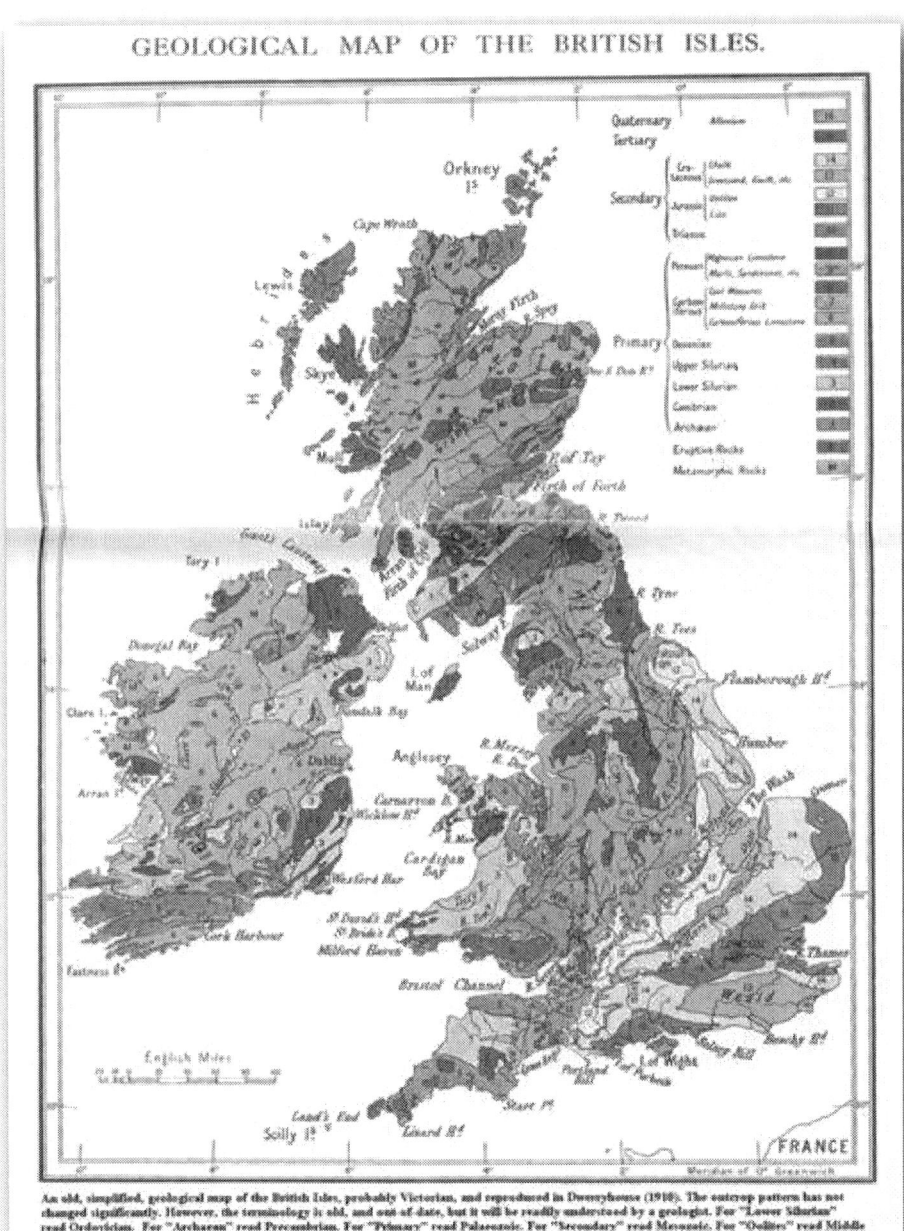

Wiki image 6/11/15

lines that transport energy. In Asia the dragon is a symbol of the living aspect of the cosmos, Earth, and nature. His abode is in the high mountains and hills, the dwelling place of the gods.

Most European churches built upon ancient sites have underground crypts and caves that serve as energy accumulators. Porsenna's Labyrinth (described by Roman scholar Pliny the Elder) is located in Siena directly underneath the main cathedral. It is formed by a close network of underground passages conceived by the Etruscans in the 6th century BC. The underground passages have different sizes and levels and are connected to the outside by wells and cisterns much like the interior of the Temple Mount at Jerusalem.

Dr. William F. Romain in *The Suppressed History of America* writes, "The Ohio Serpent Mound lies near the intersection of several fault lines, and in an area of unusual magnetic activity, combined with an area of intense gravity anomalies." *Ancient Aliens* television series reports that the Serpent Mound lies on the outline of a huge meteor strike location which infused Iridium into the soil. This created a geological conductivity discontinuity where electromagnetic and gravitational forces can appear at the surface of the ground. The massive meteor strike in the Gulf of Mexico above Yucatan appears to have opened an energy conduct that inspired the advanced science of the Olmec and Maya of that region. The Nazca Lines in Peru are said to be buzzing with energy lines underneath the geoglyphs (aligned toward Tiwanaku). Guy Underwood has dowsed the hill drawing of the White Horse of Uffington, and has presented a full diagram of the energy pattern beneath this geo-glyph.

John Michell in *Twelve-Tribe Nations* writes that the famous oracle of Apollo at Delphi is located on a geological rift in a volcanic region shaken by earthquakes. Michell continues, "Experiments with magnetometers and other instruments prove that the sites of stone circles are anomalies in the earth's energy field...Geological fault lines run below or near ever stone circle..." In the summer of 1988 a light from the sky was seen shining down on Silbury Hill near

Avebury, and the next morning rings and crop-circles were discovered in the nearby cornfields.

Michell again writes that the early settlers of Iceland choose a magical energy spot for their midsummer *Althing*, where two walls of rock had been split into a narrow chasm along Iceland's main geological fault line.

John Michell then describes the holy sanctuary of the Temple of Solomon in Jerusalem, saying that the equinoctial Sun was rising from the east behind the Mount of Olives and followed the Messianic ley-line through the Golden Gate whereupon a flash of light entered the sanctuary with a thunderous sound. The northern gateway to the Holy Land is between the parallel ridges of Mount Lebanon and Mount Hermon [where] the River Jordon is born. It winds its way south along a deep geological rift." This is along the Kidron Valley to the Jordon and Dead Sea trench connected to the Great African Rift Valley. The front cover of our book shows a depiction of Jerusalem that illustrates the deep Kidron Valley energy artery connecting down to the Jordon and beyond making this one of the most powerful energy sites on our planet. It is no wonder that Jerusalem has been one of the most desirable and contentious sites throughout all history.

In conclusion, it may be said that cosmic energy impregnates the Earth at tectonic plate boundaries where earthquake faultlines, volcanic activity, subduction zones, and many dangerous and unstable phenomena occur. Again the seductive energy draws humans toward thrilling and dangerously powerful places of tremendous vitality and energy –which ultimately destroy their civilizations.

Ancient & Modern Testimony about Energy
Diodorus Sicilus writes concerning the Oracle at Delphi that there was a cleft in the earth, where the sanctuary is now located. Every time a goat came close to the edge and peered down, it began to leap

in a curious manner and to bleat in a strange voice. Surprised at the wonder, the curious goatherd approached the cleft, and the same thing happened to him. The goats were in fact behaving like humans and fell prey to the phenomenon of 'innate joy,' and the goatherd began to predict the future.

Jean Richer, *Sacred Geography of the Ancient Greeks* writes that this joyous exaltation and dancing is practiced by the Jews at most of their festivals, especially the *Season of Our Joy* after the fruit harvest in the late autumn (Rosh Hashanah) when they dance for joy at the Wailing Wall near the site of the Temple of Solomon. There are many instances of celestial music being heard at holy sites –which would occasion joy and dancing

The ancient Asian art of *Feng Shui* relied upon masters of energy-dowsing to promote healthy habitations and salubrious environments. The Chinese drove cows and sheep into large fenced areas to see where they would sleep. Here they would build their homes which were free from geo-pathetic stress lines which the Chinese called 'Dragon Lines'. There is evidence of energy dowsing among the following peoples: Atlas Mountain tribes (6000 BC), Hebrews, Moses, Egyptians, Cleopatra, Persians, Druids, Orkney Islanders, Dartmoor people, Hopewell, Native Americans, and Inca. These tribes built their holy places above powerful energy portals, while keeping a safe distance away for their homes and habitations.

The wonderful survey by Hamish Miller and Paul Broadhurst in *The Sun and the Serpent* –concerning the *Michael and Mary lines* that cross Britain –discovered a wide spectrum of energy in the forms of ghosts, spirits, fires, and even mathematical and geometric symbols. Traditions in Ireland record that sites of standing stones have cured intense headaches and numerous other ailments. Other Irish sites were said to have attracted Jackie-the-Lantern, mad dogs, and lunatics during the full-moon.

Druidry.org (5/20/14) reports that sleep therapy was practiced at the classical Asclepian temples founded upon sacred wells and springs. Here the sick would fast and take part in rituals designed to invoke a healing dream. In Roman Britain, a dream-temple was built at Lydney Park in Gloucestershire over several springs, while records indicate St. Madron's Well was also used for this purpose. Paul Devereux, in *Earthmind*, recounts incidences where people have become unaccountably drowsy and fallen asleep at the site of a holy well. Dreaming at holy wells was also used as a method of foretelling the future. It was a custom of country girls to seek to know their future husband at the well. For example, a serving-maid of Selby could not decide which of her suitors to wed, and so sought help from the nearby *Fairy's Pin Well*, which had a reputation for divination. She drank from its water and asked the faery of the well to give her a dream of the man she should marry.

John Michell writes concerning energy lines, "At certain seasons, the lines on which they stand were believed to become animated by a current of invisible energy, and on one particular day, when the current was at its zenith, certain magic rites were performed by which the fertilizing influences were drawn through the land." Michell continues to say that the science of the Chinese geomancer's was gained through astronomy and the use of the magnetic compass –by which means the Earth's magnetic field is still measured today. The strength and direction of the current varies according to certain aspects of the Sun and Moon; for the Moon exerts the same influence upon the invisible electro-magnetic flow, as it does on the changing of the tides. The full moon produces a marked increase in magnetic activity around noon with a quiet period just before sunset.

J.A. Fleming remarks in *Terrestrial Magnetism*, "It is but natural to infer that a similar influence emanates from the planets or from the distant stars." Fleming concludes that the eclipses of the Sun or Moon substantially influence, and short-circuit the earth's magnetic field in the most dramatic fashion. This phenomenon has been addressed by ancient people beating their war-shields with spears until the eclipse abates.

The mystical Cathedral of Chartres in France is known for its design by sacred number, golden mean proportion and geometry; and especially, its foundation upon an ancient site containing a powerful node of earth-energy. Richard Heath writes in his book, *Sacred Number*, "These buildings were located upon the ancient places not just to overlay their pagan precursors but also to employ the same earth-energies in the service of God, by the sign of the dragon-slayer." St. Michael is the dragon-slayer, and angel of the Sun –the transformer of cosmic-energy to the planets and Earth. Just like many churches before the iconoclastic ravages of the French Revolution, Chartres has a famous eleven-fold labyrinth. The labyrinth of convoluted spirals was usually placed directly upon the matrix of earth-energy which had first attracted ancient people to the site.

In *Symbolism of the Celtic Cross* (1989), Derek Bryce tells us about the importance of olden "Market Crosses" which had been erected upon older sacred sites in the center of towns and villages. Amateur archaeologists began to explore the remoter parts of the west of Britain where they found sculptured stones, some of which were clearly phallic in shape. Prudish Victorians destroyed, buried, or removed these phallic stones, as they had done earlier at Avebury and in Chichen Itza in the Yucatan before the visit of Maximilian and Charlotte Empress of Mexico. Slim columns and crosses replaced the phallic stones that originally marked the energy spirals. Bryce enumerates the important activities that were carried out at these sites, such as, "Official proclamations were read out, rules for commerce such as weights and measures were laid down, justice and punishment were dispensed, and oaths were witnessed."

Guy Underwood in *Pattern of the Past* relates that animals and insects are attracted to the energy that comes from blind springs (also called fonts, portals, spirals, nodes, matrix or vortexes), and that animals use underground water currents called "track lines" for finding their directions, and locating suitable places for sleeping and raising their young. The nests of birds and the hives of bees are positioned over nodes and blind springs. Old horses like to stand over the node of an energy spiral in an open field to garner its energy, while cows congregate on the top of ancient barrows over blind springs to absorb the energy coming from the earth.

John Michell reports that the ley-lines centered above the underground water lines are said to convey fertilizing and spiritual energy to the surrounding countryside. Humans, animals, and plants likewise possess their own individual energy fields or auras whose balanced and harmonious state is essential to maintain good health. New Age dowsers have found it possible to investigate the bio-magnetic fields, or chakras of the human body to detect imbalance which leads to illness and disease. The historian Herodotus tells us that many temples were used to sleep in overnight –like a holy incubation where the cosmic energy would help to balance and cure people. Some of the temples even had a number of special sleeping cells for people to take advantage of the recuperating flow of energy.

In *Energy Secrets of Glastonbury Tor*, Nicholas R. Mann interprets the works of Victor Schauberger and Masaru Emoto saying that straight-flowing channeled water is unhappy and loses its energy. Artificially handled and stored city water rarely crystalizes on freezing but assumes random, dirty, and chaotic shapes; while pure spring water develops colorful, hexagonal, and complex crystalline forms. Natural water and water-charged atmosphere, and storms circulate with inward and outward turning spirals emulating positive and negative flowing energy. Mann also mentions that energy confined and concentrated in a centripetal vorticular system will eventually release in radiant bursts of energy and light. Perhaps the Ceque system of 42 rays radiating from the temple of the Coricancha in Cuzco is a documentation of an energy node.

The Sun and the Serpent by Miller and Broadhurst confirms that the science of earth-energy sites was passed down to the Druid, Christian, Saxon, Norman, and Elizabethan Ages, and onto the Neo-Druidism of late Victorian times. During the Golden Age, Britain instituted the *perpetual choirs* singing in tune and resonance with the music of the earth and the cosmic energy of the universe. This magical action of concord was said to cast an enchantment over the entire island to soothe, comfort, and protect its citizens through the charm of fairy music.

Miller and Broadhurst, and others suggest that ancient arts of using earth-energy were clandestinely practiced by architects, builders, and churchmen and kept alive by the Benedictines, Cistercians, Dominicans, the Knights of St John, the guild houses and lodges of the Knights Templar, and Freemasons. Ancient scientific knowledge was safeguarded in the libraries of great monasteries of Llantwit Major, Glastonbury, Bury St Edmunds, Clonard, and Lismore in Ireland. Unfortunately, many of the books of great antiquity were destroyed in the frenzy of Henry VIII's efforts to overturn the powerful monastic system of Roman Christianity by looting their libraries and treasuries as well. Whatever Henry missed was destroyed by the prudish religious-fanatic Oliver Cromwell, acting as judge and jury of culture, science, and history.

Luckily, custom and law preserved ancient sites because their power was recognized over the ages for the coronation of kings, sites of law courts, recitations of history and pedigree, declarations of war and peace, and celebrations of religious feast days and social holidays. The *All-Thing* meetings in Scandinavia were preserved for assemblies of the bards and poets, May Pole dances, as well as fairs and social gatherings. The *Gorsedd* of Wales and Brittany was reintroduced in 1792 to promote literature, poetry, and the wonderful music of ancient Druidic culture still alive within the new religion of Christianity.

In *The New View over Atlantis*, John Michell discusses the point that megalithic upright stones, rings, earth mounds, and leys were placed by design in the landscape to mark special places which manifested earth-energy. Michell claims that the original stone circle at Newgrange was roofed-over to create a special energy collector within the tumulus. He also remarks that there is a prominent ley proceeding from the southern entrance of Newgrange which is aligned with a standing stone, and proceeding further on to a mound in the distance.

Miller and Broadhurst describe the great circle of Avebury, "It was now clear that ancient people were utilizing the invisible energies of the Earth in their rites as they venerated the natural world. The current passed right through the massive barrow, surrounded by a deep ditch, forming a node point at its center…We were being drawn back to a world where this stupendous temple had been deliberately planned and constructed to take account of natural energies… Here, for the first time, marked out by rows of standing stones, was a graphic display of how the energy actually operated. It was organic… Like a river, it formed curves and eddies, all of which were accurately laid out in stone (*The Sun and the Serpent* p.103)."

Deleterious Energy

Poison may be defined as an over-dose of protein –too much protein is not healthy and may kill you. Likewise, excessive doses of energy or longtime exposure to energy may have unfortunate results. One of the major physical and psychological problems of young people is the lack of sleep. The human body needs an extensive period of complete rest in order to restore cells, blood, and tissue. *Sleep deprivation* also disturbs digestion and the proper absorption of energy from food. Sleep is one of the greatest contributors to overall health, beauty, longevity, happiness, and a sound mental attitude and constitution. "Early to bed, early to rise, makes a man healthy, wealthy, and wise," said Benjamin Franklin. The body needs to generate and replace millions of cells every night –and if you are sleeping nearby an energy font, cell regeneration is interrupted. In the long term, the energy phenomena under your bed will lead to major complications ending in cancer. Again, young people who are addicted to drugs enjoy staying up all night; but do not feel well getting up early, and consequently miss work and other vital matters; resort to further self-medication, and are totally caught up in a vicious cycle of sleep-depravation which will destroy them completely through lack of cell regeneration.

Powerful energy has mutilated innumerable sacred sites through lightning strikes, CME's from the Sun, galactic surges, fires, earthquakes, and tsunami. There is a deleterious side to the wonderful benefits derived from energy in manageable doses. Throughout the world the stones around many energy sites have been vitrified and turned into glass by powerful energy explosions, such as the many vitrified forts of Scotland. At the Mound of the Dead, Mohenjo-daro in India, there are high levels of radiation and clay vessels fused together by tremendous heat. It seems that the giant roof timbers of the circular kivas at Chaco Canyon were ignited and burned out during an energy explosion. Places like Gobekli Tepe show that the entire site was patiently dismantled with great effort and care as if the people were humbling themselves before their Creator after their temple had exploded. Strong doses of energy may stimulate prophecy, but they may also affect mental and psychological derangement from long-term exposure to cosmic and earth energy. Dr. Ibraham F. Karim validates the concept that the Egyptian pyramids were placed over sacred locations to amplify and distribute the powerful harmonizing energy of Earth and Sky. But, he has also warned about continuous exposure to energy, and encourages the practice of ancient *feng shui* to ameliorate and tone down extremely powerful cosmic forces.

In Conclusion
Galaxies throughout the universe have swept-up and inhaled the chaotic debris from cosmic collisions and explosions, and have stabilized and re-ordered these particles to operate in an organized

fashion. Equating the term 'spirit' with 'energy' does not fully convey the ancient meaning of the term *spirit*. Cosmic energy from the heavens is not a random nebulous force, but rather *intelligent* energy born of the matrix of galaxies, and traveling through integrated astronomical systems and cycles in order to arrive at the gateway of the heliosphere of the Sun –to be transferred through the Earth's electromagnetic jacket, and nurture the Earth's crust and bio-sphere with life. It is said that, "Man does not live by bread alone; but by every word (logos) that proceeds out of the mouth of God." *Logos* equals energy. Creation through speech is a common idea in many cultures. The Creator paints the world with the brush of speech which uses the pallet of energy.

Brad Olsen, *Sacred Places Europe*, retells the story of Attila Domb, an earth-energy mound near the Danube in the Hungarian Great Plain. This mound was said to be a wooden fort of Attila the Hun, but upon excavation and finding a solid *golden deer* statue turned out to be a very ancient Scythian site. The legendary and undefeated racehorse, the 'wonder mare' *Kincsem* was foaled on this property near the Heviz Spa, a large hot-spring lake. More than a century ago herdsmen noted that their horses were drawn to the site, spending long hours there, especially sick horses that would lie down for many hours. The veterinarian of the estate noted that there was less illness and higher live-foaling rates among his animals than anywhere else in Hungary. Soon rumors spread about the natural energy healing site at Attila Domb, and hundreds of people visited the site to cure their aches and pains. The area has been developed as a modern health spa authenticated by scientific analysis of beneficial energy-radiation restoring 'vitality imbalance' and pulsations of magnetism. Geologically the Earth's crust is very thin in this area making it a geological 'hot spot' in conjunction with the Saint George Dragon *ley line* crossing directly under the mound. Many cures have been reported, especially 'a feeling that the harmonious energy-flow had been restored throughout the entire body'.

CHAPTER 2

COSMIC ENERGY & FAMOUS ENERGY SITES

The Sun is composed of gaseous electro-magnetic plasma throwing out both negative and positive charged particles throughout its heliosphere which extends far beyond the planet Pluto. This heliosphere acts as a deflective shield or halo protecting the integrity of the entire solar system. The Earth as well, also has its Van Allen belts as a magnetic sheet protecting our planet from too much radiation from the Sun and universe. Earth's magnetic field is powerful and causes jet-lag to travelers whose rapid movement across electromagnetic fields has pronounced effects upon human metabolism. Jet-lag strongly affects the immune system because it disturbs the normal functions of all body systems such as melatonin, endocrine, pituitary, hypothalamus, and pineal gland.

In *The Cycle of Cosmic Catastrophes* (2006) Richard Firestone tells us that when a nearby supernova explodes it may bombard the Sun causing solar flares, as well as knock asteroids and comets out of orbit to collide with Earth. This chaos is necessary and ultimately creative, for Firestone admits that exploding supernova are responsible for the essential parts of nearly every atom in our solar system and the entire universe such as the iron atoms in our bloodstream as well as the variations in our blood type. Chaos and destruction permits energy to be liberated and recycled to renew the cosmos and defeat inertia.

In *Earth under Fire* (1997) Paul A. LaViolette advances his Galactic Explosion Hypothesis that our galaxy frequently sends out a *Galactic Super-Wave* of cosmic ray particles such as electrons, positrons, and protons. These explosions frequently reach our planet, dramatically affecting our atmosphere and climate.

When galaxies collide; enormous amounts of energy throughout the vast spectrum of electro-magnetic energies are freed from their gravitational context and released into the universe once again. This liberated dust-like energy is recaptured by younger galaxies –perhaps like dust clouds of pollen released from male trees; which is instantaneously recaptured by female trees in an electric-like flash.

Perhaps the female galaxies nurture this intergalactic pollen, add their own energy and incubate the combination to which they give birth through their matrix as infant stars and stellar dust molecules. Modern science calls this birthing a 'super-wave' of energy ejected from the galactic core. The super-wave of energy feeds our Sun which uses this energy as nourishment; and transfers it throughout the bubble-like heliosphere surrounding the solar-planetary system. This burst of energy from our Sun is called a *coronal mass ejection* (CME). LaViolette continues to say that these galactic core energy explosions present a cosmology quite different from the more publicized *big bang theory*: that all matter in the universe arose at once from a single explosion in the past.

Edward F. Malkowski in *Ancient Egypt 39,000 BC* (2010) connects the five previous extinctions in Earth's history to astronomical phenomena. He supports Adrian Melott's idea that there is paleontological evidence that a gamma-ray burst in our galaxy occurred at the end of the Ordovician period 443 million years ago. The *cosmic dust invasions* into our solar system from the direction of the Galactic Center...would have been responsible for the global climate warming that ensued. Galactic core radiation outbursts of electromagnetic particles may occur as frequently as every 13,000 and 26,000 years – when the cycle of the Precession of the Vernal equinoxes aligns with the galactic center of the Milky Way; and 13,000 years later aligns with *the anti-center of the Milky Way. The center of our galaxy is located in the direction of the* borders of Scorpio-Sagittarius. The anti-center is located in the direction of the borders of Taurus-Gemini.

Coronal Mass Ejections from the Sun

The latest work by Robert M. Schoch, *Forgotten Civilization –the Role of Solar Outbursts in Our Past and Future* (2012) presents a discussion about solar phenomena that has affected past civilizations; and will certainly affect modern civilizations which have tied their success and existence to electricity. All the evidence suggests that our single-minded infatuation with electronic power will be brief, and disastrous.

Schoch follows LaViolette's theories and proposes that Coronal Mass Ejections (CME) from the Sun may cause civilization-destroying natural disasters, as well as causing biological and mental changes. He connects cerebral activity such as hallucinations with changes in the Earth's electrical field. Ancient people called the unseen electrically-charged material in the universe by the name of *aether*, or *the cosmic ocean*. Today's watchword for this material is *plasma*.

Thomas Gould comments that a plasma energy blast carrying currents of hundreds of millions of amperes coming from the Sun could not be restrained by the Earth's magnetic field. Such a blast would fry holy sites which have been specifically designed as energy terminals –melting the crystal and sand composition of stones into glass. Archaeologists call this process 'vitrified stone'. Examples of vitrified stone are found at ancient sites in Ireland, England, France, Germany, Turkey, and Iran. Schoch reports on vitrified hill forts in Scotland and Wales; and surmises that the many olden myths about 'crystal palaces and towers of glass' may refer to vitrified-stone sites. Other theories attempted to associate *vitrification* with "Greek fire", lightening, meteor explosions, or ancient atomic warfare.

There are several places such as Chaco Canyon and Gobekli Tepe *(Hill of the Navel,* north of the Harran Plain in southeastern

Syria) which were built with tremendous effort; but subsequently dismantled and/or buried with an expenditure of even more time and human effort. If these two holy sites were destroyed by a Coronal Mass Ejection, it is likely that normal pious people would have thought that they were being reprimanded for playing with cosmic energy –and that they should faithfully dismantle these works. One cannot really conceive of any reason in the world why a culture would painstakingly disassemble a temple which had taken such great effort to build. Both sites have evidence of fire and vitrification.

Schoch writes a very interesting report on the CME of September 1, 1859 observed by the British astronomer Richard C. Carrington –namely, an unusually massive group of sun-spots which suddenly turned into intense white flashes. At the same time magnetographs at Kew Observatory detected small but abrupt disturbance in the Earth's magnetic field. Then, about 17 ½ hours later, the magnetometers went wildly off the scale recording what is now called a CME. This event produced auroral displays for the next few days. Telegraph systems were strongly affected, and 200,000 kilometers of telegraph lines suffered major disruptions and failure –becoming unusable as unwanted electrical currents flowed through the wires. Some operators were able to disconnect their transmission batteries while the free electricity moved their messages along. Other operators were electrocuted and several telegraph stations burned down. This 1859 geomagnetic storm is now referred to as the 'Carrington Event.'

The British *New Scientist* proposed a scenario later supported by NASA that a major CME could decimate electric power in the USA reducing its status to a 'developing nation.' Our high-voltage systems act as antennae attracting the destructive super-power of a CME. The fixing and rebuilding of transformers and power systems would become nearly impossible because we have focused manufacturing around electronic factories and robotics –which would have become disabled. In space our GPS, telecom, and defense satellites would be tumbling out of control because their systems are reacting to the anomalies produced by the intrusion of high-energy particles. A powerful CME would bring about a total reversal in the political power structure of our planet –where the lowly, but self-sufficient countries would dominate the electronic-based nations whose huge populations are immediately out of heat, power, food, water, air conditioning, elevators, and transportation. Electronic records, money, banking, and accounting systems would be defunct –records of property ownership and financial resources are gone forever. Some people might actually care not to survive such a catastrophe even if they were sustained and protected in secure bunkers.

The Giza Pyramid Energy Complex

Ancient caverns and passageways are found beneath most famous and ancient holy energy sites such as under the Sun Pyramid at Teotihuacan outside Mexico City, Machu Picchu in Peru, the Temple Mount at Jerusalem, and the Great Pyramid at Giza. In *Beneath the Pyramids* (2009) Andrew Collins confirms reports that Henry Salt and Giovanni Caviglia discovered a natural cave system enhanced by human hands underneath the Giza pyramid plateau. Ancient Egyptian texts dating back three thousand years tell of a secret underground chamber called the 'Underworld of the Soul and the *Shetayet*.' Information from Coptic Christian monks specifically mention a race of people long before the Great World Flood and the Great World Fire who deposited a record of its arts and sciences in subterranean corridors deep below the Giza pyramid plateau. This treasure trove of knowledge became known as the 'Hall of Records.'

Stephen Mehler (*The Land of Osiris*, 2001) writes, "The Giza Plateau is literally honey-combed with underground tunnels...right angles cut through solid bedrock with relatively smooth walls..." He further reports on the incredible network of deep underground water canals beneath Giza which connect to distant sites such as Saqqara, Abusir, and Abu Ghrob. These were shown to Mehler by Abd'El

Hakim, a native Egyptian 'wisdom keeper'. Hakim reports on some shafts being 1,000 feet deep into the earth. Your author has seen the giant, perfectly square-carved, deep rock-shaft at Saqqara which is an incredible work of monumental construction. Mehler also comments on the Serapeum at Saqqara where a thousand machine-cut stone boxes are stored in carved underground cave passages where there is insufficient space to move them around. This begs the question; how did they get there? The indigenous tradition is that these passageways and service shafts brought water from the *Western Ur Nile* which originally flowed west of Giza on the borders of Egypt and Libya, while its waters were channeled to surround the Giza Plateau with moats and lakes.

Christopher Dunn's *The Giza Power Plant* (1998) explains the pyramids as piezoelectric, acoustical and electromagnetic energy collectors. It is not possible that the pyramids supplied the energy for the power-tools that built it. Many things in history cannot be explained in reference to our own science and understanding. But, the Giza pyramids are certainly power plants that process cosmic and earth energy to convey fertility, prosperity, healing, inspiration, and well-being to the Nile Valley and its citizens. Perhaps, under certain astronomical conditions, the energy portals underneath the Giza plateau may have become amplified to an extent that masters of mind and energy control may have levitated and positioned massive stone blocks. Acoustical levitation of blocks at the Great Pyramid was suggested by Edgar Cayce and supported by his followers like Andrew Collins. It is impossible to explain these pyramids through current modes of mechanical construction. As well, without its original tightly sealed mantel of casing stones, we may never be able to re-activate the Great Pyramid to discover what it actually achieved.

Robert Schoch in *Pyramid Quest* mentions Princeton Engineering Anomalies Research (PEAR) where electronic random event generators (REGs) were developed. These tools also verified powerful anomalies in the cavern underneath the Great Pyramid. We would love to know if the cavernous energy matrix underneath the Great Pyramid is aligned to the cardinal directions as the pyramid above.

Stephen Mehler confirms that Egyptian temples built upon ancient temple sites of the *Khemit* culture were called *Per-Neter – house of energy*. Native guides were taught to 'turn the key' at these sites to open the energy matrix and allow people to experience soothing and powerful natural forces. He goes on to say that the Khemit temples were connected through crystals and streaming water to create an active energy field where people could 'get high' to experience altered states of consciousness and commune with God and the universe. This prime area of energy was later walled off and became the secret *Holy of Holies* in the temple, called a *Per-Ba, house of the spirit*.

Christopher Dunn also calls Giza a 'house of energy' –a seismic tap, resonating in harmony with the Earth's basic vibrational energy frequency, to resonate with the igneous rocks present and generate a harmonic acoustical amplification of earth-energy. The igneous rocks would be granite (mica crystals), diorite, schist, alabaster (African crystal), and basalt –mixing their qualities with highly organic sedimentary rock and limestone. The pyramid would then act as a delivery system, a power plant for the practical application of this energy. Water running through igneous rock, full of mica, caused the stone to vibrate at higher frequency.

Huge pavement stones of basalt (some as heavy as 100 tons) were laid upon limestone around the pyramids for increased resonance in harmony with the water coursing underneath. Each *Per-Neter* was tuned to a different frequency while resonating together in harmony through a myriad of tunnels like the spokes of a wheel leading to the central hub at Giza. Victor Schauberger's theories say that natural underground 'living water' exhibits vortex-dynamics and high vibratory rates that produce tremendous amounts of magnetic energy.

It may be suggested that the technology, exactness, precision, and exceptional size of the pyramids was expended in expectation of high rewards in human benefits –else these monumental projects would never have been undertaken. Beneficial and fertile energy-capture and distribution would enhance the status and fame of the ruler, assure prosperity of his people, and promote stability in government. In a parallel case; the energy pyramid at Tiwanaku has been shown to have been connected to special agricultural beds on the shores of Lake Titicaca, at elevations where food production is close to impossible. The great storehouses of the Inca Empire such as at Ollantaytambo show that abundance, fertility, and security are the foundation of great empires.

Glastonbury, an Energy Showcase

At Glastonbury, England various energy lines and spirals are reported to produce 'transformational energy, a powerful atmosphere of sanctity, a heavenly odor of burning incense, voices raised in strange cords and harmonies, dynamic weather effects, consciousness shifts, revelations, and uplifting spiritual experiences.' These extravagant commendations are supported by apparitions of the 'White Lady' (the Moon), Earth Mother, the Green Man of Nature, and St. Michael, Archangel of the Sun. Our guide, who had visited India, said that the sages of that most sacred land acknowledge Glastonbury as one of the great holy sites of the world.

Glastonbury was originally an island of a riverine-ocean swamp on the low-lying Somerset levels, an important trading center in ancient times. It was purported to be the *Isle of Avalon*, burial place of King Arthur and Queen Guinevere, and the setting of the Grail romances. Recorded visitors here include: St. Patrick, St. Bridget, St. David, and the Child Jesus and Joseph of Arimathea. Glastonbury was also noted for its exceptional library and futuristic Abbot's kitchen which supplied rich pilgrims with haute cuisine cooked at four massive fireplaces at the four corner angles of the well-ventilated structure and its banquet hall in the middle.

At the Abbey of Glastonbury the Mary and Michael lines demarcate the old church and cross at a node by the old altar site. Hamish Miller following the energy of the Michael and Mary lines up the Glastonbury Tor discovered a place where these lines formed an 'energy labyrinth' that appeared to be like a sketch of lines matting and preforming a sexual union. He and his fellow dowsers were quite embarrassed at these results fearing that some would say that this was sacrilegious. However diagrams of classical labyrinths seem to evoke this very image of sexual impregnation. Miller and Broadhurst remark that the energy pattern on the top of the Glastonbury Tor might also resemble a giant chalice symbolizing the location of the mysterious Grail Cup. The Chalice Well Garden below the Tor contains a modern well-cover displaying the Vesica Pisces.

The Magic Machine at Jerusalem

The Temple Mount at Jerusalem is one of the great holy sites in the world. Because of its power and traditional benefits various nations wish to possess and control this place where Heaven and Earth connect in one sacred union.

Philosophers like Plato and scientists believed that a holy city based upon cosmic numbers and patterns would inspire justice, harmony, and knowledge among the inhabitants. According to Frances A. Yates the 17th century Hermetic philosopher, Tommaso Campanella proclaimed that he could make a city in such a wonderful way that only by looking at it, all the sciences would be revealed.

The Temple Mount and its buildings have been destroyed by King Nebuchadnezzar of Babylon (6th century BC), Darius the Persian (2nd century BC), and by the Romans (70 AD). The Muslim Dome of the Rock was constructed in 691 AD over the sacred rocky outcrop said to be the Omphalos-navel and center of the world. The Rock of Foundation beneath the Muslim's Golden Dome is the traditional spot where Abraham bound Isaac for sacrifice, and the place where the horse al-Burak took Mohamed on his heavenly dream-journey to visit paradise. It is imagined by some that a 'New Jerusalem' will be the greater temple of a new divinely-governed world order. According to many reports there is a sacred quality in the light surrounding Jerusalem and the Temple Mount. And while Jerusalem means 'Holy Peace,' it certainly does not signify 'Worldly Peace' because it has been invaded by countless nations making it a scene of bloody slaughters and devastation.

In *The New View Over Atlantis* Michell writes about holy sites saying that, "At certain seasons, the lines on which they stand were believed to become animated by a current of invisible energy, and on one particular day, when the current was at its zenith, certain magic rites were performed by which the fertilizing influences were drawn through the land." In *The Dimensions of Paradise* John Michell explains that the Universal Spirit at the site of the Temple Mount at Jerusalem manifested itself as, "The light that streamed out of the holy of holies at seasons when the electrical currents of the atmosphere were fused together with the magnetic energies of the Earth Spirit at the Temple of Jerusalem." In the same work Michell affirms that Jerusalem continues to be the Omphalos of the globe, the seat of both the Earthly Temple and the Heavenly Jerusalem. It continues to be the focus of prayers and traditions of three of the world's major religions.

The Temple Mount certainly fulfills all the aforementioned requisites of a true holy site: It is oriented to the equinoxes and sits upon a stone fabric of natural and artificial subterranean channels, chambers, quarries, stables, cisterns, water courses, pools, and super-megalithic stonework at the foundations underground. As well, the Temple Mount in Jerusalem is connected to one of the greatest fault-lines on the planet as it lies at the head of the long Kidron Valley which precipitates from a height down into the Jordon Valley and the Dead Sea. The Jordon Valley is connected to the Great Rift Valley which runs deep into Africa. This is the great fault-line through which cosmic energy is conducted to Jerusalem and many parts of the Middle East.

In a special tour called 'Behind the Walls' it is possible to be guided deep underneath the Temple Mount. Opposite the large area in front of the Wailing Praying Wall, there is a passage way behind the great walls revealing the cavernous nature of the Mount. At one point one may see megalithic stones set without mortar of incredible size in precise courses sixty feet below as foundations supporting the great walls of the Mount. These particular stones are called the work of Herod; but they are the deepest stones of the foundation, too ancient, and trimmed in the Phoenician fashion with an indented dropped-border all around their edges. This same work is said to exist at Baalbek in Phoenicia. Hebrew tradition attests that Solomon employed Hiram, king of Phoenicia, as the contractor of lumber, supplies, artisans, masons, and engineers for the building of the first Temple of Jerusalem.

John Michell uses the evidence from Dr. A.S. Kaufman to affirm that the Temple of Solomon was oriented east-west, and facing the Mount of Olives toward the rising Sun at both the spring and autumn equinoxes. Also, the wall to the east was lower than the rest to allow the rays of the Sun to enter the Temple. The Holy of Holies of the Temple of Solomon stood under the Dome of the Spirits on the northern edge of the Dome of the Rock (p.189). Ezekiel 43 writes:

> Behold, the glory of the God of Israel came from the way of the east: and his voice was like the noise of many waters: and the earth shined with his glory...And the glory of the Lord came into the house by way of the gate whose prospect is toward the east.

Michell describes the holy sanctuary of the Temple of Solomon in Jerusalem, saying that, "The equinoctial Sun was rising from the east behind the Mount of Olives and followed the Messianic ley-line through the Golden Gate whereupon a flash of light entered the sanctuary with a thunderous sound. A twenty cubit cube (20 x 20 x 20 x 18" = 144,000) made of special woods and metals stood at the heart of the Holy of Holies where the walls and ceilings were lined with gold, and on the Rock of Foundation stood the Ark of the Covenant, and above it a pair of golden angels protecting it with outstretched wings as an energy circuit over the ark. Thus the Shekinah Glory, the Divine Presence, the light and spirit of Israel, hovered above the Ark. This spirit of fertility then spread out through the veins and fissures in the earth to all parts of the country...the Temple ritual evidently gave people a feeling of well-being. They were happy and prosperous and filled with high spirits and good health. The function of the Temple was to marry the forces of heaven and Earth for the benefit of human spirits and the fertility of the countryside." The laws and the legends of the Temple at Jerusalem all represent that this site was an instrument of an elaborate sacred science.

John Michell had written, "A legend of the temple at Jerusalem says that it was the center of a network of underground water channels, which spread outward to all parts of the country." Again he writes, "The cosmically proportioned temple spread the holy energy of the Ark throughout the country, and peace and happiness prevailed." Michell says that this joyous exaltation and dancing is practiced by the Jews at most of their festivals, especially the Season of Our Joy after the fruit harvest in the late autumn."

Many kings and priests who officiated at these Temples of Heaven and Earth wore a special 'star-mantel' of sky-blue color ornamented with myriads of stars. This costume is reported to have been worn by Imhotep, the Grand-vizier of King Zoser of Saqqara. Unfortunately, these holy costumes were mimicked by the many charlatan imposters who made money through holy astrologic prophecy and divine magic. The great kings of the Maya dressed in the star-flower blossoms of the sacred Ceiba tree in impersonation of the Milky Way Galaxy, Our Holy Mother, who suckles us with the milk of cosmic energy.

In conclusion, it must be said that the 1859 Carrington Event that fried the British telegraph system certainly gives credence to vitrified stones at ancient sites suffering a similar blast of cosmic energy. The Giza pyramids, Glastonbury, and the Temple Mount at Jerusalem present traditions of the management of cosmic energy for the benefit of the fertility of agriculture, the mental and physical health of humanity, as well as the extraordinary accomplishments of rulers such as King Arthur and Queen Guinevere of the Grail saga and the great statesmen and poets such as King David and King Solomon.

CHAPTER 3

ENERGY ART & SYMBOLS

All around the world the symbol for the Earth is a square, and the symbol for Heaven is a circle. The logo for the Freemasons, who adopted the ancient traditions of the Knights of the Temple of Solomon, is the right-angled set-square (representing the square symbol of the Earth) and the compass for drawing circles (representing the circle of the Heavens). Compass and square appear in ancient China as the symbols of the philosophy of the wisdom of Heaven and Earth.

The 'G' in the center of the Freemason's logo is said to represent geometry, the science that God used to design the universe.

During the rebuilding of a very ancient bridge called Baal Bridge, near Limerick, in Ireland, an old brass stone-mason's *trying square* with the date 1517 was found under the foundation-stone with the following inscription, "I will strive to live with love and care, upon the level, by the square." The 'square deal' and 'being on the level (plumb)' are expressions that have passed down from the instruments of carpentry and masonry to signify justice, balance, and order in the universe (phoenixmasonry.org).

Egyptian and Mesopotamian art shows gods traveling in boats upon a cosmic ocean decorated with zigzag energy patterns as may be seen on the remains of the Circular Zodiac of Dendera from Egypt. The zigzag pattern appears to show high vibrations of energy, such as lightning. The ocean of cosmic energy has been called by many names such as aether, radiation, pneuma, plasma, spirit, air, and light.

In the culture of bees, a small percentage of scouts prospect the countryside for a new hive location for the new swarm that will leave the original nest and form another colony around mid-summer. The bee-scouts return to the swarm and communicate by dance the

Temple of Heaven & Earth

direction of their prospective new site, by describing an angle in relation to the sun and the distance away. The bee-scouts then do a waggle-dance which closely resembles the zigzag pattern illustrated in Egyptian art. For reasons unknown to date –the intensity and duration of this zigzag waggle-dance by a scout convinces the other scouts to check out the site; and upon their return they will validate through an intense waggle-dance of their own their approval of this location –or they will not dance or tepidly complete only a few waggles. I believe that the waggle-dance is the scout-bee's intuitive and scientific estimation of the beneficial energy at the new site. Since other scouts confirm or invalidate this energy estimate –a decision about this site is immediate and irrevocable –a strange curiosity that has baffled bee-keepers. The bee's existence is based upon energy management, such that they shuffle-dance, slowly rotating around the hive during the cold of winter to maintain a specific core temperature for the survival of the hive.

The Aberlemno Stone in Scotland also depicts the zigzag or lightning energy pattern. The snake above the energy pattern is the universal icon of wisdom, knowledge, and energy. Another stone at the same site shows the zigzag pattern over the doorway of a small temple which appears to radiate energy spirals.

The Art of the Picts –Sculpture and Metalwork in Early Medieval Scotland by George and Isabel Henderson shows the energy zigzag (*figures* 31, 71, 85, 272) intertwined over and under a snake in *figure* 80; and across a temple; and intertwined with the double disc under the 'V-rod' & sickle Moon (*figure* 186, shown on the left, and also in *figures* 188, 246, and 259).

<u>Please notice</u> that the double discs on the left are brimming with seven energy spirals –seemingly activated by the quarter-Moon and its 'V-rod' in partnership with the 'Z-rod' between the double discs. Guy Underwood says, "The water line and *aquastat* both produce spirals of 7, and multiples of 7 coils, and never any other number (p.41)."

Temple of Heaven & Earth

Of course, in ancient astronomy there are 7 days during the four weeks of the four phases of the Moon equaling 28 days times 13 months in the lunar year (13 x 28 =364 days). This lunar year system is found in ancient astronomical sites around the entire globe.

Please look above, at image #259 at the 'Z-rod' below the foot of the cross and between two (+ & -) energy spirals (usually depicted as double discs) which are sharing energy with one another. To the right of the cross is single energy spiral spewing forth energy. Celtic knot-work appears as an energy network in the form of tapestry design. Image 80, on the left shows the energy 'Z-rod' (second panel from the top) in the middle inspiring a tall temple structure.

Image 31 shows the energy serpent in the middle of the energy zigzag, which again appears to the right of the cross in image 272 (third image from the bottom right). The double disc symbol above the Z-rod and snake (image 31) may be their 'duality of the universe symbol' which encompasses all dualities: Sun and Moon, yin and yang, night and day, chaos and order, positive and negative, male and female, and all such dichotomies. Below the cross (image 259), the double discs are counter-opposed in positive and negative fashion – and appear to be sharing or in conflict through their energies. The double disc may be the forerunner of our infinity symbol (∞).

Temple of Heaven & Earth

Thomas Karl Dietrich

The Medieval Alchemists

The alchemist, Fulcanelli in *Le Mystere des Cathedrales* tells us that the pious Gothic Cathedrals were built by medieval Freemasons in order to insure the transmission of hermetic symbols and doctrine. The churches were clothed in an esoteric mantel of stained-glass and stone art illuminating "The Great Work" a code-phrase for the principles behind God's Creation. One of the great and enduring symbols of energy was the winged-dragon. Fulcanelli shows a

photo of the Portal of Saint Anne at Notre-Dame, Paris where there was an old pillar stone of St. Marcellus touching the mouth of a dragon who is born from tongues of flames of energy coming from the subterranean earth. St. Marcellus is shown in a tranquil attitude giving a blessing with his right hand. The message appears to be that the saint is not in conflict with the energy-dragon.

The image has been widened to better show detail. It is not the original but a modern renovation of the pillar of St. Marcellus in Notre-Dame, Paris which had lost much of its detail through weathering. This contemporary statue does not show the flying dragon having any connection to the flames of energy emitted from the ground as the original stone image explicitly showed.

This context of saints and energy-dragons is constantly repeated in Christian art and story where saints take over the ancient holy sites of the people of the Golden Age whose cosmology and science centered upon the use, reverence, and ritual of cosmic energy from the heavens. The icon of St. George over-powering the winged-dragon is again a memento of the church adopting ancient holy places. The legend says that the dragon lived in a cave and harassed the locality. The energy symbol 'wings' means cosmic energy, while 'cave' means subterranean earth energy. At Mont St. Michael in Brittany St. Michael dominates the energy dragon at this extraordinary sea island estuary location which is on another Michael ley line (aka. Apollo-Athena) extending from Skellig Michael in Ireland to Mount Carmel in the Holy Land. The story of Cadmus also has its foundation myth of slaying the dragon at Thebes in Greece.

Fulcanelli also mentions the myths of Apollo killing the dragon-monster Python who guarded the oracle of Delphi, and Jason destroying the dragon of Colchis. Fulcanelli shows an image from the Cathedral of Amiens in which cosmic energy from the sky is vivifying matter on earth. The material on earth is depicted full of swirls and energy spirals as shown on the ancient iconic stones above.

Understanding Polarity in Energy Spirals

The universe produces energy through the dichotomy of opposite forces, such as night and day, summer and winter, order and chaos, male and female, positive and negative, and so on *ad infinitum*. These contentious opposites provide change and motion to keep the cosmos alive and free from the death march toward entropy.

Dualism exists in both the Heavens and upon the Earth. There is an abundance of positive cosmic energy captured at the large openings of caverns and fault-lines in the Earth. This positive heavenly energy is mixed with the negative polarity of the Earth to become a hybrid called earth-energy. At the source and fountain-head of these subterranean channels the earth-energy blossoms forth to dance with the positive cosmic energy in a sacred and balanced union of physics combining the virtues of Earth and sky. Most often this union is not consummated but held in balanced tension between negative and positive electromagnetic spirals. Sometimes, even triple spirals appear half-way, as a shadowy apparition of attempting to form a union which is vacillating between the frequency and constant tension of these opposite polarities.

The consummated union of Earth and sky creates a larger phenomenon which extends far outward from the center of the energy-portal. Dowsers and water-diviners sense the limits of this great unified energy spiral which extends an equal distance under the earth as it does into the sky. This shows that the one-dimensional spiral is really a three-dimensional orb.

In general terms, Yang is the bright positive energy of heaven; while Yin is the dark negative energy of earth. But yet, the landscape is filled with positive and negative spirals –just as the atmosphere is positive; but full of negative (leftward-spinning counter-clockwise) low-pressure centers, storms, tornados, and hurricanes –pushing and confronting positive high-pressure formations (rightward-spinning clockwise). On the negative earth there are **positive** energy tracklines used by animals and positive aquastats prevalent at holy sites. Places where positive and negative energy mingle and coexist are the meeting places of Heaven and Earth. And these places are congenial to human nature because we are a union of spirit and matter. In fact, all creatures in life are a product of this holy union with varying proportions of matter and intelligence.

Guy Underwood in *The Pattern of the Past* confirms, through his own personal energy dowsing, that both positive and negative spirals are found near to one another at ancient holy sites such as: White Horse and Dragon Hill at Uffington, Stonehenge in Salisbury Plain, Merlin's Mound, and in the genitals of the Cerne Abbas Giant. This Giant also has a positive and a negative spiral on his chest. One of the names that Underwood has heard water dowsers employ at blind springs where two water lines cross is Beth-El, 'House of God.'

Others agree concerning the physics of positive and negative poles of energy. Nicholas R. Mann in *Energy Secrets of Glastonbury Tor* explains the geophysical reason for Glastonbury's holy precinct saying, "There is an unusual three-dimensional subterranean formation of the caverns and aquifer under the conical hill of Glastonbury Tor. This geological system generates a positive charge to the water near the surface which interacts with the usual negative charge of the earth forming a series of vortex spirals turning outward and inward between the opposing positive and negative electromagnetic energies."

In many of the world's cosmologies the male (+) Sky god impregnates the female (-) Earth. In other ancient cosmologies like the Egyptian, the Sky god is female and is impregnated from below by the male Earth god. Astronomers tell us of polarity changes in the Sun. It is reasonable to assume that all bodies in motion will cycle through periods of positive and negative polarity.

At Birney Hill, England, a double-spiral presents the dual nature of the universe and the dual polarity found at most ancient energy sites where positive and negative intertwine. We also notice some straight lines that communicate directly with the centers of the spirals. This phenomenon is described and diagramed by Guy Underwood under the heading of 'combined water, aquastat, and track lines' where the aquastat splits into two straight lines, one entering and the other emerging from a spiral. The double spiral above shows just such lines cutting across the spirals and communicating directly with the centers, like some 'grounded' electrical circuit.

Further testimony of double opposed spirals comes from Guy Underwood in the *Pattern of the Past* through his own personal dowsing experience, confirms that both energy and energetic water spirals are both left and right-handed; and also discloses a wide variety of energy patterns such as loops, arcs, necklaces, geo-spirals, halos, and shadows.

Nicholas R. Mann also writes that the red and white dragons of Merlin are the red and white springs of Glastonbury, "Two simultaneous centripetal, counter-rotating…coming to a point of stillness at the center of the core…a descending and ascending dragon…or serpent-like forms of colors moving through mists that build into a shining spherical tunnel or doorway." Mann also recounts the testimony of the local resident, Ella Portman, "I learnt that the water that runs through the labyrinth under the Tor is energized by it like an accumulator…formed by the dance of male and female energies… the power of both creation and destruction."

The classical labyrinth is seven coils with passage ways turning right and left toward the goal. It should be noted that the labyrinth is found throughout the world. The exercise of walking the larger labyrinths is to find the goal by exploring numerous contrary paths; and return by liberating oneself from the cycles and polarities of the universe –for a brief psychological and intellectual moment. The labyrinth represents the larger composite union of two opposite spirals; as it guides the dance of balance and mixture of Earth and sky energy. An energy dowser with a crystal pendulum positioned at the center of the site will alternately pick up one and then the other of the two opposite natured spirals. Using a hazel rod or copper wire loop; the dowser will pick-up the larger coils of the entire precinct as he crosses them upon entering or leaving the site. Because of the polar dichotomy of Earth and sky, good and evil, night and day; Buddha and the Stoic philosophers recommend a middle path that is neither excessively happy, nor terribly sad between the extremes of religious devotion and carnal delights. This golden straight-path is frequently the choice of many of us who have been disappointed or injured by life.

Bernard Roger in *The Initiatory Path in Fairy Tales –the Alchemical Secrets of Mother Goose* Tells us that Mother Goose comes from the Egyptian cackler-goose who laid the golden egg of the universe which became mother to us all. In both Egypt and China the goose is considered to be a messenger between heaven and earth. People have noticed this great migrator who carves its flight nearly from North to South Pole and return again. Roger also comments upon the promiscuous images of the Sheela-na-gig (a world-wide cultural image) with her pendant breasts and her open sexual organ representing the cosmic genetrix of energy and life. There exist primitive ancient statues of a well-goddess with water flowing from her breasts. The goddess Anna in Britany, Jana in Sardinia, and Diana in Rome represent the Moon. Perhaps the unusual *Sheila na Gig* portray the waters of life and creation flowing from the vagina of this ancient woman goddess?

Spiral Art in Physics
Ancient art in stone is not primitive art; but rather, it depicts the fine nuances in energy, astronomy, and physics. The spiral art at Gavrinis Island in the Gulf of Morbihan is imaginative, impressionistic, and identical to the art of Newgrange in Ireland. Brittany's legends, music, and language are closely allied to the culture of Ireland.

The stones at Gavrinis appear to speak about eruptions of energy from the Earth as explicit as a modern video documentary.

Temple of Heaven & Earth

The drawings from Martin Brennan capture the dynamic flows of right and left-handed spirals of earth-energy conveyed to sacred monuments by aquifers, fault lines, and caverns.

The diagrams and photographs above seem to show powerful and dynamic flows of energy at specific sites. These flows are scientifically categorized by Guy Underwood in his seminal work *The Pattern of the Past* (1969) where he describes and tests the manifold windings of the spirals and explains many of their special medical, psychological, and spiritual effects.

The Earth Spirit by John Michell describes earth-energy as "A stream of magnetic current, fertilizing, and accompanied by manifestations of spirit...and on certain days, its seasons determined by the positions of the heavenly bodies."

Cosmic Energy brings food, life, and joy to our planet. The symbols of this extraordinary unity of Heaven and Earth were often terrestrial animals such as snakes and dragons –often adorned with wings and feathers to signify their mixture with the celestial realm. Birds were symbols for stars. Asian Flying dragons of the Milky Way, winged or feathered-serpents, and the Egyptian winged solar disc and serpents are, of course, the icons of heavenly wisdom transferred through waves of energy from the sky. Miller and Broadhurst called the Earth, "An intelligence that responded to the energies of the heavens."

Finally, the geometric images of crop circles found around the world on every continent must be considered as energy art, since energy manifestations have created them (N.B. the Heavenly-circle and the square-Earth motif). There are numerous eye-witness accounts of a lightning-fast ball of light quickly carving these crop circle into astoundingly accurate shapes and designs.

Finally, there is a key symbol of energy art from Chichen Itza concerning a Chac Mool image which exactly depicts the union of the square of Earth and the circle of Heaven. The Chac Mool has the circle on top of his head which is his connection with the Cosmic Mind. The square is upon his midsection representing his material nature precisely like Da Vinci's icon of the Cosmic Man, surrounded by the square focused upon his mid-region. The photo comes from *Genesis de la Cultura Andina* (2008) by Carlos Milla Villena:

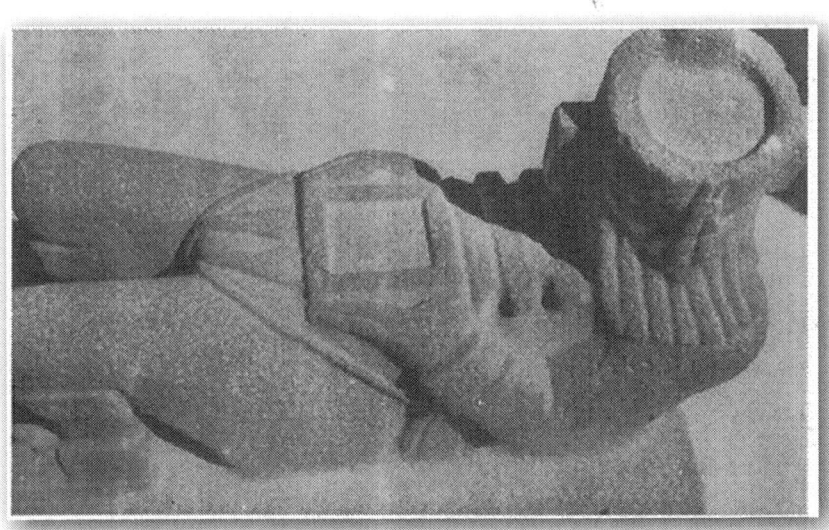

CHAPTER 4

ASTRONOMY IS THE MOTHER OF ALL SCIENCE

Ever since a bolt of lightning ignited fire upon the earth, humankind has looked to Heaven and Earth for help, knowledge, and inspiration. Astronomy has been our guide and teacher giving us the concept of time and the seasons, the great mythological ages of the zodiac cycle, global measurement, cosmic numbers, geometry, physics, the cosmology of the duality of yin yang, and all the other sciences. Many of these energy sites were discovered where a lightning strike had felled an ancient oak. Other sites were brought to notice by seeking out the special birthing places of animals, and the hives of bees whose society is totally based upon energy management. During the Age of Milk, Mead and Honey in the 'Golden Age' –it was recorded that mankind spoke 'the language of birds and animals' being more in-tuned to nature and the interconnectedness of everything in the universe. Principles of the Golden Age mixed with contemporary ideas were the basis of every Renaissance that ever restored wisdom and culture to society and civilization.

Astronomy is the Holy Grail in the Sky, the Tree of Knowledge, and the Key to All Mystery. Sky-watching created 'the scientific method' of observation in a structured and calibrated setting of wooden and stone circles where recordation, analysis, repeated review and continual observation led to the development of theories based upon observation of fact. Recordation of astronomical phenomena required the invention of symbols and numbers. The construction of observatories required geometry and measurement.

The passing down of astronomical traditions certainly inspired art in weaving, painting, and engraving symbols on bones, wood, and stone. The connection of Earth and Sky begins with wooden posts to serve as back-sights to align the heavens with an observatory, and establish the primal order of our position in the universe. This reinventing of the order of 'place within time' consecrates the observatory as the social and governmental center, and a temple of a new society. Civilization needs astronomy to lay out cities, manage agriculture, navigation, and trade. Festivals and rituals to the creative spirit of God are defined through astronomy. Social and governmental meetings, fairs and celebrations, are designed according to the cycles of the heavens. Pagan celebrations were absolutely based upon equinoxes, solstices, and cross-quarter days which were totally adopted by all modern religions for their rituals, celebrations, and needs.

Ancient people called the planets *'angelus,'* Latin for 'angel or messenger.' The planets of the solar system were regarded to be the conductors of cycles of change in politics, religion, and climate. The Egyptians regarded birds as symbols of stars and the sky. Many cultures claim to have been taught by sacred birds such as the Egyptian Phoenix, ibis, and falcon; the Hyperborean swan, and the Mexica-Maya-Andean quetzal. The ancient serpent of wisdom was elevated to the sky and clad with wings as the *Olmec Sky-dragon, the Winged-Serpent of Quetzalcoatl, the Greek and European Flying-Dragon, and the Chinese Golden Sky-Dragons of the Milky Way.*

The advent of the new Messiah was prophesized by a junction of planets, or a blazing star in the sky. The philosophy of cosmology proclaims the physics of heaven create events here on Earth. "On Earth as it is in Heaven," says Hermes, the spirit of the planet Mercury and all Hermetic knowledge. When the Greek historian Herodotus visited Egypt in the 5th century BC, the priest of the Temple of Divine Wisdom chided him and called the Greeks "children who had not one science hoary with age." Indeed, astronomy is that science which accompanied mankind in his darkest hour and helped to restore civilization after all catastrophes. Astronomy is truly the mother of all science, initiating the tools of investigations and research.

Astronomy and the Cosmological Worldview

The physics of the spinning Earth transitioning between night and day is one of the most powerful physical and psychological events in nature. The advent of darkness, night, and fear of the unseen is a monumental moment in every life. While, the softness of the first light of day slowly breaking into a symphony of pastel colors, followed by the triumphant explosion of light brings exhilaration, comfort, and hope for new beginnings –drawing its curtain over the disappointments of yesterday and the past. These primal experiences of night and day, the waxing and waning phases of the Moon and the seasons of growth and harvesting of the year seem so basic and natural that we do not realize the powerful impression that they create upon our sensibilities and mind. I think that it was Goethe who said that those who have lost their appreciation of the cycle of the seasons begin to approach insanity. The cycles of astronomy strongly determine our worldview and impression of life:

> Night & Day leads us to realizations of duality and dichotomy such as yin yang, Heaven and Earth, male and female good and evil, and order and chaos.
>
> The seasons of spring, summer, autumn, and winter make us appreciate the four-fold cycle of thermal changes of moist-hot-dry-cold inherent in all things from birth, maturity, decline, and death. The west gets storms and moisture from the jet stream; north receives the hot rays of the summer sun, east gets the early morning dry solar winds, south is cold because of the declining arc of the winter solstice Sun

in the Northern Hemisphere. The fruitful and maturing seasons further divide the duality into quarters.

Our observations of the motions, cycles, conjunctions, oppositions, and interrelationships of the planets of our solar system with each other, and the Sun and Moon –generates numbers, geometry, triangles, pentagons, hexagons, and divine golden proportions.

Through this Cosmology of understanding astronomical motion, cycles, and physics; we ascend to the highest level of truth and understanding that both order and chaos are necessary to create energy and motion; and therefore life. Once we appreciate the dichotomy –we see the burgeoning order in all things and the working of the Cosmic Mind. Because our mind is an element of the Cosmic Mind we are allowed to ask for help in discovering all matters in the universe. People have raised their faces and hands in prayer using this principle since the beginning of time.

Knowledge of the cosmos introduces us to the physics that regulate life here on Earth, and all our pursuits and disciplines from science to government, health, and religion.

Astronomy and the Great Dichotomy

One of the aspects of the dichotomy of opposites is the symbol of the mirror image. Everything in the cosmos has a double image. In order for good to exist; there must be evil –if there is light; there must be darkness –if love is present; there also is war. Fairy tales are propaganda to instill concepts of paradox, enigma, duality, dichotomy, and mirror-image relationships into the imagination and consciousness of children. Some religions profess that Jesus and the Devil are brothers. The Roman Church says that the first man, Adam instigated 'original sin.' Both of these shocking claims are examples of an effort to express the Great Dichotomy of the universe in which both good and evil exist in a world of creatures of dual nature, woven out of matter and spirit (negative and positive forms of energy).

Bernard Roger in *The Initiatory Path in Fairy Tales –the Alchemical Secrets of Mother Goose* (2013) looks at this curious dichotomy which is every present in fairy tales:

> One of the rules in fairy tales is that the most humble, modest, and weak of creatures like the decrepit old crone, a dwarf, ducks, fish, bees, ants, or ravens guide the seeker to the Golden Apples of Life and Knowledge. Why the most humble? Because the most humble was the most enlightened –who knew that all inspiration comes from on high and the *Language of the Birds*. In *The Crystal Ball* the young seeker finds the ugly, grey, wrinkled, princess with the red hair. She places a mirror in his hand in which he sees her as the most beautiful and desirable maiden in the entire world. In another tale, false is true when, "All the birds will answer: It's me, it's me. Only one will say: It isn't me. This is the one you must take." The secret of the crystal ball allows the seer to look into the depth of the crystal globe which is like the round universe. This entrance into the Golden Palace of the Sun is the ability to find the potentiality of order out of the chaos, *Ordo ab Chao*.

So, according to the alchemists, the dichotomy of the universe contains the secret of life and death: the transmigration of the energy of the human soul through material death into the cycle of life again and again. Each and every cult throughout history requires its initiates to imitate death in order to be reborn again. In Freemasonry, the president of the lodge proclaims, "All together, the living and the dead assure the permanence of the [Great] Work."

Coyolxauhqui is the Mexican goddess of the Milky Way Galaxy. She is life, yet she carries the skull of death upon her belt. She brings the cycle of life and death, creation and destruction to the galaxy. After a very long period of time she has been overthrown by her brother and is offered up to the universe. 'The Great Work' that the Knights Templar, Rosicrucian's, and Freemasons speak about is about the creation of 'energy' through chaos, change, and motion. All the esoteric mystery cults derive their foundation from the physics of the cosmos and the cycles of astronomy because they are demonstrated in the sky for all to see.

Testimony of the Astronomers
The works of Norman Lockyer, *The Dawn of Astronomy* (1894) and *Stonehenge and other British Stone Monuments Astronomically Considered* (1906), took over 100 years to gain academic and public acceptance –for their simple proposal that ancient megalithic temples were aligned to the motions of the Sun, Moon, Earth, and stars. He also proposed that the Egyptians knew that the skies were moving and ultimately changing over time. Most importantly, Lockyer determined that Egyptian temples had been rebuilt to accommodate the change in new astronomical alignments. He believed that this fact would lead to the most accurate dating of construction and renovation of all structures.

After examining the Stonehenge complex, the noted astronomer Fred Hoyle wrote *On Stonehenge* (1977) that a *simpler* structure would have sufficed to meet the purposes of a seasonal and agricultural calendar for farmers. Hoyle questioned why the stone observatory was more precise than it needed to be? If we are correct in saying that astronomy transports energy and modulates its intensity –then there are ample reasons why astronomical accuracy should be of a very high standard.

The Sun has eleven year cycles of alternating positive and negative polarities. The Moon and planets participate in the strength of the transmission of the energy from the Sun. This explains the necessity for rigorous observation to determine solstices, equinoxes, eclipses, and the conjunctions and oppositions of the many heavenly bodies, stars, and asterisms which enhance the power and flow of the cosmic energy. The necessity of 'precision observation' was needed to monitor the wide range of cosmic phenomena, especially long term climate cycles which would affect comfortable habitation and sufficient food production.

Robert Schoch in *Pyramid Quest* writes that the astronomers and builders of the Great Pyramid, "Have made the north pole of the earth and the north pole of the sky one and the same in direction." The synchronization of Earth and Sky initiates the union of heavenly events with events here on Earth. The Egyptian depictions at Edfu show the surveyor gods Seshat and Thoth who proclaims, "I hold the peg. I grasp the handle of the club and grip the measuring cord with Sehat. I turn my eyes to the movement of the stars…I make firm the corners of thy temple." Lockyer comments on Egyptian precision in that the apertures and separating walls of Egyptian temples *exactly* represent the diaphragms of modern telescopes, "A narrow beam of sunlight coming through a narrow entrance some 500 yards away from the door of the Holy of Holies…at the moment of sunrise… practically flash into the sanctuary and remain there for a couple of minutes."

The priest astronomers watch the heavens and calculate the rising flood of the Nile, the very best time to plant and when to reap. They keep the sacred knowledge of the heavenly cycles in their temple books and teach them to their initiates. They determine the sacred and the social festivals that bring joy to the people and reverence for the universe, source of the divine energy that sustains all life. The astronomers have created a cosmological worldview, science, and religion through studying the recurrence of the cycles of the Earth, Sun, Moon, planets, and galaxy. They have established laws and canons based upon the physics of the astronomical bodies and the universe –which is the absolute truth of life, death, resurrection and all things. As other kingdoms sink into corruption, and empires do not last beyond 500 or 1000 years at most; the Egyptians have endured over tens of thousands of circuits of the Sun.

Quickly Rebuilding Civilization at the Stone-Age Observatory

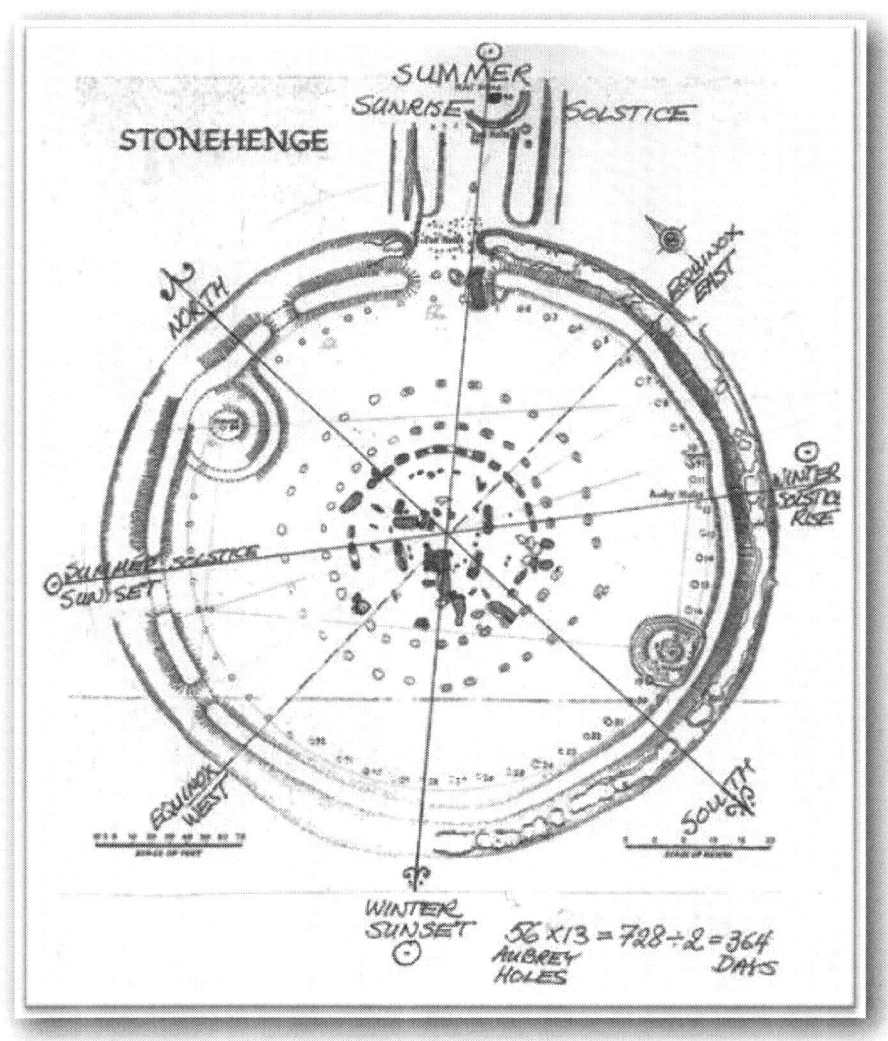

It is recorded in all human traditions that civilizations have been destroyed by tsunami, flood, drought, fire, volcanic eruption, earthquakes, hurricanes, tornadoes, corruption, wars, pestilence, and hunger. Some cities never rise again, but some quickly revive to rebuild, refashion, and restore the world that they had enjoyed by employing the help of astronomy. This is possible because astronomy has all the tools that create civilization and culture in the beginning.

The above diagram of the alignments of the Stone-Age observatory at Stonehenge shows how quickly time and space can be restored in less than a few months within a degree of fine accuracy. This involves tracking and recording the movements of the Sun, Moon, and planets that promote all human pursuits from farming, fishing, navigation, geographic and calendric survey, government, law, and religion. The first act of reconstruction is to restore the connection between Heaven and Earth. This will define the movements of the Sun and Moon in relation to our own geographical longitude and latitude —because these positions regulate the seasons, the growth of nature, the tides, and even the balance of the human psyche. The site for these observations of the heavenly realm requires a central energy portal to inspire observers to focus properly, calibrate correctly, and formulate inspired conclusions. As well, the site should be slightly elevated and southward sloping to promote good foresights and back-sights of clear horizons.

The north-south axis can quickly be marked by <u>bisecting</u> the angle of any day's rising position of the Sun on the eastern horizon, and the setting position of the Sun on the same day on the western horizon. Around the observation center, poles must be made ready to mark the extreme Sun rises and Sun sets of the summer solstices and winter solstices. Again, by bisecting the angle of these solar extremes, the cardinal direction of the east-west axis will be determined —which will exactly represent both the spring and autumn equinoxes.

Sometimes a berm of earth may be thrown up around the perimeter of the observation site to create a regular man-made horizon called a henge as a middle-sight between the foresight and the natural horizons of mountains and sea. Bisecting the aforesaid angles can be quite accurately achieved by using tightly woven ropes of grasses, fiber, and hair.

The establishment of the Four Cardinal directions of north-south-east-west is important for cities and holy sites to receive the optimal benefits of sunlight, solar power, and cosmic energy. This is a simple fact of physics concerning the astrological relationship of the Sun and the Earth. Holy sites will not function to their highest advantage, and cities laid out in grid will not receive the most balanced dispensation of sunlight and fresh winds over the course of the year if they are not aligned to the cardinal points.

After about a year of rechecking the various alignments, a very accurate instrument of solar observation is achieved. Once the cardinal directions, solstices, and equinoxes are confirmed, a pattern or mandala of the temple site is developed upon a square divided into nine boxes; or a circle defined by the six arcs of its radius drawn upon its circumference. Many temples are founded upon a square, surmounted by an octagon, upon which circular structures are then elevated. It is now important to track the extreme risings and setting positions of the Moon which will change along the horizon over a complete cycle of the lunar nodes in 18.618 years, or 6800 days (It is easy to remember the number 18.618 because 3 x 6 = 18 {the number of inches in a cosmic cubit}; and .618 is the Golden Mean Ratio φ.

The Flower of Life is the simplest and most accurate blueprint for an astronomical temple observatory, once True North has been established. First, a circle is drawn upon the energy-matrix large enough to encompass the main energy spiral. Begin your second circle where the first circumference intersects the North-South longitudinal line. Keeping all the radii equal, now draw the third circle where the North-South line intersects the original circle. Now draw circles on all the new points of intersection. The entire figure is called 'the Flower of Life' and was found on the extremely ancient (3,000+ BC) Osiris Temple at Abydos, Egypt about 50 feet below the level of the semi-ancient Egyptian temple complex. This flower pattern has also been found in China, Japan, Spain, Ireland, and India.

Cycle of the Vernal Equinoxes & Rotation of the Milky Way

Norman Lockyer found the worship of the constellation of the Bull and Scorpion throughout the culture of astronomy from the earliest time of the pyramid age. This is because the borders of Taurus-Gemini and Scorpio-Sagittarius are the points where the Milky Way Galaxy crosses the zodiac (the yearly path of the Sun). The galaxy or river of stars, crossing the zodiac path of the Sun was a powerful astronomical image which all of mankind saw and appreciated. For ancient people the crossing of the Milky Way at the zodiac sign of Scorpio-Sagittarius represented the portal of the souls returning to heaven; while the crossing at Taurus-Gemini was the entrance of souls from the Milky Way being reborn to the Earth.

The Precession of the spring (vernal) equinox completes its cycle over 25,920 years (26,000 according to the Maya). Precession moves clockwise through each one of the twelve signs of the zodiac in 2160 years –a figure which has become a holy number in Vedic cultures. The rotation of the Milky Way Galaxy around the circuit of the zodiac is possibly completed in 216 million years, which is 18 million years from sign to sign. The cycle of Pangaea corresponds to 216 million years.

Joseph Selbie, *The Yugas* (2010), notes that all cultures tell of Higher Advanced Ages ruled by the gods which have degenerated from a Golden Age to Silver, Bronze, and Iron Age. Selbie finds it interesting that nowhere is there a myth to be found recording *human progress*. History only tells of the fall from a higher state. The

Egyptologist, Schwaller de Lubicz noted several periods of decline in Egyptian art and technology; which he synchronized with the Cycle of Precession of the Vernal Equinoxes. Yet, every period of decline was resurrected by a Renaissance in which the old was mixed with the new. The admixture of the old with the new was a principle of the cosmological worldview –called Hermetic wisdom after the planet Mercury which taught humankind about the movements of the Sun, Moon, and planets.

Change of the Tilt of the Earth's Axis affecting the Cardinal Alignment of Temples & Holy Sites

The 'Cardinal Alignment' means directly to the north-south polar axis, as well as the east-west axis. Holy sites function at their optimal best when their energy channels align to the cardinal directions. Astronomy regulates the power of energy at a holy site; and functions strongest during solstices, equinoxes, and to a somewhat lesser degree during the Cross-Quarter-Days (which occur between the equinoxes and the solstices).

Alignments depend upon the tilt of the Earth's polar axis changing its tilt angle over a cycle of about 41,000 years from 21.5° to 24.5° during a period of 20,500 years, and from 24.5° back again to 21.5° in another 20,500 years. This change in the tilt of the Earth's axis disturbs all past cardinal alignments (The disruption of temple alignments has nothing whatsoever to do with the cycle of the Precession of the Vernal Equinoxes).

Norman Lockyer in *The Dawn of Astronomy* says that St. Peter's Basilica in Rome is indeed orientated to the sunrise of the spring equinox at which time Easter occurs. Orientation means *toward the east*. However, in the 9th Century AD there was a reaction to orientation declaring, "God is everywhere." Lockyer says that the great Egyptian temple of Amen-Ra at Karnak, aligned to the sunset of the summer solstice, "Forms a scientific instrument of very high precision, as by it the length of the year could be determined with the greatest possible accuracy through the brief appearance of a beam of light that would illuminate their sacred deity-image at the end of dark corridors on a sacred and significant day –as an epiphany of that heavenly body." He cautions that not every temple in Egypt was orientated to the Sun; but many were directed to stars and constellations. Lockyer comments that stellar alignment is brief and only holds true for about 200-300 years. He cites as evidence the adjustments and realignment of the axis of several temples.

N.R. Mann tells us that at Glastonbury, local legend says that a **dragon** regularly flew between Aller Hill and Curry Rivel, as well as The Mary Chapel –a path that lies directly upon the solstice alignment. Also, Dod Lane (the Way of the Dead) is exactly aligned to the rising and setting of the Sun at equinox.

All geographies located upon and nearby to 51° north latitude such as Stonehenge, present the special condition that summer and winter solstice (the extremes of solar energy and light) intersect at an almost perfect angle of 90°.

Sun, Moon, and planets rising or setting upon the horizons or appearing directly overhead in the mid-heavens experience variations in their powers –increasing at rising, highest at zenith, and lessening at their setting. The word 'Religion' comes from the Latin word for 'binding', as in the binding together of Heaven and Earth. Some astral religions worship heavenly bodies as conveyors of cosmic energy –whose true source is the universe.

Anthony F. Aveni in *Skywatchers* tells us that the pyramid of the Sun at Teotihuacan by Mexico City is set 15° 21' north of west. Some suggest that long-term continental drift has caused the deviation from true north. Brad Olsen reports that the Avenue of the Dead is 7920 feet long. The diameter of the Earth is 7920 miles.

Some Greek temples are said to have been aligned to the star *Spica* in the constellation of Virgo, alluded to in the *Book of Revelation;* and recognized by Mexica-Maya-Andean astronomy as a great power-point in the sky called 'the Great Attractor'. The astronomies of the Americas, such as the Maya, are closely focused upon the rising of the Milky Way and its culmination overhead at midnight during the course of the year. Modern science confirms that Virgo is the focal direction in which our galaxy and its cluster group are traveling in the universe.

The Gifts of Astronomy

Astronomy measures solar, lunar, and Earth time periods by calculating the revolution of night and day into 24 hours, the monthly phases of the Moon from New Moon to Full Moon and back to New Moon, and the calendar length of the year of about 365.2425 days. The ancient cosmologers created the zodiac of animal and human images along the annular path of the Sun. Many cultures also depicted the 28 mansions of the Moon's cycle through the sky. The cosmologers established pictures of the gods, heroes, and benefactors of the human race across the Heavenly sphere that told a mythological history from the Golden, Silver, and Copper Ages. These Great Ages were linked to the rotation of the Milky Way galaxy where it touched and cycled through the houses of the zodiac over 216 million years. Confusing years and calculations were not necessary when everything could be checked and dated from the clock in the sky. This remarkable and accurate chronographic system could be consulted every night in the sky, amplified by stories and myth, and complimented by lessons in astronomy, geometry, and math without the need for books or writing instruments. Every nation on Earth adopted astronomy as their common understanding and language of science.

The equinoxes (March & September) and the solstices (June & December) became the high feasts of religion, kings and queens, and the royal priesthood who perpetuated science and culture. These equinoxes and solstices are also called the **Quarter Days** because they portion the year into four quarters. The Hebrew feast of

Passover is the observation of the first sliver of the New Moon on the sunset that falls after the spring equinox. Christian Easter is the first Sunday after the Full Moon following the spring equinox. Rosh Hashanah is the first sight of the New Moon that occurs after the autumnal equinox. Yom Kippur falls ten days after Rosh Hashanah. Christmas follows the winter solstice.

Exactly between the solstices and equinoxes come the **Cross-Quarter Days** which are the social festivals of the people, sailors, farmers, builders, merchants, and administrators of local government. These festivals and fairs were for trading goods, match-making, paying and hiring servants and workers, discharging debts, contracting leases of properties, political meetings, and assemblies of courts of law and justice. With the help of astronomy, life had become more organized and secure. People could share tips on the best times for planting, harvesting, preserving foods, breeding animals, and the auspicious times for the best fishing, hunting, and times for safe navigation. The Cross-Quarter days highlight the agricultural year of blossoming fruit, May flowers, and the abundant harvests in August. Lockyer cites Devoir concerning the alignments of Lagatjar (Le Menec in Brittany) where both the May and August alignments were represented by rough stones; while the solstical stones were carefully trimmed, tooled, and occasionally polished.

Astronomy Measures Temple, City, & Countryside. The main temple of ancient cities was typically upon a high fortified position, an *acropolis*, oftentimes a volcanic stack endowed with portals of energy seeping through the caverns and subterranean geology. Often these locations were coincidentally aligned in the directions of solstices and equinoxes thereby affecting a special union between Heaven and Earth.

Since the accurate bisection of sunrise and sunset of the solstices establishes the true north-south cardinal line; and since the equinox sunrise and sunset is always the east-west line –astronomy guarantees the most accurate and indisputable survey of land, precincts, and building sites which can easily be checked and calibrated. This fact strongly encourages permanence of habitations, respect for law and order, the creation and retention of wealth through Real Estate over great periods of time. Such divine order encourages loyalty and trust in the community and the creation and stability of nations. Permanence and order promote long-lasting prosperity and investment in nation, territory, and city. Accurate division of land into estates, farms, villages, and cities contributes to a lasting and just civilization; the organization of law and society; and a tax basis to support both government and religion.

Astronomy invents written symbols, language, and number. Laird Scranton, *China's Cosmological Prehistory*, writes that the imperative to record and keep astronomical records prompted the development of the earliest forms of Chinese writing and hieroglyphic forms. He continues to say that the *Na-khi* system of writing was developed primarily to record cosmological traditions –and that their earliest symbols seem to have been adopted from an already-existing cosmology.

Astronomy is responsible for all Climate Cycles on Earth. The universe is a cosmic ballet of exquisite heavenly bodies spinning, while gracefully rotating around objects which are themselves revolving around far away centers of gravitational mass. If we look at the Earth, it is spinning like a top, while circling around the Sun which is moving around the Milky Way galaxy speeding toward a point in the direction of the constellation Virgo.

The Earth is by design affiliated with the movements of the universe, the Milky Way Galaxy and its cluster galaxies, the Sun, Moon, and other planets of the solar system. All of these factors create the dynamics of the Earth's axis tilt, wobble, orbital eccentricity and inclination, orbital relativity to the orbits of the other planets, and many other variables. The ancient Hindu cosmologers even said that the Earth changes in size. Working upon the researches of Adhemar and Croll; the Serbian scientist Milankovitch proposed in the 1920's that every one of these astronomical factors would naturally influence changes in the climate of the earth –because they create variations in the amount of sunlight and energy that reaches different areas of our planet. These findings were disregarded for 50 years until 1976 when deep-sea sediment cores revealed a 450,000 year record of climate change which matched Milankovitch's theories.

The Milankovitch Cycles:

Eccentricity of the Earth's Orbit changes from an almost perfect circle (e = 0.0005) to somewhat elliptical (e = 0.06) completing a full cycle in 100,000 years. At this moment, the orbit is elliptical –and the entire orbit rotates around the sun in a matter of about 21,600 years. The inclination of the Earth's orbit also drifts up and down relative to its present orbit with a cycle of 70,000 years. Numerous variations occur over a period of 413,000 years producing a general cycle of about 100,000 years to the invariable plane of the solar system, which coincides with our theoretical cycle of the Ice Ages. These changes also mutate the length of the cycle of the Precession of the Vernal Equinoxes. The difference between the current 6.8% solar radiation and the future 23% solar radiation would result in a totally different climate here upon earth –producing a completely new variety of flora and fauna.

The Cycle of the Obliquity of the Earth's Ecliptic: The inclination of the Earth's axis cycles between 22.1° and 24.5°, completing a full cycle from 22.1° to 24.5° and back again to

22.1° in about 41,000 years. The present tilt is about halfway between the extremes which may account for the high yields in food production which in turn are responsible for overpopulation and excessive pollution. The greater the tilt of the axis –the more severe the seasons resulting in solar radiation extremes causing great changes in food production, as well as the ability for humans to work long hours during inclement seasons. Colder summers would allow more ice and snow accumulation near the Polar Regions. Obliquity changes the position of cardinal directions on Earth, and therefore the alignments of temples and megalithic structures.

The Precession of the Vernal Equinoxes is the rotation of the Earth's axis around a celestial northern pole in about 25,920 years. Precession and Eccentricity increases the seasonal contrast in one hemisphere –with a like decrease in the other hemisphere, such that during the cold winter time the Northern Hemisphere is closest (perihelion) to the warmth of the Sun. In another 13,000 years, the Northern Hemisphere will experience aphelion during its winter time (making winter much colder), while the Southern Hemisphere will experience winter during perihelion (making it more balanced and less cold). Precession is due to the combined motions and gravitational pull of the Earth, Moon, Sun, Mercury, Jupiter, Saturn, and the other planets which are all revolving and rotating while the Sun itself is subject to larger forces in a greater context.

Dust & Debris: It has been proposed that a disk of dust and other debris is in the invariable plane, and this affects the Earth's climate through several possible means. The Earth presently moves through this plane around January 9 and July 9. Earth also moves faster when one focus of its ellipse is the perihelion. All these minute variations combine over time to manifest significant astrologic influence on climate and life upon our planet.

(The above information comes from George Kaplan of the US Naval Observatory, Astronomical Applications Department. Other information comes from National Climate Data Center (NCDC), UCD Paleoclimatology, National Environmental Satellite Data Information Service (NESDIS), and NOAA).

Astronomy is one of the major factors of our humanity because it develops and expands our mind, heart, reason, and intuitive faculties. Astronomy causes us to blossom forth by making us aware and responsive to science, religion, and philosophy. It guides us to investigate the movements of the stars and the heavens, and to appreciate the cycles of life and nature. Astronomy encourages us to look at numbers, geometry, and proportions; to research concepts about light and energy, environmental balance, and the laws and interrelationships of Earth, the solar system, and the universe.

Quotations about Ancient Astronomy

Omar Khayyam (1048-1131AD), the Persian polymath, philosopher, poet, and astronomer, spoke of 'That inverted bowl we call the sky'. Interpreting his meaning one might say that Astronomy is the up-turned Cup of the Holy Grail in the Sky –dispensing life and energy onto the Earth.

Hermes Trismegistus said, "Egypt is an image of Heaven, or to speak more exactly, in Egypt all the operations of the powers which rule and work in Heaven are present in the Earth below. In fact it should be said that the whole cosmos dwells in this our land as in a sanctuary...There will come a time when it will have been in vain... The gods will return from Earth to Heaven...And in that day men will be weary of life, and they will cease to think the universe worthy of reverent wonder and worship...no one will raise his eyes to heaven; the pious will be deemed insane –Asclepius III, *Hermetica* (600 BC–200 AD)."

Claudius Ptolemy (called the 'Divine Ptolemy'), Alexandrian astronomer and geographer (100-178 AD) wrote, "Of the means of prediction through astronomy...is that whereby we apprehend the aspects of the movements of the Sun, Moon, and stars in relation to each other and to the Earth, as they occur from time to time...the passages of the fixed stars and the planets often signify hot, windy, and snowy conditions of the air."

King Cormac of Cashel (10th century AD) reports that four great fires were lighted on the four great festivals of the Druids in **February** (Candlemas, the end of Winter), **May** (beginning of Spring), **August** (end of Summer), and **November** (beginning of Winter). These four yearly fires marked the Cross-Quarter Days of the calendar. The May fire of ***Baltine*** was celebrated by great double bonfires between which the cattle, livestock, and young people paraded to bless and purify them for the upcoming New Year. In Irish *Bal* is god, *tine* is fire. This national festival also involved rekindling multitudes of home fires, symbolizing new spirit, and energy throughout the nation, its government, and people. The important rekindling would also burn away sin, misdeeds, curses, charms, and the evil-eye. The celebration involved dancing and music at sacred trees and wells near to the astronomically aligned stones. Norman Lockyer says that the year god in Babylon was Baal, while in Egypt the year god was Thoth who was named Hermes in Greece, and Mercury in Rome.

Norman Lockyer's books, *The Dawn of Astronomy* (1894) and *Stonehenge and Other British Stone Monuments Astronomically Considered* (1906) announced the science of astronomical temple alignment.

Lockyer said that knowledge of astronomy was common among the ordinary people, farmers, and Druids of ancient Britain, while today, "We now go into a shop, and for a penny buy an almanac which gives us everything we want to know about the year, the month and the day –and we think that we have command of astronomy." Lockyer wrote that astronomy and the development of the calendar gave the Egyptian priests, "Great power; in that they were able to tell on what particular day of what particular month the Nile would rise each year, because they alone knew in which part of the cycle they were in [since their temples were aligned to the summer solstice when the Nile flood came to Egypt]."

Lockyer demonstrated that the Temple of Jerusalem, the Pyramids of Giza, St. Peter's Church in Rome, as well as countless Egyptian and Maya temples were orientated to the spring and autumn equinox and the cardinal directions. Lockyer also proved that ancient monuments such as Avebury and Stonehenge in Britain were aligned to the solstices (June 21 & Dec.21) as well as the equinoxes (Mar. 20 & Sept. 22). In addition, Norman Lockyer discovered that there were alignments to the Cross-Quarter-Days at many very ancient stone circles. While the solstices and equinoxes marked the mid-point and height of the seasons –the cross-quarter-days marked the beginning and ends of the agricultural seasons of sowing seed, blossoming, ripening, and harvesting.

Alexander Thom, *Megalithic Sites in Britain* (1967) contemplates, "It is remarkable that 1000 years before the earliest mathematicians of classical Greece, people in these islands [England, Ireland & Scotland] not only had a practical knowledge of geometry and were capable of setting out elaborate geometrical designs but could also set out ellipses based on Pythagorean triangles." He also wondered that one of the largest henges in Europe, namely, Avebury was set out with an accuracy of 1 in 1000; and that ancient Irish, Britons, and Scots had set up stations for observing the 18.618 year Metonic cycle of the lunar nodes; which contemporary scholars still claim to be of Greek origin.

Fred Hoyle, *On Stonehenge* (1977) stated, "An attempt to explain the structure of Stonehenge in less complex terms, as a means of keeping track of the seasons, for example, seems less plausible, since a much simpler structure would suffice for this simpler purpose." Hoyle concludes that the main feature of Stonehenge was that of precise eclipse prediction, saying that, "Predictions of eclipses of the Sun & Moon would have conferred power and prestige."

Christopher Knight and **Robert Lomas** talk about control in society in *Uriel's Machine* (1999), "Knowledge of astronomy remains a source of considerable social power…The key to our rapid modern scientific progress is our ability to record, access, and use information…only a tiny proportion of people in the world really understands the science that makes our society work, and this elite often uses its knowledge to control those who do not have it."

Robin Heath, *Sun, Moon, & Earth* (1999), laments, "Most people know almost nothing about the Sun, Moon, and Earth system, despite our total dependence on its rhythms" He regrets that modern science is so devoutly shackled to corporate funding, and has become "academically corporatized."

Fritz Zimmerman, *Nephilim Chronicles* (2010) clearly demonstrates that a race of ancient Native Americans constructed and surveyed countless sites aligned to the solstices and equinoxes, including the Metonic cycle of the Moon's nodes over 18.618 years. These ancient giants used measurements from the sexagesimal system and constructing astronomical henges *exactly* as large as Avebury in England (1250 feet in diameter). Giants, Vedic sexagesimal astronomy, colossal cardinally-aligned henges in America cannot be explained by the current scientific models of human development. These facts do however concur with ancient cosmological myth concerning the *Golden Age*. It is also true that President Abraham Lincoln viewed one of these giants and their astronomical sites, and commented upon it officially saying, "The eyes of that species of extinct giants, whose bones fill the mounds of America, have gazed upon the Niagara, as ours do now."

Stone-Age Calendar & Eclipse Prediction

Fred Hoyle showed how ancient sites were accurate yearly calendars and eclipse predictors. He says that both the Sun and Moon strongly influence the activities of agriculture, hunting, and fishing. Yet their movements are difficult to harmonize into one calendar mechanism. European and African sites along the Atlantic Ocean, as well as North, Middle, and South American sites and Canadian Medicine Wheels and Sun Lodges were arranged in divisions of 28 or 56 (28 + 28) stone pillars in stone circles which approximate the 28 day cycle from New Moon to New Moon, or Full Moon to Full Moon. Thirteen of theses cycles of the Moon's phases over 28 days come very close to the full cycle of the Earth's yearly revolution around the Sun (13 moons x 28 days = 364 days). For an example, the El Castillo pyramid at Chichen Itza in Yucatan has 4 staircases of 91 steps (4 x 91 = 364 days in a year = 13 x 28 = 364).

At the 28-stone circles, depressions are found in the ground behind these upright stones. A round Moon-stone was moved *counter-clockwise* one place-marker each day (= cycle of 28 days). The Sun-stone marker was moved *counter-clockwise* one hole every 13 days (13 x 28 = 364 days).

At the 56-stone circle; the Moon-stone was advanced two stones every day (2 x 28 = 56) to complete a full monthly cycle of the Moon around the circle. The Sun-stone was moved two holes every thirteen days (56 x 13 = 728 ÷ 2 = 364 days).

Hoyle cautions that close observation of the Full Moons should be made to check and rectify the positions of the Sun-stone and Moon-stone; and that Sun-stone corrections should also be made at midsummer solstice and midwinter solstice.

Eclipse Prediction

Hoyle tells us that in order to make eclipse predictions you really need to have a circle of 56 stones and holes as just described above. The Stone-Age astronomer needs to have two additional round-stone markers for designating the nodes (*nodes N and N'*) where the Moon's orbit crosses the zodiac path of the Sun. The additional two stones are placed opposite each other, and are moved *clockwise* 3 holes per year (56 stones ÷ 3 = 18.66 years, which is close to the accurate revolution of the lunar nodes of 18.618 years).

With this system, a nearly accurate calendar of the movements of the Sun, Moon, and the Nodes of the Moon's orbit is established. Hawkins originally discovered that the Aubrey circle was a perfect eclipse predictor, and was astonished at the precision of this most ancient device. Indeed some of the Atlantic stone circles in Brittany are found to track the 0.9° periodic deviation of the Moon which was not rediscovered until Tycho Brahe in the seventeenth century (Michell p.87). Astronomer Fred Hoyle has used the design of the *Aubrey Circle* of 56 holes around Stonehenge to produce hundreds of replica models in order to teach astronomy to students.

Robin Heath in *Sun, Moon & Earth* (1999) describes stone circles which are definitely *not* circular, and appear to be flattened. Many of these are extremely old with an occasional stone knocked out of alignment. Because of their extreme age they appear to be rustic and quaint, rather than the instruments of high science that they prove to be. The geometry of the flattened circles is based upon crossed lines –a north-south axis at right-angle to an east-west axis. Upon this cross of the both axis –stretch a tight rope to the west and place a marker. Swing this tight rope to the east and place a marker (A recognizable standard distance could be 6 feet, or 4 yards, or 13 cubits, or any other standard of your choosing to become your standard for your site (standard = #2 [1 + 1] in the diagram). The distance between these two markers becomes the radius for circle *B* on the west marker, as well as the radius for circle *C* on the east marker.

These two identical circles form the *Vesica Pisces* (fish-plate or fish-bladder) directly upon the north-south axis. Then a tight rope is stretched from the crossing of the north-south axis and the east-west axis. Now the radius AB is added to BO is swung down to south on the north-south axis. Now PB represents the solar year (19.618 x 18.618 = 365.24 days), PO represents the eclipse year (18.618 x 18.618 = 346.62 days). ***Image, analysis, and description by Robin Heath in Sun, Moon & Earth***

Then stones may be arranged to mark Sun rises and sets on the summer and winter solstices and the equinoxes. Also the extreme Moon sets and rises during its 18.618 year rotation of the Moon's nodes may also be marked by stones. This simple method creates a calendar clock which is perfectly accurate for the latitude of the site because of the physical observation of the rise and set points of Sun and Moon at that precise location.

Robin Heath now says, "This most beautiful analogue of the Sun, Moon, and Earth system stores their key constants *and* ancient metrology all within itself as ratios. An awesome glimpse of an ancient wisdom is now finally revealed." Heath says this because the interior triangle, BCP, imposed upon a circle of 360° simply and correctly creates the very complex expression of the eclipse year, the solar year, and the year of 13 moons:

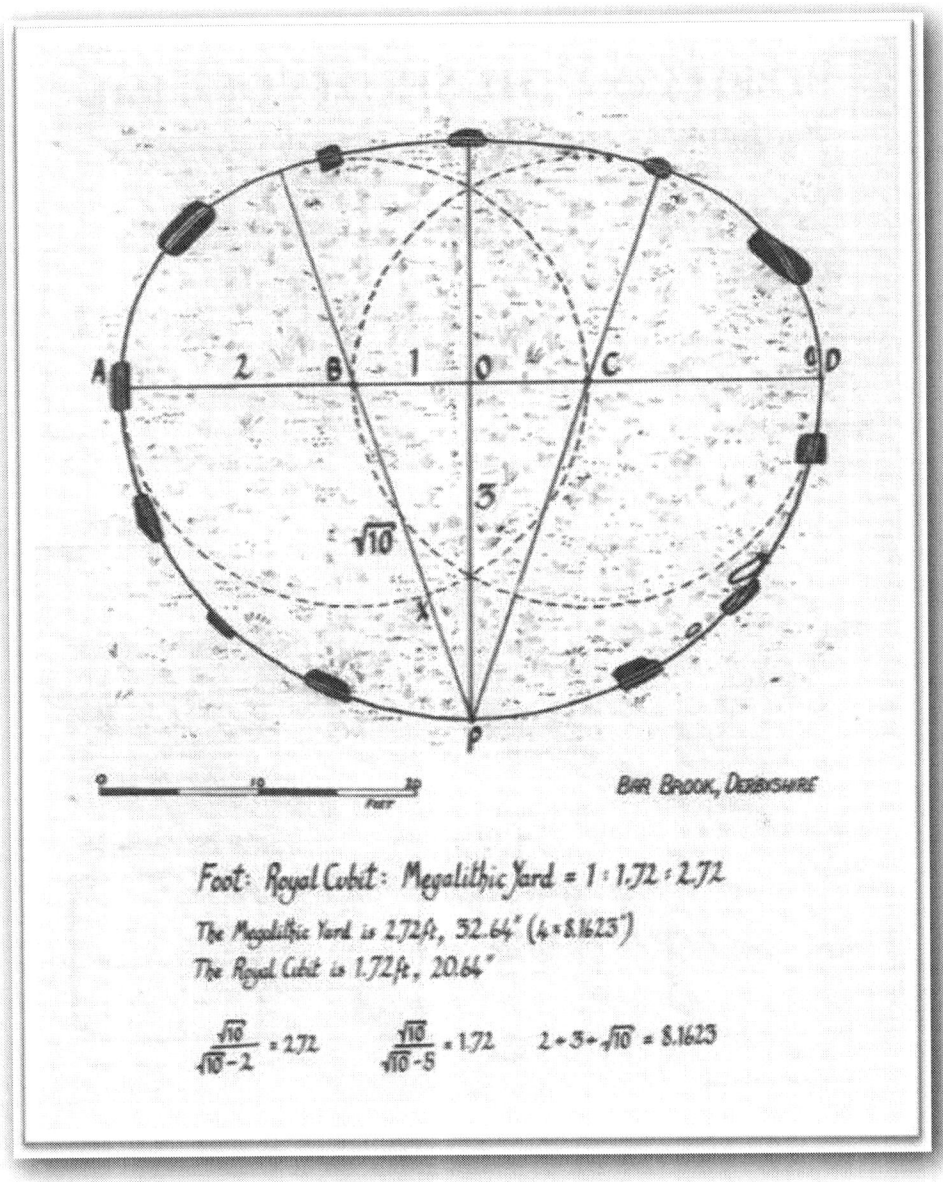

BAR BROOK, DERBYSHIRE

Foot : Royal Cubit : Megalithic Yard = 1 : 1.72 : 2.72

The Megalithic Yard is 2.72ft, 32.64" (4 × 8.1623")
The Royal Cubit is 1.72ft, 20.64"

$$\frac{\sqrt{10}}{\sqrt{10}-2} = 2.72 \qquad \frac{\sqrt{10}}{\sqrt{10}-3} = 1.72 \qquad 2+3+\sqrt{10} = 8.1623$$

18.618 x 18.618 = 346.62 days (the eclipse year)
18.618 x 19.618 = 365.24 days (the solar year)
18.618 x 20.618 = 383.86 days (13 lunation's of the Moon)

The difference between each of these three periods is almost about 18.618 days

The astronomical observatory is the first act of joining Heaven and Earth by pulling the cycles of the Sun, Moon, planets, and stars down from the sky and *marking* them with precision upon the Earth. Thus, order and justice originates in this union of Heaven and Earth – from which springs civilization and culture, philosophy, science, and religion.

CHAPTER 5

CYCLES OF CHANGE & THE FOUR SEASONS

From the time that we were children, middle-aged, and then mature, until we reached our golden years we experienced the cycle of the four seasons: the moisture and rebirth of spring, the heat of summer, the dryness of fall and ripening fruit, and the cold and death of winter. We and every living thing respond to this rejuvenating cycle which is the primal physics of life and the universe. Each day follows this cycle of moisture at dawn, heat at mid-day, dryness in the afternoon, and cold at night. We ourselves are moist when young, hot in our prime, dry in our maturity and cold in old age.

These cycles are the physics of the material nature of the universe that spirit or intelligent energy endows with form. Again we have to review that the universe is continually moving and changing through a dichotomy of opposite opposing forces: darkness and light, night and day, woman and man, good and evil, and so on. Ancient philosophers agree that the universe is formed by the opposites of Chaos and Order. Heraclitus' view is that the cosmos is in constant conflict. The composition of opposites sustains everything in nature. Good and evil, just and unjust are simply mirror images or the opposite sides of the same single thing. John Michell calls cosmic duality –"dynamic equilibrium…and…the complementary and reflexive nature of the universe" The Asian philosophers never call Yin and Yang –but always say Yin Yang because the forces are complimentary and responsive. This implies that energy is held in tension between two opposites that promote the vibration necessary to move energy.

This principle of physics is beautifully illustrated in the ancient book of Chinese wisdom, the *I Ching, Book of Change*. Yin Yang describe the astronomical cycles of Heaven and Earth.

Yin is dark, negative, female, Moon and Earth, wet and cold, revolving counter-clockwise on Earth and across the sky.

Yang is bright, positive, male, Sun and Heaven, dry and warm, revolving clockwise on Earth and across the sky.

Taoist Master Alfred Huang in his definitive translation of *The Complete I Ching* (1998) tells us that this 'Heavenly Book' was banned by the Communist government which took over China in 1949. According to the *I Ching*, "Every country has its destiny and every person has his or her fate, but everyone still has freedom to make their own choices...when events proceed to their extremes they give birth to their opposites." This holy book of ancient wisdom concerns the cosmology of the union of Heaven and Earth. The 'Ancient Classic Truth' or *I Ching* dates back to 2500 BC in a Golden Age when its language was simple and easy to understand when the number of Chinese characters was small. Master Alfred Huang says that at first, the I Ching was purely a handbook for divination in that people consulted the will of Heaven and Earth before approaching any important decision.

Originally, Master Fu Xi reported on the dichotomy of yin yang surrounded by eight trigrams of only three lines representing the rising and falling thermal energy sequence of cyclical change like that of morning-noon-evening-night; spring-summer-autumn-winter, New Moon-First Quarter-Full Moon-Last Quarter, and so on. It seems evident that the I Ching is directly derived from astronomy, such as the equinoxes and solstices, and the eight cardinal directions of the compass. King Wen of the Zhou Dynasty increased the three-line *Gua* trigrams into hexagrams of six lines introducing more subtleties into the system. Since the I Ching is a diagnostic tool for examining change based upon the number eight, this factor of eight (8, 16, 32, 40, 48, 56, 64...888) has become a lucky symbol in Chinese culture.

Master Alfred Huang says that according to the I Ching, two of the main tenants of change are that, "Everything is in a continuous process of change...when situations proceed beyond their extremes, they alternate to their opposites."

The Wikipedia writer says that one should never say yin *and* yang; but only *yin yang* because these opposite and contrary forces are so *complimentary* and flow into and out of one another (4/25/16). This is a reference to cosmological principles of the universe which moves and changes, yet lasts forever. The only problem of a *complimentary* yin yang icon is that it is revolving *clockwise* only and not in both directions.

The Astronomical Cycles

Astronomy creates temperature variations of moist-hot-dry-cold in **counter-clockwise** cycles. Astronomy creates cycles of cold-dry-hot-moist in **clockwise** cycles. The Yang *yao* are represented by the number nine, while the Yin *yao* are represented by the number six.

The Northern Hemisphere of the Earth spins (rotates) **counter-clockwise** every day and therefore the dawn is moist, mid-day is hot, afternoon is dry, and night is cold.

Every day from our perspective, the Sun appears to move **clockwise** across the sky.

The Moon appears in the west and moves daily about 13° **counter-clockwise** across the sky. Therefore, New Moon is moist, First-quarter is hot, Full-Moon is dry, and Last-quarter is cold.

During the 12 months of the year the Sun appears to move **counter-clockwise** through the signs of the zodiac. Therefore, spring is moist, summer is hot, autumn is dry, and winter is cold. The I Ching refers to the cycle of the seasons as: originating, developing, maturing, and declining.

During the Precession of the Vernal Equinox the Sun moves **clockwise** through the zodiac during a complete cycle of 25,920 years (2160 years per sign). Therefore, the ages change from cold-dry-hot-moist.

The Milky Way Galaxy spins **counter-clockwise** (moist-hot-dry-cold) through the houses of the zodiac in 216 million years.

Most likely, the revolution of the Milky Way Galaxy would be **clockwise** through the universe.

These counter-opposed cycles rotating clockwise and counter-clockwise ensure a balanced sequence of climate variations upon the Earth. Because the universe is a dichotomy of chaos and order, most philosophies recommend stoicism, balance, harmony, and the safe path in the middle. The I Ching also adopts the Confucian Doctrine of the Mean (Chung Yung) –being without inclination to either side; to remain central. By blending the energies of yin yang they believe that they achieve harmony. The Trigons of the Conjunctions of Jupiter and Saturn, the Shekinah Cycle of Mercury and Venus, and all astronomical cycles conform either the physics of moist-hot-dry-cold or, cold-dry-hot-moist cycle.

There are over 200 versions from different cultures concerning the Great World Flood, from the story of Noah landing on Mt. Ararat, to the Peruvian version of the ark full of animals landing on the Island of the Sun at Lake Titicaca. Ancient Vedic and Chaldean cosmologers, as well as the Hopi Anasazi of the Americas record that there were great cataclysms of destruction during the extensive period of the cycles of the Milky Way Galaxy (*The Culture of*

Astronomy). Traditions report that the Earth itself has gone through the four great cataclysmic events of Global Fire, the World Drought, the Great Flood, and a forthcoming Worldwide Ice Age –to counteract the general cycle of moist-hot-dry-cold. Hindu cosmology speaks of the beginning of the sleeping stage of Brahma: *The whole world dries up, and Vishnu becomes the wind, the cosmic life-breath, and pulls out of all creatures the enlivening air. Finally Vishnu becomes fire, then water; and all elements* (*The Mythic Image*, Joseph Campbell). This great cosmic cycle is about 216 million years long producing a great variety of change. But, even during the shorter 25,920 year cycle of Precession, the seat of world power appears to move gradually around the globe.

Yin Yang, and the eight Trigrams characterize the primordial elements of water, fire, earth, and air, as well as the clockwise and counter-clockwise flow of the opposed astronomical cycles. In the diagram below the <u>clockwise</u> cycle of elements is: moist-Lake, hot-Thunder, dry-Mountain, cold-Wind. The <u>counter-clockwise</u> cycle of elements is: moist-Water, hot-Heaven, dry-Fire, cold-Earth, completing the eight trigrams.

LAKE moist

HEAVEN (hot)

WIND cold

FIRE (dry)

WATER (moist)

THUNDER hot

EARTH (cold)

MOUNTAIN dry

The I Ching and *Feng-Shui* are based upon astronomy, beginning with alignments to the four cardinal directions north-south-east-west; as well as the winter and summer solstices, and the equinoxes. A system of cardinal rules was actually formulated for builders concerning the alignments of cities, houses, temples, and graveyards. The main idea is the location of energy spots, and creating a perfect balance (Qi or Ch'i) between the negative and positive polarities of the energy of yin and yang.

Testimony Concerning the Duality of the Cosmos
In the *Book of Genesis* Moses (1393-1273 BC) confirms that God separated the light from the darkness. The cosmos is based upon opposites, just as the cycles of the swinging pendulum brings fame and fortune as well as sorrow and suffering into every life.

Zoroaster (6000 or 625 BC) believed in ethical dualism, the struggle between truth and lies, right and wrong, and order and chaos.

Hesiod (750-650 BC) says that first there was Chaos of whom were born Darkness and Night. And the goddess Night gave birth to the Day whose light filled the universe.

Pythagoras (570-495 BC) says that the universe has antipodes of up and down. He also says that light and darkness, and hot and cold have equal parts in the universe.

Heraclitus (535-475 BC) said that conflict and war are the mother and father of all things.

Protagoras of Abdera (490-420 BC) who said that 'Man is the Measure of All things' affirmed that in any and every question that two opposing arguments can be constructed to support either side.

Epicurus (341-270 BC) of Greece spoke of *"ataraxia"*, the tranquility and the imperturbable soul. His watchword was keeping things in balance, and that pleasure is the absence of suffering and pain.

In *Aztec and Maya Myths* Karl Taube writes that, "To the Aztec, creation is the result of complimentary opposition and conflict. Much like a dialogue between two individuals, the interaction and exchange between opposites constitute a creative act. The concept of interdependent opposition is embedded in the great creator god, *Ometeotl*, God of Duality, who resides in the uppermost thirteenth heaven of *Omeyocam*, Place of Duality." This location possessed both male and female creative principles.

Ancient stories of the duality and union of Heaven and Earth are found among the nations of the world: Egyptian Nut the Heaven-goddess spreading herself out over Geb the Earth-god; Aztec Coatlique being impregnated by a ball of feathers from the sky; Greek Ge (Earth) and Uranus (Heaven) joining in union; Hebrew angels consummating with the daughters of men; and Chinese Yin (Earth) mixing with Yang (Heaven).

In Egypt, creation begins with the Monad splitting itself into two equal parts, like cell-division.

Day and night, summer and winter originate in astronomy, and constitute an undeniable logic and physics of nature and the universe. But it is Yin and Yang that portray the most sophisticated versions of duality and motion. Though they split apart, each retains the seed of the other as a dot of white in black yin, and a dot of black in white yang. Creation begins through opposites –positive and negative polarity in motion and cycles. This is the physics that drives the universe.

The Chinese *Book of Change* revels the cosmic cycles created by the swirling symbols of Yin Yang which stand for all polarities and the cycles of motion such as male and female, day and night, summer and winter, and Heaven and Earth. Laird Scranton, *China's Cosmological Prehistory*, details the cosmology of opposites: Earth versus Sky, wind versus still air, fire versus wood, and water is aligned opposite dryness and drought.

Laird Scranton, *China's Cosmological Prehistory*, cites Richard Smith who calls the Book of Change, "An effective microcosm of the fundamental process of the universe." Scranton writes that the first of the Sage and Virtuous Emperors were the mythical couple: Fu-xi shown with a carpenter's square (to measure the square-ness of the Earth) and his wife, Nu-wa shown with a carpenter's compass (to measure the roundness of the Heavens). Apparently there is nothing new under the Sun, since the symbols of the Freemason's are the carpenter's compass and square. Scranton equates Nu-wa with the

From China's Cosmological Prehistory, Nu-wa and Fu-xi holding the tools of creation –a compass and a right angled square – later adopted by the Freemason's as their prime symbol. The god and goddess' lower bodies are the tails of the Heavenly Serpent of all knowledge. God and goddess weave chains of stars from two circles, one at their heads and another at their tails.

Egyptian goddess Neith, credited with having woven matter. He also writes that one of the fundamental processes of creation involves the initial conception of the two realms of Heaven and Earth. In some traditions, the separation is sustained by four pillars which separate and distinguish Heaven from Earth.

Testimony of the Four Elements & the Ogdad of Eight

In Egypt, Moustafa Gadalla, *Egyptian Divinities*, tells us that the fabulous cities of Memphis, Heliopolis, Thebes-Luxor, and Hermupolis, all worshiped the *Ogdad* of eight deities who were the four dual-gendered twins. These were the four primordial forces of Nun, the great cosmic ocean, split as twins, *one male and one female.* The four males were symbolized as frogs, while the four females were represented as snakes.

In Asia Minor, Heraclitus (c.535 BC) of Ephesus proclaimed, "Everything is change –everything flows (*Panta Rei* and *Omnia mutatur*) –nothing stays at rest." The Eastern philosophies also support these ideas such as the Japanese concept of the changing river (*Hojoki*), and the Buddhist doctrine of impermanence. Many of our ideas about health revolve around balance and harmony. Heraclitus (nicknamed 'the Riddler') said, "All entities are characterized by pairs of contrary opposites...all things come into being by the conflict of opposites...strife is justice...all things come to pass from logos...the path up and down are one and the same...we are and are not...no man steps into the same river twice...the upward-downward path goes on simultaneously and instantly, and results in hidden harmony."

In India, Wilkins in *Hindu Mythology* says that *Purusha*, the soul of the universe was all alone and did not enjoy happiness; and therefore into two parts, such as husband and wife. Other accounts say that *Purusha* first created the waters and threw a seed into them which became a golden egg of luster equal to the Sun; in it *Purusha* was born as Brahma, parent of the entire world. After dwelling for a year in the egg, the glorious being, through contemplation, split in twain, half male and half female.

In Sicily, Pythagoras divided man's life into four seasons: 20 years a boy (spring), 20 years a youth (summer), 20 years a young man (autumn), 20 years an old man (winter). He proclaims that the principle of all things is the Monad. From the Monad springs the undefined Dyad; and from these two entities spring numbers, points, lines, figures, solid figures, bodies, elements of fire, water, earth, air –which interchange into one another completely, and combine to produce the universe.

In North America the Hopi recognized the destructions of the world by fire, drought, water, and ice.

In Central America, Hunbatz Men, *The 8 Calanders of the Maya*, describes the "Aztec Calendar Stone" which was originally positioned in the center of ancient Mexico City (*Tenochtitlan*) in the central square called the *Zocalo*. The renowned Mexican astronomer and archaeologist Don Antonio de Leon y Gama (1735-1802) determined that the stone showed the eight cardinal points around the circle: north, summer solstice rise, equinox rise, winter solstice rise, south, winter solstice set, equinox set, and summer solstice set. The stone is also called *Tonal Machiotl*, Stone of the Sun –The Diagram of the Suns that Have Been and Will Be.

LaViolette in *Earth under Fire* recognizes what he calls the *zodiac cipher*; the 12 houses of the zodiac following the pattern of moist-hot-dry-cold. The twelve signs of the zodiac are divided into three triangles of the four elementary natures ($12 \div 4 = 3$):

Moist: Scorpio, Pisces, Cancer
Hot: Aries, Leo, Sagittarius
Dry: Taurus, Virgo, Capricorn
Cold: Libra, Aquarius, Gemini

These energetic cycles of moist-hot-dry-cold in constant motion apply to every phase and condition of life:

Birth-maturity-decline-death
Beginning-growth-corruption-dissolution
Friendship-love-hate-separation

Youth is moist, supple & fresh
Middle age is hot, eager, and on fire
Maturity is dry, stable & formed
Old age is cold, stiff & inflexible

Morning is moist with the dew-fall.
Noon is hot with the overhead Sun.
Afternoon is dry as all moisture has evaporated from the air.
Night is cold as warmth and light disappear.

New-Moon to first-quarter is productive of *moisture*.
First-Quarter till full-moon is *hot*.
Full-Moon to last-quarter is *dry*.
Last-quarter to new-moon is *cold*.

Spring is moist. Simmer is hot. Autumn is dry. Winter is cold.

Even the 'four-stroke, internal combustion engine' is modeled upon the cycles of moist-hot-dry-cold: wet fuel –ignition by fire –expansion by dry air –retraction of the cylinder by cold vacuum.

IMAGES OF THE FOUR ELEMENTARY NATURES
The Four Evangelists represent the zodiac signs: Scorpio, as an eagle (Moist), Leo the lion (Hot), Taurus the bull (Dry), and Aquarius the man (Cold). The mythical monster called the griffin has the head

and chest of an eagle (Scorpio-moist) and the body of a lion (Leo-fire) representing the duality of heaven and earth.

The Riddle of the Sphinx at Delphi
Paul LaViolette begins *Earth under Fire* by solving the great riddle of antiquity about the body of the Sphinx in Delphi and the Sphinx card of the Tarot. This Sphinx has the hindquarters of a bull (Taurus-dry), the foreparts of a lion (Leo-hot), the wings of an eagle (old version of Scorpio-moist), and the head of a human (Aquarius-cold). The

Sphinx therefore represents the physics of the cosmos and the astronomical cycles of moist-hot-dry-cold. Again, Paul A. LaViolette in *Genesis of the Cosmos* (p.177) reports that during a lecture in 1785, Alessandro Cagliostro, a renowned Sicilian scholar of the esoteric, stated that the ancient Magi wore the Rose Cross around their necks on a golden chain. Its origin was attributed to the god Hermes-Thoth founder of the order of the Magi. The ancient secret letters around the cross were replaced by the bull (Taurus), lion (Leo), eagle (Scorpio), and water-bearer (Aquarius).

The Etruscan Chimaera has the head of a lion (Leo-hot), the tail of a snake, and a goat's head on its back (Capricorn-dry). The Hittite Chimaera has the head of a human (Aquarius-cold).

Feng-Shui & Geo-Pathic Stress

Feng-Shui means "wind and water" and discusses buildings and environments in terms of the elementary forces of energy that bind universe, Earth, and humans together. The ancient Chinese art of Feng-Shui deals with electro-magnetic radiation and anomalies in the environment. Feng-Shui identifies places of unhealthy imbalance between positive and negative forces, and attempts to mollify and redirect these forces to promote a healthy environment. In our Energy chapter we have already mentioned how the Chinese drove cows and sheep into large fenced areas to see where they would lie down to rest, sleep, and give birth. Here they would build their homes which were free from Geopathic Stress lines (GS lines).

The magnetic compass was especially created for centering the balance of *Feng-Shui* because it determined the astronomical directions in terms of the electro-magnetic flows of energy from the Sun. East was designated as the Green Dragon of the Spring Equinox, shown by the star *a' Scorpionis*. South was the Red Phoenix of the Summer Solstice, and the star, *a' Hydrae*. West was represented by the White Tiger of the Autumn Equinox, and the star *a' Tauri* in the Pleiades. North came under the auspices of the Dark Turtle and the

Winter Solstice, and the stars *a',b' Aquarii*. Throughout China there still remain some pockets of the old preserved *feng-shui* forests –the earliest examples of environmentalism. It is interesting to note that the star *a' Scorpionis* and the star *a' Tauri* were the Spring and Autumn Equinox during the cycle of the Precession of the Vernal Equinoxes between the time of 17,280 BC to 15,120 BC.

During 1928-1929 Gustav von Pol organized his fellow citizens armed with dowsing apparatus to map a field survey of electro-magnetic forces in their South German home village of Vilsbiburg to identify places of potential harmful radiation. He wrote a book, *Earth Radiation as Cause of Cancer and other Illnesses* (1932, *Earth Currents* in English). In 1969, Guy Underwood, *Pattern of the Past*, wrote that animals would not use these energy sites unless they offered health-giving and restorative properties. Underwood specifically mentions a doctor friend who 'had found that sufferers had been sleeping over water lines, and that their condition improved immediately when their beds were moved'.

The Irish energy-dowser Brendan Murphy has catalogued thousands of cases of cancer causing sites, and has attempted to gain recognition for his findings by the Irish Cancer Society, but in vain. Brendan Murphy is featured in the *Geopathic Stress Documentary* (2012, posted on YouTube.com by Siobhan Croke). Murphy gives a very simple and compelling explanation of the cancer-causing effects of direct exposure to electro-magnetic radiation. The human body loses on average about 500 million cells every day. During undisturbed restful sleep the brain sends signals to the body to initiate the process of mitosis in which cells split and divide to replenish the destroyed cells of each day. Imbalanced electro-magnetic radiation interferes with this vital process of cell restoration and places the immune system in exceptional danger.

Murphy and his college, an English scientist, examined Johnstown Castle and Castle Barrow –and found that the 18th century builder had managed to neutralize all energy lines entering both properties. The English scientist confirmed every location of energy lines and geo-magnetic anomalies with a modern scientific apparatus called a geo-magnetometer. He also said that these force lines –being electro-magnetic in nature –can be diminished by magnets, large pieces of iron placed over them in the ground, or deflected by copper rods. The geo-magnetometer distinguishes Curry Lines, which appear over subterranean water, from Hartman Lines which are associated with mineral deposits. It has long been confirmed by water dowsers that fruit trees over certain energy spirals bare limited and small fruit. Geopathic Stress lines have also been associated with infertility.

Geopathic Stress Lines

New Age Dowsers recognize Earth-energy lines that are overloaded with negative energy. These *Geopathic Stress Lines* are out of balance and create harmful environments that produce cancer and other ills. Dr. Joseph Kopp illustrates these lines by left-handed tree-malformation winding, tree cancers, trees which have become lightning magnets, vegetation decay, harmful sleeping places, and 'accident black spots' where motorists have repeatedly swerved and lost control of their vehicles.

Richard Creightmore (*web-pages. Isabel Barros. Wexford, Ireland*) writes about *Feng-shui* as follows: When the British wished to construct a railway line over the sacred Lung Mai, or 'dragon veins' around Shanghai –Chinese geomancers petitioned local businessmen to buy and dismantle this disruptive outrage upon the *Feng Shui* of their city. In British culture there is no general outcry with environmental pollution, scarring from railway and motorway cuttings, bridges, quarries, tunnels, mines and underground bunkers, steel pilings, gas, electricity and water mains, sewers, and building foundations.

The resulting etheric disharmony manifests as a lowered quality of the local natural life forces, often through the medium of what have been known in European geomancy as 'Black Streams' —local capillary meridians of energy associated with streams of underground water flow whose yin yang balance has been distorted on the side of excessive yin. Ascendance of degenerative over generative and regenerative influences occurs in places lying directly over such streams. These 'black streams' are known in the Feng Shui tradition as lines of underground '*Sha*' or toxic energy, in contradistinction to the 'white streams' that carry healthy, generative and regenerative energy or '*Sheng Qi*'.

Just as local geology determines the local soil and vegetation; it also affects human consciousness. People who live and work on clay soils are different to those on chalk soils. People in river valleys are different from those on hilltops in their vision of life. Many of the centers of concentration of holistic thinkers in Britain today lie in sandstone districts where the higher quartz content of sandstone perhaps amplifies the spiritual possibilities of human consciousness. The anciently-venerated sacred places of Delos (Greece) and Deya (Majorca) are both set in rings of hills high in ironstone. Granite districts are relatively high in natural radioactive elements, such that the exposure to background ionizing radiation of dwellers in moorland Cornwall or North-East Scotland is estimated at 25% above the United Kingdom national average and 300% more for those who live in houses built of granite blocks. Underground water streams and geological faults are known to have an effect on the geomagnetic and etheric fields around them. The new science of geo-pathology is growing. Dowsers, physicists and engineers are presenting information couched in terms of electromagnetism. The etheric earth forces present a lower-octave reflex geomagnetic fields measurable with electromagnetic instruments. Where local disturbances in the geomagnetic flux occur, so-called areas of geopathic disturbance, there appears also some disruption to the biological regulating mechanisms of living organisms. The importance of the natural geomagnetic background to body equilibrium was comprehended in the early manned space flights. Geopathicly disturbed zones may differ from surrounding regions in the degree of ionization, from altered electro-magnetic field charges; in AC changes; in enhanced electrical resistance; in altered acoustic levels and radio reception; and in increased gamma radiation. Associated also with such areas are increased 'occult' phenomena. The relationship between haunted houses and ley-line crossings is well known. Astral projection is easier and stronger along the paths of ley-lines. As the Earth rotates on its axis, it functions as an electro-magnet, generating electrical currents in the molten metals found within its core, and an electromagnetic field on the surface which oscillates at an average frequency of 7.83 Hz, which is almost identical to the range of alpha human brainwaves. Life on earth has evolved with this background magnetic field, and creatures are accustomed to living within its presence and are able to cope with the slight fluctuations over time caused by electrical storms and the sun's activity. The Physicist W.O. Schumann identified this frequency in 1952, and it has become known as 'brainwaves' or Schumann Waves. The space agency NASA has had to build Schumann Resonators into their space shuttles in order to artificially generate this electromagnetic frequency, which is known to safeguard the health of astronauts when they are beyond the influence of the earth's vital frequency. Geopathic stress (GS) represents a distortion of this natural frequency by weak electromagnetic fields created by streams of water flowing underground, geological fault lines, underground caverns, and certain mineral deposits (notably coal, oil, and iron). For example, where the inner Earth's vibration of 7.83 Hz crosses a water vein 200 – 500 feet below ground, stress lines vibrating at up to 250 Hz can be created. Man-made disturbances to the earth's surface can give rise to further distortions, including quarries and mines; road and rail cuttings and embankments; building foundations, especially tall buildings with steel pilings; tunnels, sewers, drains, buried utility pipes and wires; as well as artificially created electromagnetic fields from overhead or underground cables and electricity-generating stations and sub-stations. Any distortion of this 7.83 Hz level creates a stress with the potential to weaken the immune system of any mammal living above the distortion, leading to greater susceptibility to viruses, bacteria, parasites, environmental pollution, degenerative disease, and a wide range of health problems. Many dowsers use a 0 – 16 scale known as the Von Pohl scale to measure the strength of geopathic stress, in which 0 represents the healthy 7.83 Hz Schumann frequency, and 16 an extremely strong locus corresponding to 250 Hz. For example, people who are sleeping on a GS locus of 9 or more (perhaps a combined score from the presence of several geopathic features) are likely to develop cancer.

Sleep Deprivation

As noted above, Geopathic Stress interferers with overnight cell reproduction –which will destroy the entire human body over time. It also stands to reason that any lack of sleep will have a profound effect upon physical and mental health, personality, attitude, and longevity. Young people addicted to marijuana or alcohol like to stay up late at night watching television and playing video games. The next morning they have difficulty waking up to the alarm clock for work. They do not feel so well because of the lack of sleep; and resort to self-medication with more drugs. Another day is wasted, and they slip into a vortex of degeneration. Fulcanelli the alchemist directs that the philosopher should always respect the properties of opposites. He writes, "A portion of the first chaos has remained in the world." Night is as important as day –because recuperation takes place in the darkness. Cell production, metabolism, digestion, transformation into blood and organic substance occurs during the tranquil sleep of night. Here too, the sacred dew falls from the sky producing divine nourishment from heaven as the jelly-like *Nostoc* and Manna. Indeed, one of the most powerful cycles in the universe is the ordinary rotation of night and day. This is because all our hopes and dreams about life are enacted upon this simple revolution. The cycle of the seasons of the year provides April's moist showers to bring May flowers, and the warmth of the summer Sun, as well as the dryness of autumn firming the ripening fruit and crops, till the cold winter allows nature to sleep, lie fallow, and rejuvenate again. Those who have lost their connection with the cycles and the seasons –are lost indeed.

Sleep and Diet

In regard to the above mentioned benefits of sleep, it is also appropriate to turn to the subject of diet and health from a cosmological viewpoint. In the Golden Age people understood that energy is available at holy sites, through sunlight, at dawn, through sleep and rest, and countless other avenues. Energy through food and drink is just an extra for soldiers, athletes, hard-working farmers, sailors, and tradesmen, and rescue workers.

Therefore, when you wake up –you don't need to fill up the tank or recharge the battery because you are already recharged. A glass of water and a banana will get you where you are going. With this in mind either stick to three tiny meals a day, or go on an 'energy as needed' regime. Again, you are full of holy energy in your bones, muscle, and body; as well as extra energy from restful deep sleep. You really need to eat at sundown. This is a cosmic diet and you should align yourself to the Sun, Moon, planets, and stars. Get up before dawn and go to bed maybe an hour after sunset. From New Moon to Full Moon eat even less than you are accustomed to eat. From Full Moon to New Moon, make up for what you missed from New Moon to Full. Check the current and correct positions of the planets –not the false 'astrologic' positions based upon a vernal equinox that does not move in cycle. If you see Mars and Saturn together in a dry house and unrelated house like Virgo –you should slightly increase your intake of fluids and food to counter balance the dry cosmic conditions. Of course all this is subject to debate. I used to reward myself with a smoke of tobacco when I was working and creating something good. Now I use food as a reward. I am eating right now as I type. Do not punish yourself. Old habits die hard, and life is worth enjoying, so go ahead and splurge an extra meal which you promise to do without in the near future. Also take note of the seasons, and cut-back on you intake during summer and autumn – which you must make-up during winter and spring.

You must learn to cook all meals for yourself, and never eat processed food again. Forget vitamins, supplements, and all additives which are sending the wrong message to your body. Buy only the best organic remembering all the money that you have saved on medicines.

I have grossly repeated myself numerous times in this chapter about cycles and change through the elementary natures of moist-hot-dry-cold. But, you must realize how fundamental this basic physics is to all aspects of life and the cosmos –as well as our deepest understanding of health and happiness.

CHAPTER 6

CREATION OF NUMBERS & GEOMETRY

After the people of the Golden Age discovered energy-portals they came to recognize that energy was being modified and delivered to Earth through the Sun, Moon, planets, and stars. This prompted them to study and observe astronomy in great detail. Sky-watching turned out to be a wonderful pleasure as the Heavenly bodies were great teachers showing off their cycles to mankind which in turn revealed geometry, numbers, and proportions. Furthermore, the geometry, numbers, and proportions in the Heavens appeared in nature here on Earth as if the Heavenly models had created them by design. Later astronomers called the wandering planets *angels*, or 'messengers.'

Norman Lockyer was one of the first modern scientists to demonstrate that ancient holy sites and temples were properly aligned to the solstices and equinoxes, correctly counted the days of the year, and calibrated the extreme risings and settings of the Moon. The so-called 'Holy Numbers' are simply the completion numbers of astronomical cycles. For example, the Precession of the cycle of the Vernal Equinoxes in sexagesimal terms of Vedic astronomy is 25,920 years, or 2160 years per each of the 12 signs of the zodiac. 216 is a Vedic holy number stemming from this cycle. The Judeo-Christian *Book of Revelation* writes that 666 is the mark of the Beast or Devil. Yet, 6 x 6 x 6 = 216, the diameter of the Moon is 2160 miles, and 6" + 6" + 6" = 18" the cosmic cubit of measurement as may be seen by Da Vinci's iconic Vitruvian Man in the square and the circle. The

Masonic inspired and designed Washington Memorial is 555.5 feet tall x 12" inches = 6666" inches.

Testimony about Numbers

Dr. John Dee (1527-1608), astrologer and physician to Queen Elizabeth I, wrote in *Merlin's Secret*, "The stars which agree with their reproductions on the ground follow the celestial path of the Sun, Moon, and planets…thus is astrology and astronomy carefully and exactly married and measured in a scientific reconstruction of the heavens…"

John Michell in *The View over Atlantis* beautifully connects the universe with the Earth by saying, "The mathematical laws to which all natural growth conforms were known to prevail both in the greatest cycles of celestial motion and in the development of life from the smallest germ of a cell. These laws can be studied throughout nature, in the regular logarithmic spirals to which a budding fern unfolds, or precisely illustrated in the arrangement of seeds on a sunflower, in sea shells, and ammonites. The geometrical patterns of universal growth and form, the pentagon of a rose, the hexagon of a snowflake or of a honeycomb, all the regular shapes to which nature conforms, are present throughout the universe in every scale and dimension."

China has always preserved their culture of *feng shui* and the sacred landscape. E.J. Eitel writes, "Everything that exists on Earth is but a transient form of appearance of some celestial agency. Everything terrestrial has its prototype, its primordial cause, its ruling agency in Heaven…the mountain peaks formed by the stars, the rivers and oceans answer to the Milky Way (*The Science of Sacred Landscape in Old China* 1873)."

Ancient Stone-Age astronomy is the true fountain of all Hermetic wisdom. For, do not the followers of Hermes say, "On Earth as it is in Heaven." Our understanding of physics comes directly from the cycles, numbers, and proportions of the Heavens. Every true student of history has seen the 'Rise and Fall' of all civilizations and empires. So too do our lives follow the cycles of birth, maturity, our prime –followed by deterioration, decay and death. Progression and devolution are not ends but realities in the frequencies within the flagellations of the cycles.

The apparent retrograde movement of the planets as seen from our Earth orbiting the Sun made the planets appear to weave backward and forward in the sky –wherefore they were called the 'frolicsome, capricious goats'; while some saw them as the 'weavers of fate' or the 'the heavenly choirs' and even the maleficent 'singing Sirens' who lured sailors to their death among the shoals. On the whole, people regarded the planets as messengers and teachers of mankind –and this is the real source of so-called 'extra-terrestrial inspiration'.

Ancient people believed in 'the logic of the stars.' Our viewing perspective from a moving heavenly body is by definition 'astrologic and geo-centric'. For example, the planet Venus does not draw a pentagram in the sky; because Venus is orbiting around the Sun. But, from our vantage point, Venus does indeed and truly draw a 5-pointed pentagram star in the sky during 13 of her orbits in the same time as 8 Earth years. The 5-8-13 relationship of Earth-Venus is part of the physics of the creation of life on our planet. It is part of the Fibonacci series of numbers that produces the Golden Mean Ratio which is the most creative force in the universe.

Again, from our perspective and position in the solar system; the Sun and Moon appear to be the same size in the sky. This is because the Sun is 400 times larger than the Moon, while it is 400 times farther away from the Earth than the Moon. This enables the Moon to eclipse the disc of the Sun. The Moon exhibits astrology as it draws upon the tides of the ocean, as well as the physiological and psychological tides of the organs, nervous system, blood, and arteries of the human body and mind. The Moon even raises the crust of the Earth about one foot in height each time she passes over our head.

Even though the new Copernican solar system of the Renaissance placed the Sun at the center of the orbiting planets –for us, the Sun still rises in the east and the Moon sets in the west. With the acknowledgement of the Milankovitch Climate Cycles as the primary cause of climate change; it became necessary to re-examine the gravitational forces of Jupiter, Saturn, Mars, Venus, and Mercury as changing the dynamics of the Earth's cycle. These dynamics are the tilt and precession of the Earth's axis, and the shape and tilt of its orbit; which all create change in the amount of solar light, heat, and energy reaching different parts of the globe. Life cannot be sustained on Earth without the complete partnership of the Sun, Moon, planets, and stars.

The Drama & Dichotomy of Day & Night, and the rebirth of a new Day

From our geo-centric observatory, the Sun appears to be extinguished in the west, and born anew each day in the east. Psychologically, the most dramatic and freighting journey to which we are exposed is our revolution through night and day. The darkness engenders the fear of termination and oblivion. The appearance of light brings joy, rebirth, and hope for a new beginning where 'Tomorrow is another day'. Our Earth creates the numbers of 1 day, 1 night, 1 new day ($1 + 1 = 2 + 1 = 3$ days confirming the cycle of day and night, followed by a new day.

Earth and Sky Create the Number Four & its Multiples

All ancient cultures use the circle as the symbol of Heaven, and the square as the symbol of Earth. This symbolism comes from the construction of the astronomical observatory as a circle and a square using the vertical bisections of the sunrise and sunset markers of the summer and winter solstices to create the true north-south axis. The horizontal bisection establishes the east-west axis of the rising and setting of the equinoxes. Early nautical compasses and compass-roses on sea charts were based upon the four corners of the Earth, the quadratic numbers, 4-8-16-32-48-64. The circle of the early and modern compass is divided into 64 directions: North = 64/0, East = 16, South = 32, and West = 48. Ancient directions and sightlines were pecked-out upon natural rock outcroppings and observation points at Teotihuacan and Machu Picchu marking the four cardinal directions, which were then quartered to form eight lines, and which were then divided again to form sixteen sightlines around a central dot.

John Michell writes, "The combination of circle and square, heaven and earth, spirit and matter provides the foundation pattern of temples universally...it is the basic plan of historical cities, laid out on cosmological principles by the priestly geomancers with their ritualized science of land-surveying." Michell says that Romulus marked out the ground plan of Rome as a circle and a square combined. The *Book of Revelation* speaks of 4 beasts and that the New Jerusalem was envisaged to be a city foursquare. Ancient Central-Americans have their four gods called *Pauahtun* who reside at the four corners of the world holding up the sky and maintaining order by preserving the separation and distance between Heaven and Earth. In China the four-legged turtle with his hemispheric shell was regarded as a symbol of Earth floating through the cosmic ocean. Four represents the division of the year into the Cycle of the Four Seasons and the four elementary temperatures of moist-hot-dry-cold. The deck of cards is divided into four suits: hearts-priests, clubs-farmers, diamonds-merchants, spades-soldiers. Four suits of 13 cards each equal 52 weeks of the year.

The Sun and the Sexagesimal System, concerning the number Six

The radius of every circle will cut six perfect arcs upon the circumference of its circle. Therefore every circle intrinsically expresses

Above is a sliced Pomegranate exhibiting the creative power of six.

the number six. The circle was held to be a symbol of the Heavens. The number six is a fundamental proportion of the human body and found throughout nature in snowflakes, honey combs, and crystals.

As already noted, the mystical number **666** is the foundation of the sexagesimal system of astronomical numbers. 666 can be interpreted as 6 x 6 x 6 = 216, the sexagesimal cube. Also, 6 + 6 + 6 = 18, the number of inches in the ancient cosmic cubit. The Earth orbits the Sun at the incredible speed of 66,666 miles per hour at a distance of about 108 (half of 216) solar diameters (RbH). 666 is the sum of all the numbers from 1-36 added together. Even the first six Roman numerals add up to 666 (I,V,X,L,C,D). The ancient Pacific site of Nan Mandol is said to have been built by 333 men, which is half of 666. John Michell writes that the canonical *sexagesimal* measures: 108-216-432-864-1296-1728 were found at the Sun & Moon Pyramids of Teotihuacan near Mexico City. The cosmic cube of the universe measured 12 x 12 x 12 = 1728. The distance from the Earth to the Moon is 6 x 60 x 660 = 237,600 miles.

400 Moons of 2160 miles diameter fit into the 864,000 mile diameter of the Sun (864,000 ÷ 400 = 2160). The Sun is 400 times farther away from the Earth than is the Moon. That is why Sun and Moon appears to be the same size in the sky. The Earth orbits 108 x 864,000 (solar diameters) away from the Sun = 93,312,000 miles away. The Dvapara-Yuga Period of 864,000 years equals the diameter of the Sun. Also, the diameter of the Sun, 864,000 ÷ the sexagesimal 6 = 360, the number of degrees in a circle.

Mystics say that the number 666 represents light and the Sun, and that 1080 is the radius of the Moon in miles. John Michell says that combining 666 + 1080 = 1746 achieves a number known as *The Treasury of Spirit* and the *Pearl of Wisdom* called the balance of powers between Heaven and Earth. To show the prevalence of these special numbers, the *Salamanca MS.* Of the life of the Irish Saint Cuanna (c 590 AD) says, "Great numbers of saints and monks were soon attracted to Kilcooney by the fame of its learned and holy founder. In fact we are told that on one occasion no less than 1746 (Sun 666 + 1080 radius Moon) of these holy men assembled in conference in a beautiful meadow near the church, and there entered into a league of holy friendship with each other –surely a beautiful spectacle before angels and men in that rude and barbarous age." It is not uncommon to find these *canonical* numbers in contexts where complex numbers appear too detailed, and where general approximations could better apply. In the ancient *Book of Fenagh* by St. Caillin (before 1300 AD) the canonical numbers of 1440 (12 x 120) and 4320 (12 x 360) appear as guests at Caillin's feast.

The Eight Subdivisions of the Square creates the Octagon

The Octagon was used in the architecture of the Knights Templar. The octagon is a symbol of the eight directions of the winds as shown by the Temple of the Winds in Athens. The octagon is formed by three boxes on the horizontal with one box above and another below the middle box.

Other examples of the use of the number eight are: Minarets which are octagonal shaped domes, the Holy Ogdad in Egypt, Eight immortals of China, The Eightfold Path of the Wheel of Time, Freedom Tower, and numerous Lighthouses. There are eight octaves in music, and 88 keys on the piano. Goethe's theory of color related to music. The Cupola Dome in Florence, US Capitol 88 feet from the Potomac. Washington Monument has 8 windows and was opened in 1888. The Crab, scorpion, spider, and octopus, have eight arms. There are eight trigrams of Yin Yang, chessboard of 8 x 8 squares, 8 elite pieces, and 8 pawns. There are 8 furlongs in a mile. A "bit" is the smallest unit of data signifying Yes or No. A "byte" is equal to 8 "bits" which can represent 256 states of information (Four to the 4th power = 256; while four to the 5th power = 1024). *Sagrada Familia* is founded upon a square base evolving into an octagon, San Vitale in Ravenna is an octagon, Carolingian Octagon church in Aachen, and Little Hagia Sophia.

The planet Venus creates the numbers 5-8-13

During 8 Earth years, the planet Venus draws a 5-pointed star in the sky as she revolves 13 times around the Sun. The pentagram star is made up of lines that are all in Golden Mean proportions: 0.382 and 0.618 φ, and 1.0 and 1.618 Φ.

On Earth there are innumerable forms, flowers, and shapes like that of the starfish which follow the pentagram pattern of Venus. A horizontal slice of apple shows five seeds arranged in a pentagram pattern. The mythological beauty contest on Mt. Ida between Hera, Aphrodite, and Athena was won by Aphrodite (Venus) who received a golden apple as the trophy. The number five and the pentagram have always been associated with the planet Venus.

Temple of Heaven & Earth

Jupiter & Saturn create the Numbers 12, 20, 30, 360 & 800

Jupiter travels around the 12 signs of the zodiac in about 12 years; about one sign every year. Saturn travels around the zodiac in about 30 years. While each is traveling, they meet in conjunction about every 20 years in the sky. During 60 years they meet in three different places in the sky separated by a perfect equilateral triangle of their conjunctions. In addition to this, Jupiter and Saturn are exactly opposite to one another (opposition) again every 20 years forming another equilateral triangle of oppositions in the sky over 60 years. When this *opposition triangle* is superimposed upon the *conjunction triangle*; together they form a perfect hexagram star which Jews call the Star of David. Because everything moves in the universe –a point of this hexagram star slowly advances around the entire zodiac in a cycle of 800 years. Therefore Jupiter and Saturn create the numbers 12-20-30-40-60-800, as well as the geometry of the equilateral triangle; and the beautiful hexagram star. Synchronizing the 12 year cycle of Jupiter with the 30 year cycle of Saturn creates a 360° degree circle (12 x 30 = 360°) which perfectly accommodates the movements of these bright, *highly-visible* giant planets regarded as the time-keepers or 'chronologers' of the sky.

Mercury communicates the numbers 3 and 6, the Triangle, Hexagram & the Proportion of Pi π 3.142

Mercury creates an equilateral triangle of three *inferior* conjunctions with the Sun in 116 days. Mercury also makes an equilateral triangle of three *superior* conjunctions with the Sun in another 116 days. If these two triangles are superimposed they make a hexagon like the hexagon of the conjunctions and oppositions of Jupiter and Saturn. The planet Mercury and the Earth kiss in conjunction 22 times during 7 years (22 ÷ 7 = 3.142857→) producing the ancient canonical value of pie π.

In nature hexagonal columns are found at the Giant's Causeway in Ireland, six-sided cells construct the beehive, and human skin cells are hexagonal. Richard Heath *(Sacred Number)* quotes Robert Temple who says that hexagonal cells are found in many surfaces especially where there are energy transformations such as melting or freezing. Earth's atmosphere often forms hexagonal convection cells, which are echoes of those created on the solar surface. The honeycomb of the European bee is built out of six-sided cells. Darwin also remarks on the existence of three-sided cells in the honeycomb of some bee types

The Moon communicates the numbers 7, 14, 21, 28 & 56

The median cycle of the Moon traveling around the Earth is about 28 days. The four phases of the Moon from New Moon to First Quarter, to Full Moon to Last Quarter and back to New Moon divide the 28 days into four weeks of seven days each (4 x 7 = 28). Every culture celebrates the Moon and the number seven:

> Seven golden candlesticks, the seven days of the Creation of the world, the seven churches in Asia, seven stars of the Rishis, seven angels, seven plagues, seven seals, seven seas, seven blessings, seven notes on a musical scale, seven shepherds, six orbs of similar size fit around a seventh at the center, seven entrances to the old City of Jerusalem, the seven hills of Rome and Athens, seven circuits around Jericho, seven circuits of swans around Delos, and San Francisco which is 7 miles x 7 miles square (= 49 square miles). Their football team is called the 49ers after the 1849 Gold Rush.

In ancient cosmology there are seven cardinal directions: north, south, east, west, the Underworld, the Middle World under the Moon, and the Upper World of the heavens above. 7 x 6 x 5 x 4 x 3 x 2 x 1 = 5040 = 7 x 8 x 9 x 10 is Plato's ideal number of citizens in his ideal heavenly city on Earth spoken of in his book of *Laws*. It is marvelous that the seven days of the week with the names of the seven heavenly bodies have been universally used around the world from Bolivia to Europe to Australia since ancient times. In many cosmologies there are seven heavens, seven stars around the North Pole, and seven stars of the Pleiades (13 stars in Cuzco).

Seven is the Sabbath, 7 weeks from Passover to Pentecost. 7 x 7 is a jubilee. Gucumatz spent 7 days in the sky, 7 days in the Underworld of Xibalba, 7 days as a snake, 7 as an eagle, 7 as a jaguar, 7 as a clot of blood (7 x 6 = 42, the holy number of the Egyptians). The angels of God divided the language of the people of the Tower of Babel in 70 (or 72) different languages. Egyptians mourned the dead for 70 days.

The oldest and original symbol of the Jewish faith is the seven-branched candlestick. The Shabbat is the seventh day of rest and worship dedicated to the Creator. The seventh year, or sabbatical, is a time of rest for humans and the land which should lay fallow every seventh year. Melchizedek, also known as Melch-Zedok was an angel of the Phoenicians, said to be the father of the seven Elohim (hafapea.com 12/24/12). The *Sutra of Amitabha* describes the mystical world of 'Utmost Happiness' surrounded by seven tiers of embankments, seven layers of veiling, seven rows of trees, seven pools of crystals of every kind where heavenly music plays continually.

The number seven mixing with other numbers creates the recurrent series of 142857→. Adding these numbers together equals 27. When 27 is reversed it is 72 which is 360° ÷ 5 (the Venus number).

$1 \div 7 = .142857$ $2 \div 7 = .285714$ $3 \div 7 = .428571$ $4 \div 7 = .571428$ $5 \div 7 = .714285$

$6 \div 7 = .857142$ $7 \div 7 = 1$ $8 \div 7 = 1.142857$ $9 \div 7 = 1.285714$ $10 \div 7 = 1.42857$

$11 \div 7 = 1.57142$ $12 \div 7 = 1.714285$ $13 \div 7 = 1.857142$ $14 \div 7 = 2$ $15 \div 7 = 2.142857$

The Number 2 x 7 = Fourteen

Matthew 1:1 says that there were 14 generations from Abraham to David, 14 generations from David to the Babylonian Captivity, and 14 generations from Babylon to Christ (14 + 14 + 14 = 42, the Egyptian holy number). However, the count of persons equals 40 including Jesus (14 + 13 + 13 = 40). Luke 3:23 says that there were 77 generations from and including God and Adam, until Jesus.

The number 14 is a *fortnight* –half of the Moon cycle which emulates the creation cycle of New Moon to Full Moon, like the progression from darkness to light. The number 14 also appears as an ancient measurement of weight: one stone = 14 pounds weight. The Egyptian god Osiris was cut into 14 parts by the 14 conspirators who killed him. There are 14 Stations of the Cross in Christian churches.

The number 777 is a most important and revered astronomical number. Many sacred numbers are hidden in holy texts. In his *Aryan Invasion Debate* (p.109) Koenraad Elst tells that the *Books of Genesis* encoded astronomy into their holy writ. For example Lamech's age is 777 which equals Jupiter's synodic period of 399 plus that of Saturn's at 378 (399 + 378 = 777). Mahalalel's age is 895 = 116 (Mercury's synodic cycle) + 779 (Mars' synodic cycle). Yared's age is 962 = 584 (Venus' synodic cycle) + 378 (Saturn's synodic cycle). Important numbers in the Old and New Testament are 12 and 13 which express the monthly cycles of the Moon: namely 12 sons of Jacob plus one daughter, 12 Tribes of Israel plus the priestly tribe of Levi, 12 apostles plus Jesus. The 13 petal'd rose is the symbol of the Talmudic Torah. This manner of placing special mathematical and astronomical numbers into religious texts continued onto the New Testament where the number of fish caught in Simon Peter's net was 153, which is equal to the sum of the third powers of its own constituent figures (1 [1x1x1] + 125 [5x5x5] + 27 [3x3x3] = 153).

The Number Twenty-Eight

There are 28 lunar houses of the Chinese zodiac of 28 animals. A woman's menstrual cycle averages 28 days. Men reach their full growth and strength at 28 years of age. Ecclesiastics mentions 28 dualities in 7 verses (*a time for giving birth, a time for dying...a time for war, and a time for peace*), a priest crosses himself 28 times during Mass (*ridingthebeast.com* 7/28/12).

Sun & Moon create the Numbers and Sequence 13, 26, 52

The Earth, Moon, and Sun are all in motion. Within this system the Moon manages to travel about 13° every day from our perspective on Earth. For this same reason of multiple astronomical movements, there are about 13 New Moons and Full Moons during the course of the solar year. Ancient astronomers reconciled the relationship of the Sun and Moon by building circular observatories of 28 or 56 stones (2 x 28). 13 months of 28 days = 364 days in a year –a close and workable approximation of the length of the year based on watching the cycles of the Moon and Sun. The Temple of Inscriptions at Palenque contained 13 corbeled vaults leading to the burial chamber, representing the 13 levels of heaven; while the 9 levels of the pyramid symbolized the nine levels of the Underworld.

Sacred Number 42 of the Egyptians

Forty-two is a sacred number of the Egyptians who have 42 Nomes (city territories), gods, tribes, and sacred commandments. There are 42 rays radiating from the temple of the Coricancha in Cuzco. Six is the Vedic holy number of the Sun, while seven is the holy number of the Moon. 7 + 6 = 13 the holy number of Mexica-Maya-Andean astronomy. Equally important is the fact that 7 x 6 = 42. Egypt is a land of sixes and sevens because it is ruled by a queen who represents the Moon, and a king who represents the Sun. In ancient Abydos, the Flower of life diagram is six circles inscribed around a central circle encompassed by a greater circle creating the geometry of six and seven, and eight by including the outermost circle. Geoffrey Chaucer (1380's AD) wrote, "To set the world on six and seven." Shakespeare said, "All is uneven and everything is left at six and seven." An ancient Chinese saying holds that seven and eight imply chaos. Egyptians believed in the holiness and unity of the universe. At the last judgment of an Egyptian person's soul –they needed to recite a confession of purity; that they had not transgressed against Ma'at, divine justice, and the 42 Commandments of the 42 gods. According to Brad Olsen, Cairn L at Loughcrew, Ireland has six internal chambers encircled by 42 massive kerbstones. This site is older than

Newgrange and also uses quartzite stones. A three dimensional (3 x 3 x 3) magic cube contains three magic squares with the numbers 7, 14, 21 in their centers, and their horizontals and verticals all add up to 42, but not their diagonals. The circle of 360 ÷ 42 = 8.57142→. The reverse of 42 is 24, a two year Sun cycle, and the hours of night and day. Each die has 21 pips (1+2+3+4+5+6), and both dice together have 42 pips. Buddhist scripture has 42 sections. The Kabbalah says that God used the number 42 to create the infinite, eternal, and endless universe. Technology programming also uses the number 42. There are 42 minutes in the fall of an object through the center of the Earth, called the 'gravity train'.

Venus & Earth create the Numbers and Sequence 5, 8, 13

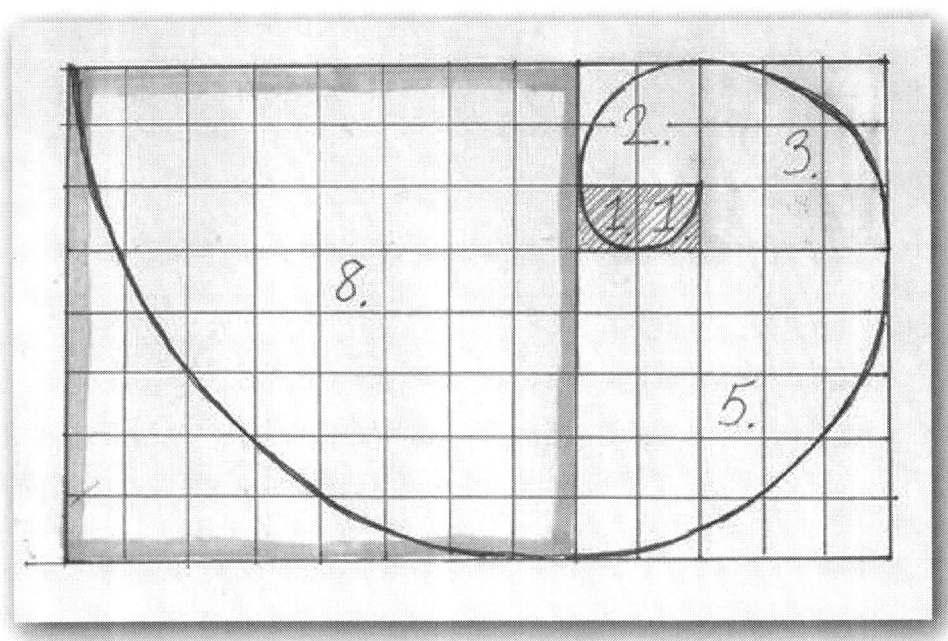

It is necessary to review the Venus numbers to properly show their relationship to the Earth and Sun. Long-term observation of the

Sun, Moon, and planets along the zodiac shows that Venus draws a 5-pointed pentagram star during 13 of her revolutions around the Sun during the course of 8 Earth years. At Delphi, the Venus festival of the 'rose mandala' was held every eight years. As said above, the interior angles of this Venus pentagram-star produce angles of 36°-72°-108° (added together = 216) which correlate with sexagesimal (6) astronomical cycles and the circle based upon 360°.

Fibonacci numbers are very sexagesimal in nature, and grow toward the Golden Mean: as for example: 2 ÷ 3 = .666, and 8 ÷ 13 = .615, while 34 ÷ 55 = .6181818, and 89 ÷ 144 = 0.6180; almost approximating the true value of the Golden Mean φ 0.618.

Because of Venus's 13 revolutions (creating a pentagram) around the Sun, Venus has an affinity with the Moon –which produces 13 New and Full Moons during a year. The number 13 appears in science based on the observation of astronomy and nature: The apparitions at Fatima came on the 13th day of the month. There are 13 Heavens in Maya cosmology. There are 13 scutes on the common turtle's shell. 13 days in a Maya week, and 13 signs of the Maya zodiac. The fundamentals of Maya astronomy are based upon the number 13, and it's doubling to 26, and another doubling to 52, followed by another doubling to 104. The synchronization of several Maya calendars running at the same time created the most accurate astronomical time machine every devised by humans.

Venus synthesizes the Numbers 5 & 6

Venus creates the number five through her *Grand Quintile*, a five-pointed star-pentagram. Yet, the observable motions of Venus *nearly* follow thirty-six (6 x 6) day cycles, and 216 (6 x 6 x 6) day cycles between her *inferior conjunctions* with the Sun, Venus' Greatest Eastern Elongation (GEE) of 47.5° away from the Sun, Venus' *superior conjunction*, Venus' 47.5° Greatest Western Elongation (GWE) from the Sun, and finally her return to *inferior conjunction* with the

Sun. In Greek tradition, the pentagram was an ancient sacred sign of having attained astronomical wisdom. Pythagoras adopted this sign after visiting Egypt –where the five-pointed star is a common motif in art and hieroglyphs.

The Number Nine

Temple I, *Pyramid of the Jaguar* at Tikal, Pyramid at Chichen Itza, Pyramid *Temple of the Inscriptions* at Palenque all have nine distinct levels corresponding to the nine levels of the past ages of the Underworld. There are nine storied pagodas in the Far East. There are nine months in human gestation period, and nine gates of the human body. There were nine, French Knights Templar who hid their secrets at Chartres. Jericho dating from 8,300 BC is surrounded by a wall and a moat 27 (3 x 9) feet across and 9 feet deep. The Island of Nan Madol is in the Pacific Ocean where 333 warriors created a system of district chiefs which is still in existence in modern times. The Sun Temple at Peking is orientated to the winter solstice, and is arranged according to the number nine. The altar is ascended by 27 steps. The circular roofed structure is 99 feet tall. On the pavement are nine circles of as many heavens, consisting of nine stones, then a circle of 18 stones, and then a circle of 27 stones.

The Number 16

Sixteen is the square of a square, namely: 2 squared = 4 and, 4 squared = 16. Dividing a circle into eight geographical fields of N-S-E-W and North-East, North-West, South-East, and South-West –creates a compass-rose sub-division, which allows further sub-divisions of eight into 16, 32, 48, and 64 points of the compass. The Viking alphabet had only 16 symbols. In 128 years (2 x 64) the Sun, Moon, and Venus come into conjunction 16 times (128 ÷ 8 = 16). Therefore, 16 pentagrams of Venus occur during 128 years.

Maya Astronomy 13-26-52-104

When Western scientists examined the calendar and astronomy of the Maya they were amazed at the unbelievable accuracy over thousands of years that they had achieved. This incredible accomplishment was achieved by the Maya through multiple astronomical cycles and calendars running concurrently. The Maya matched and interlinked many calendars every 52 and 104 years on a small scale, and every 5200 years (26,000 ÷ 5 = 5200) on an intermediate scale. The Maya called the Precession of the Vernal Equinoxes, the Cycle of the Pleiades which they reconciled every 26,000 years.

Maya astronomy is said to have come from the Olmec; but this unique astronomy has been in use for a very long time, and is common to the Mexica, Maya, and Andean cultures. There were separate cycles of the 260-day Mountain-Corn cycle which equaled the 260 day Human Gestation period (Milbrath, p.30). There were the Vague Solar year at 365 days, cycles of the Moon, cycles of Mars, conjunctions of Jupiter and Saturn –and many more coincidental periods when different cycles matched up perfectly. There is no clock more accurate than the Sun, Moon, and planets –because the heavens themselves are the ultimate clock. No chronometer can equal the *star-clock* of the cosmos.

Mexica-Maya-Andean astronomy began by adding the number thirteen to itself:

13 + 13 = 26
260 day human gestation cycle = 9 moons
260 day cycle of mountain corn maturation = 9 moons
260 days x 3 = **780-day synodic period of Mars** (780 = 13 x 60)
260 days = the 'trecena' of 13 cycles of 20 day names
260 years = 13 x **20-year conjunctions of Jupiter and Saturn**
26,000-year return of the Pleiades cycle, or one full precession of the vernal equinoxes around the zodiac

26 + 26 = 52

Every 52 years, or 18,980 days the 260-day cycle and the 365-day cycle coincided on the identical month and day (52 x 365 = 18,980 = 260 x 73). This was called the *Calendar Round* and the festival of the *New Fire*. It was symbolized by a bundle of 52 sticks tied together. Tompkins in *Mexican Pyramids* (p.289) writes that 13 days were added to the calendar (of 365 days) every 52 years to accomplish our leap-year correction.

520 years account for **26 conjunctions of Jupiter and Saturn.**

520 = 5 x 8 x 13

5,200 years marked the completion of 100 x 52 year Calendar Rounds –during which the *Maya Long Count* cycle was completed. This period is one-fifth of their Precessional cycle called *"Return of the Pleiades"* (26,000 ÷ 5 = 5,200).

26,000 ÷ 52 = 500 years. Curiously, 500 years coincides with the Egyptian **Cycle of the Phoenix** at Heliopolis. The Akapana pyramid in Tiwanaku is 650 feet on each side (650 x 4 = 2600). Bru na Boinne in Ireland is 260 feet in diameter.

52 + 52 = 104

Every 104 years heralds the *Double Calendar Round* when both the 260- and 365-day cycles *again* coincided with each other, with the addition of the *Venus Round* of 104 years (8 x 13 revolutions of Venus drawing eight pentagrams in the sky).

Mexica-Maya-Andean cosmology synthesized numbers within the human birth cycle, human menstrual cycle, native Mountain Corn ripening, Moon cycles, Venus' star-pattern cycles, Mars cycles, conjunctions of Jupiter and Saturn, Precession of the Vernal Equinoxes, and many other *yet-to-be-discovered* synchronicities into one of the most impressive unification systems of cosmic order ever devised by humans.

After long analysis of the Maya cycle numbers of 949 and 819, the famous scholar Lounsbury discovered the 1,195,740 day linkage between the Maya 73 x 16,380 days (derives from Venus, Sun, Haab & Tzolkin cycles), and the 63 x 18,980 days cycles (derive from Saturn, Jupiter & Tzolkin cycles). Forestmann's studies amplified by Lounsbury discovered the amazing **1,366,560 day cycle** that reconciles seven major astronomical cycles from the Dresden Codex. These reconciliations include synchronisms between Venus synodic, Mars synodic, human gestation cycle, the agricultural cycle, the 260 day cycle, the vague solar year of 365 days, the 52 year Calendar Round, the 360 day year and 360° zodiac, and the movements of Jupiter and Saturn.

Cycle of the Shekinah

Solomon's Power Brokers –Secrets of Freemasonry, The Church, and The Illuminati (2007) by Christopher Knight and Alan Butler refers to an ancient astronomical cycle called the Cycle of the Shekinah recorded in Hebrew traditions.

As was said several times over, Venus draws a perfect pentagram-star along five points of the circle of the zodiac; completing one pentagram every eight Earth years. Every 40 Earth years, Venus traces 5 of these pentagrams on the zodiac. During 1440 years, Venus completes 180 pentagrams in the sky. The number 1440 appears frequently in cosmological traditions, and is also the number of minutes in a day (60 x 24 = 1440).

Most importantly, every 480 years Venus completes 60 pentagrams on the zodiac, and also makes an extremely close conjunction with the planet Mercury –so close that Venus and Mercury together look like one very bright heavenly object. The Hebrew cosmologers reckoned that the Shekinah **480 year** *close-conjunctions* of Venus and Mercury heralded the great moments in their history, traditions, and mythology:

> 4320 BC (*Shekinah synchronizes with Precession in Gemini, the Sign of the Age of Adam*)

3840 BC
    3360 BC
        2880 BC *(360 ♀ pentagrams)*
2400 BC Noah and the Great Flood *(3 x 800 year Trigons =5 x 480 year M+V conjunctions)*
    1920 BC
        1440 BC Moses and the parting of the Red Sea
960 BC Building of the First Temple of Solomon (967 BC)
        480 (487) BC Second Temple rebuilt by Zerubbabel upon the return from Babylon. Hebrew authors compiled and wrote down all their traditions
            0 (8) BC Expectation of the Messiah *(Precession Aries/Pisces)*
480 AD *(60 ♀ pentagrams)*
    960 AD *(120 ♀ pentagrams)*
        1440 AD *(180 ♀pentagrams)* Building Rosslyn Chapel, Scotland
1920 AD
    2400 AD *(3 x 800 year Trigons = 5 x 480 year M+V conjunctions)*
        2880 AD *(360 ♀ pentagrams)*

The brilliant light that the Magi astrologers were following *could* conceivably have been one of the 480 year Shekinah close-conjunctions of Venus and Mercury. It may also have been a close conjunction of Mars, Jupiter, and Saturn –which are called 'the three kings' when they appear together in the sky. The Magi, as the three kings, may also refer to the stars in Orion's belt.

Trigons of the Conjunctions of Jupiter and Saturn over 800 years

The conjunctions and oppositions of Jupiter and Saturn occur every 20 years forming an equilateral triangle of conjunctions, and an equilateral triangle of oppositions. When these two triangles are overlaid; a hexagram-star is produced upon the zodiac. The hexagram-star revolves counterclockwise around the entire zodiac during 800 years (40 x 20 = 800 years). After a complete cycle of 800 years, the next first conjunction will have moved about 9° further along the zodiac. The triangle of Jupiter and Saturn conjunctions stays within the *same triangle of elementary signs* (moist-hot-dry-cold) for a period of about 66.6 years; producing a regular and noticeable climate variation for this period of time. At this moment (2016 AD) the triangle is moving through Aries-Leo-Sagittarius (hot); which would indicate a rise in global temperatures. Because of the relative positions of Earth, Saturn, and Jupiter; triple conjunctions of Jupiter and Saturn can occur in a single year. From our moving vantage point here on Earth, both the planets Saturn and Jupiter move retrograde, then forward, then retrograde again over the course of a 13-month period. A Babylonian clay tablet in the British Museum predicted such a triple conjunction in Pisces on May 27, October 6, December 1, during 7 BC (iastate.edu/triple, 1/24/11).

It may be appreciated that the individual planets convey cosmic numbers, geometry, and proportions to the Earth. It may also be seen that planets working in unison, through long term cycles achieve complex woven patterns –which ancient people symbolized as *Fates* weaving the fortunes of the world upon a loom. The accurate definitions of time, traditions, and climate in Maya cosmology, cycles of the Trigons of Jupiter and Saturn, and the Shekinah cycles bespeak an astronomical sophistication among ancient peoples of an extraordinarily advanced standard, far exceeding our expectations.

The Precession of the Vernal Equinoxes
Gravitational attraction between the Earth, Sun, and planets while they are all in motion causes the Earth's axis to wobble around its true north celestial pole over a period of 25,920 (Vedic) years, or

26,000 (Maya) years. Today in 2016 AD, the Vernal Equinox, circling clockwise through the zodiac, has moved through almost all of Pisces, and will approach the border of Aquarius in the year of 2160 AD. This event is the much heralded *Age of Aquarius*, anticipated by the Hippie generation of *the Flower Children*. This Precessional Age is a very minor cycle as compared to the Cycle of the Milky Way Galaxy over 216 million years which prompts the famous mythical Golden, Silver, Bronze, and Iron Ages; the break-up of Pangaea and its reformation, and the Great Catastrophes of Fire *(Ekpyrosis)*, Drought, Flood, and Ice –recorded in the cosmologies of ancient peoples from around the globe.

One-fifth of Maya Precession equals 5200 years

In 2012 AD certain publicity-seekers forecast numerous apocalyptic events. Their reasons were that the last Maya Long-Count cycle began in 3188 BC. If one adds 3188 + 2012, this particular Long-Count terminated in 2012 AD. The Long-Count is one of numerous Maya calendar reconciliations within their Cycle of the Pleiades (Precession). A Maya council of Elders met in Antigua, Guatemala and unanimously confirmed that the end of the Long-Count of 2012 AD was not going to be a cataclysmic event in this cycle.

The Rotation of the Milky Way Galaxy

Our home, the Milky Way Spiral Galaxy is like a river of billions of stars and stardust across the dark night sky. This star-stream crosses the zodiac on the borders of Scorpio/Sagittarius and flows upward and across the borders of Taurus/Gemini at an angle of about 60° to the plane of the zodiac. Ancient people all around the world have recognized that the rotation of the Milky Way is our most powerful cosmic cycle affecting life on our planet. It is truly a real revolving cycle of creation and destruction upon which the Phoenicians, Egyptians,

Mexica, Maya, Andeans, Hebrews, Irish, Indians, Chinese, Japanese, Greeks, and Romans based their cosmic myths and culture. Indeed, the myth structure of this great cycle has been borrowed, adopted, and translated forward by all ancient nations as a common *great history* of humanity.

The 137.52° Fine Structure Constant in the Universe

The Fine Structure Constant will be discussed in chapter eight, but because of its importance it must be included here. Mario Livio in *The Golden Ratio* tells us that the universe, its galaxies, and the Milky Way generate the 1/137 constant called *the fine structure constant*. The properties of the universe, atoms, and galaxies are determined by a few numbers known as constants of nature. These measure the strength of gravitational, electromagnetic, and two nuclear forces. Where does this odd number come from? It comes from the creation of spirals by the Golden Angle which is 360° x 0.618 φ = 222.48°. The reciprocal of 222.48° is 137.52° (360° - 222.48° = 137.52°). This is the foundation of the cosmic design of our Milky Way Galaxy through the Golden Ratio proportion.

More Information on the Number Thirteen

The number Thirteen is especially regarded throughout diverse cultures of our globe. The number continues to have an unparalleled fascination for humans. The reason for this is that Thirteen is a premier cosmic number created by the Moon, Venus, Earth, Precession; and has shown itself to be a synchronic vehicle among the other planets of our solar system.

The Mexica, Maya, and Andean cosmology discovered the universality of the cosmic number thirteen. The Maya zodiac was divided into 13 star groups with Sagittarius divided into two constellations

(Milbrath, p.250). This division creates 13 months of 28 days. Taube and Miller (p.53) speak of the 13 levels of Heaven and the 13 bird patrons of the daytime hours, and 13 night-time hours. Susan Milbrath cites (p.254) the Postclassical Paris Codex, "Long recognized as a form of zodiac representing thirteen star groups." Thirteen star groups also appear on the Madrid Codex, although not in a formal zodiac sequence. 28 days x 13 months equals 364 days a year –a system repeated at astronomical sites around the world. The icon of Andean cosmology is a special cross, called the *Chakana*, with 13 fields surmounted by a condor (symbol of heaven) at the top, pumas at the sides (symbols of this world), and a snake (symbol of the underworld) at the bottom.

Curiously the Maya Era Base for the *Long Count* hinges upon the completion of several cycles all finishing in the number thirteen: 13.13.13.13.13. The *Long Count* is finalized after the completed cycle of 13 Baktuns of 400 years which equal 5,200 years (13 x 400 = 5,200). Thirteen Baktuns of 400 years must be completed five times to finish the Cycle of the Pleiades (13 x 400 x 5 = 26,000 years of Mayan Precession).

Robert Graves in *The White Goddess* quotes Hyginus who says that the original thirteen-consonant alphabet (with five vowels) was taken by Thoth-Mercury into Egypt, brought by Cadmus into Greece, and taken by Evander the Arcadian into Italy. Graves says that the Etruscans-Tyrrhenians were Cretan stock.

As cited above, in Hebrew tradition, the number 13 is highly esteemed. Thirteen is the number of deities in the centerpiece of the Chinese mandala; and there are thirteen terraces at the Inca water gardens at Tipon, 13 miles from Cusco. Aveni cites (p.310) the diagram of Pachacuti at the Coricancha (*Temple of the Sun*) at Cuzco where there are 13 stars depicted in the Pleiades star group. Strangely, Cuzco is also 13° south of the equator. There are 13 members of a witches coven, 13 original colonies of the USA, and income tax, the IRS, and the Federal Reserve were instituted in 1913 (*AR#115*).

In *Solomon's Treasure*, Tracy R. Twyman reports on all the 13's found on The Great Seal of the United States of America. The American Dollar paper currency shows: a pyramid with 13 layers, 13 pentagonal stars above the eagle's head arranged in a six pointed star shape, 13 leaves on the olive branch in the right talon of the eagle, 13 "Jonathon arrows" in the left talon, 13 vertical divisions on the eagle's shield, 13 letters in 'E Pluribus Unum', 13 letters in 'Annuit Coeptis', and there are also 13 stars on the chevron of the seal of the Treasury Department overlaying the word 'ONE'. There are doubled sets of 13 (13 x 2 = 26) on the bill: surrounding Washington's portrait are two sets of eight leaves and five berries (8 + 5 = 13 x 2 = 26). The words on the front of the note: FEDERAL RESERVE NOTE, THE UNITED STATES OF AMERICA, THIS NOTE IS LEGAL TENDER FOR ALL DEBTS PUBLIC AND PRIVATE, WASHINGTON D.C., ONE, TREASURER OF THE UNITED STATES, SECRETARY OF THE TREASURY, ONE DOLLAR, and WASHINGTON all add up to 169 letters which is 13 squared. There are 13 examples of the use of 13 on the back of the note if you include the letter count of 'IN GOD WE TRUST' = 12 + 'ONE' below the motto = 13. The large number '1' in the corners are 13 cm apart as is the internal framework on the front of the bill. The motto in the eagle's beak *E Pluribus Unum* refers to the union of the 13 states into one nation.

The design of the Great Seal came from contributions by Benjamin Franklin, Thomas Jefferson, William Barton, Charles Thompson, and Eugene du Simitiere; and all but one were Freemasons. Robert Scot, a Freemason, cut the metal die for the Seal.

The design of the current Dollar Bill which incorporates the above Great Seal was a collaboration of President Franklin D. Roosevelt, Secretary of Agriculture Henry A. Wallace, and Secretary of the Treasury Henry Morgenthau. The design was executed by the Bureau of Engraving and Printing which employed 13 engravers.

Thirteen in Numerology

13 refers to the death of matter, and the birth of spirit
13 is the snake, dragon, and Satan
13 is associated with the Virgin Mary
13 at the Last Supper
13th on a Friday, Christ died on the cross; and Eve tempted Adam
13 dogmas of the Jewish Faith according to Maimonides
13 doctrines of the Witnesses of Jehovah
13 is a holy number of the Mexica-Maya-Andean cosmology
13 segments of the sacred cord of the Druids
13 constellations of the Sumerian zodiac and 26 major stars
13 is the number in a witch's coven
13 gates of a woman's body
13 chords of the Japanese harp
13 constants of physics
13 ancient cantons of Switzerland
13 states of the Federal German Republic
13 original states of America
13 x 2 = 26 characters of Jehovah
13 is Chaos
13 times does the word "star" appear in the Koran
13 is a Fibonacci number
13 is the sixth prime number
13 is the second star number
13 are the circles in a Metatron's cube.
13 factors in the Ostervald Bible (taken from crystal inks.com; *ridingthebeast.com* 12/5/10)
13 scutes on the tortoise of Cancer on the Asian zodiac
13th of October 1307, Friday (Venus day), slaughter of the Knights Templar
13 Jesus, King Arthur, and Kukulcan all had 12 followers + themselves
13 is the diagonal of the 5 x 12 rectangle layout of the four station stones at Stonehenge, as well as the proportions of the Temple of Solomon, according Robin Heath. 5-12-13 is one of the true Pythagorean triangles.

Other Interesting Astronomical Numbers

1728 (12 x 12 x 12) is said to be the sacred altar cube of the Heavenly City of Jerusalem as a model of eternity and a mandala of the universe. Half of this number equals **864**, a fraction of the Sun's diameter of 864,000 miles.

The Royal Mile in Edinburgh is supposed to be a version of the Egyptian Royal Mile said to be 8/7 x 5280 feet = 6034.2857 feet. These 6034 foot miles are said to make up the cube layout of Washington D.C., such as the distance between the White House and the Jefferson Memorial (Richard Heath, *Sacred Number*).

The Master numbers: 11, 22, 33

The numbers 11, 22, and 33 are called *Master Numbers*. The Sun creates the number eleven in the polarity reversal of its magnetic field every 11 years. Many ancient cultures and secret societies venerate these numbers which appear to be exponents of the sexagesimal system (11+22+33 = 66).

The highest degree of the Scottish Rite Freemasons is that of the 33rd degree. According to William B. Stoecker (*Atlantis Rising #115*) there are 33 vertebrae in the human spine, DNA has 33 turns, 33 muscles in the human foot, and the UN symbol is divided into 33 sections. Some historically significant modern and ancient cities are located upon or very close to the 33rd degree north latitude or south latitude (redicecreations.com & W.B. Stoecker). Of course, in general terms of astronomy and climate, the position of 30° to 36° would give inhabitants of these latitudes the fairest and most stable year-round temperatures at sea level.

Let us look at 90° x 0.618 = **55.62°** and 90° - 55.62° = **34.38°** north or south latitude where some interesting, historical, and significant cities are located within one degree north and south such as:

54.62° - 56.62° north latitude: Derry Ireland, Edinburgh, Glasgow, Riga Latvia, Moscow and many Russian cities, Copenhagen and many cities in Denmark and Sweden, and Kazan.

54.62° - 56.62° south latitude: Puerto Toro, Chile

33.38° - 35.38° north latitude: Albuquerque, Oklahoma City, Memphis, Birmingham, Little Rock, Charlotte NC, Atlanta, Wilmington NC, Nicosia Cyprus, Kabul, Islamabad, Kirkuk, Tripoli, Beirut, Palmyra, Rabat, Santa Barbara, Riverside, Los Angeles, Hiroshima & many cities in Japan,

33.38° - 35.38° south latitude: Sydney, Cape Town, Buenos Aires, Montevideo, Adelaide, Canberra

Conclusion

Most of the astronomical numbers and cycles are created from our geo-centric position on Earth looking outward into the universe. For example, Venus does not draw a pentagram in the sky. Venus only draws a pentagram in the sky as seen from our vantage-point here on Earth. Venus takes 225 (sidereal) days to orbit the Sun; but observed from the Earth, it takes Venus 584 (synodic) days to circle the Sun. Also, the Sun makes a complete spin on its axis in 25 days —yet seen from the Earth the Sun's spin takes a full 28 days to complete. It is a matter of our perspective and position on our moving and spinning Earth, tied to the Sun which is itself rotating in the galaxy. Yet, we see a cosmic creation taking place here on Earth through the numbers, geometry, and proportions from space directly to our planet.

CHAPTER 7

COSMIC MAN & THE GREAT PYRAMID

Humans are special because they can choose the direction of their lives; they have 'freedom of will' to make their own choices. The cosmological worldview from the Golden Age defines humans as dualistic creatures existing between Heaven and Earth, and composed of equal parts of matter and spirit from these two realms. This is why they can choose. Below, we will see that Leonardo Da Vinci uses the dual symbols of the 'square' of the Earth and the 'circle' of the heavens in his demonstration of the form of man, and his numbers and proportions. He clearly defines man as a combination of Heaven and Earth, and notes that his source was Vitruvius who has said that his information came from very old sources, indeed.

Leonardo Da Vinci's drawing of the Vitruvian, or *Cosmic Man*, is taken from the geometry of the Earth-Moon-Pyramid diagram interpreted from ancient sources and drawn by Robin Heath. However, Leonardo has moved the large Sub-Lunar circle that goes through the Moon to the base of the square around the Earth. Why has he done this?

The explanation for Da Vinci's adjustment is that he wanted to express the dual nature of Man —a creature composed of equal parts of matter and spirit. Da Vinci placed man's height and reach in the 'material' square surrounding the Earth. The center of this square is the man's sexual gateway. Da Vinci then focused the center of the heavenly 'spiritual' circle upon the Man's navel, the viaduct of nutrition, flowing from our mother. The circumference of the circle

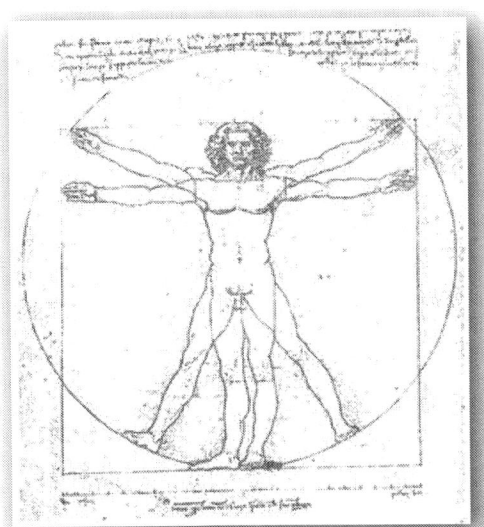
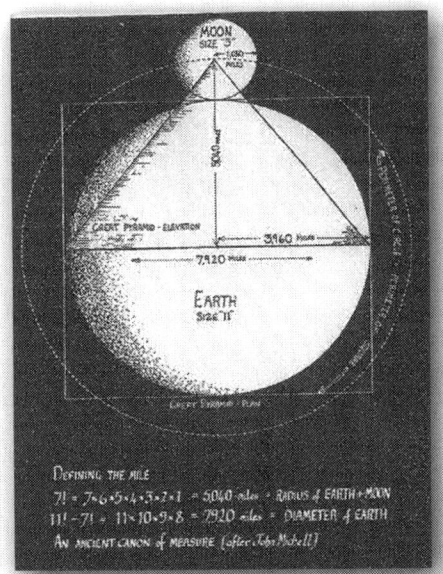

The VITRUVIAN MAN
by Da Vinci

EARTH-MOON-PYRAMID
by Robin Heath

'squares' and equals the perimeter of the square. The function of the circle is to represent the energetic halo or aura of the Earth, which the ancients called the *Sub-Lunar* circle. We live in this aura where life happens to exist upon the crust of the Earth and into the atmosphere, realm of storms, clouds, winds, and birds.

The Roman architect Marcus Vitruvius Pollio (70-25 BC) took his ideas from ancient sources when he wrote, "In the human body the central point is naturally the navel, for if a man be placed flat on his back, with his hands and feet extended, and a pair of compass centered at his navel, the fingers and toes of his two hands and feet will touch the circumference of the circle described therefrom." The Renaissance genius, Leonardo Da Vinci beautifully translated this written description into the world's most recognized icon.

But long before Vitruvius and the Romans –the Greeks and Hebrews held an exalted and cosmic notion of mankind. In the Book of Moses (*Genesis 1.26*), the *Elohim* proclaimed, "Let us make man in our image, after our likeness." Protagoras of Abdera (490–420 BC) announced, *"Man is the measure of all things!"* The *Pythoness* of the Oracle at Delphi exclaimed, "Man, know thyself; and thou shalt know the universe and the gods." Man is understood to be a microcosmic creature in the form and measure of the universe –expressing both the divine and material realms such as order and chaos, creation and destruction, the dichotomy of the opposing forces of Horus and Seth, Lugh and Crom Cruach, the creative and disruptive forces of Shiva, and the contention of Heraclitus' strife between love and war. Man can be both Heaven and Earth, and all the shades of combinations that lie between.

Cosmic Numbers from the Universe implanted in Man

A six-sided hexagram drawn upon a square of sixteen boxes around the Man –demonstrates how numbers, geometry, and proportions generated in the universe are expressed in the human body. The hexagram star drawn in that box epitomizes the number six of the sexagesimal astronomical system of numbers.

The square drawn around the Man was taken from the square drawn around the Earth to shown man's connection with the material nature of our planet. The square is divided into four boxes in length and four boxes in height centered on the man's groin. Each box is one cubit in width by one cubit in height. We know this because Da Vinci has shown us that the man's elbow (*cubitum*) to his fingertips spans the length of one of the boxes, which is the definition of the 'cubit' –elbow to fingertip. The cosmic and geographic cubit is 6"+ 6"+ 6" = 18 inches in length. The man's height and reach is four cubits (4 x 18" = 72" or 6 feet). The inside measure of the length of the King's coffer in the Great Pyramid is 78.06 inches, which accommodates a 72 inch (6 foot) person with 3.03 additional inches at the head and at the foot.

The Man's foot is 12 inches long (drawn in profile) multiplied by six, equals his height 72 inches (6 x 12" = 72"). The man is six feet tall. The number 72 is significant in all cultures because it is a number implanted within Man and astronomy. The important cycle of the Precession of the Vernal Equinoxes moves one degree every 72 years (25,920 ÷ 360° = 72 years per degree). Many of the references below were collected by *Genesisveracity.com* (4/9/10):

72 disciples of Jesus Christ
72 disciples of Confucius
72 virgins of Islam
72 immortals of Taoism, and 36 hells and 36 heavens
72 conspirators of Seth-Typhon against Osiris
72 Seth cuts the body of Osiris into 72 parts
72 angels and 72 demons of the Cabbalists
72 races from Noah: 15 Japheth, 30 Cham, and 27 Shem
72 languages confused at the Tower of Babel
72 names of God in the Hebrew Kabbalah
72 arrangements of the four Hebrew letters in the name of God
72 is the number of 70 elders + Moses and Aaron
72 old men of the synagogue in the Zohar
72 translators of the Hebrew Torah (Old Testament) at Alexandria. The version of the Bible called the Septuagint comes from the time of Ptolemy Philadelphus who gathered 72 Rabbi in separate chambers who produced identical Torah in 72 days.
72 sicknesses according to Mohamed
72 Norse warriors of Valhalla
72 x 7 = 504 doors at Valhalla, the Norse Heaven
72 chapters in the old version of the Book of Revelation
72 members of the Convent of St. Bridgette of Sweden
72 malevolent stars in Chinese astrology + 36 benevolent =108
72 skulls on the necklace of Kali, the Hindu goddess of Destruction
72 linens of the Parsee

72 is the relationship between the mass of Moon to Earth to Saturn

72 x 150 = 10,800 bricks in the Indian fire altar.

72nd part of a 360 day year. Hermes wins 1/72 of the year from the Moon goddess, so that 5 holy days are added to the 360-day year = 365 days

72° x 5 = 360°

72 x 360 = 25,920 years (Vedic precession of the vernal equinoxes)

.7222 = 260 ÷ 360

.272727→ relationship of the diameter of the Moon to the Earth: 2160 ÷ 7920 = .272727

27 the numbers 142857 added together = 27

7.2° Eratosthenes' angle at Alexandria to measure the Earth

720 = 2 x 360, or a circle divided into ½ degrees (c. Great Pyramid)

720 = 1 x 2 x 3 x 4 x 5 x 6

72 inches tall –the Cosmic Man of Vitruvius, 6 feet in height (6' x 12" = 72")

72 statues of Buddha around on the main dome of Borobudur in central Java

72 stars on the inside of the Capitol Rotunda dome at Washington D.C.

1/7200 is the size of Man compared to the Great Pyramid at Giza

If humans are fundamentally six feet tall, how come there are giants and little people? Whatever height that you are; you are usually six times the length of one of your feet. Some researchers have said that the different degrees of latitude away from the equator influence height; and therefore measurement standards. Indeed, latitude changes many things. A pendulum clock at the North or South Pole would measure 24 hours exactly; while the same clock would be disturbed by Coriolis force at different latitudes coming up with results like 34 hours in a day. A pendulum would just swing back and forth if placed exactly upon the Equator. Human size and the length of the human foot change *–but the proportion of that foot to the height and reach of a human* do not change. Humans are usually six times as tall as their foot.

The Circle of Six Arcs

Above we saw the man in the square of sixteen boxes (4 x 4). We can now understand why Leonardo Da Vinci chose to shift the center of the sacred circle away from the groin-center of the square representing the *material* nature of man. Da Vinci slid the Sub-Lunar circle upward to be centered upon the man's navel in order to represent the *spiritual* half of human nature.

The navel is the baby's connection to energy and sustenance from the mother's body. In another context this serves as an analogy to the human condition, that even when we are mature we need sacred energy from our Mother in Heaven. In ancient art, the heavenly sky goddess is portrayed with pendant breasts to represent the Heavenly Mother of the Milky Way Galaxy who offers us her milk as divine energy. And truly we receive light and energy from our Sun that receives energy from the Milky Way.

The essence of a circle is its central point and the radius which produces the number six. This is because the radius of a circle describes six equal arcs around the circumference of its circle. Six arcs of 60° make up the circle of 360°. The Vedic-Hindu astronomical cycles are all based upon the sexagesimal system which has evolved from the circle of six arcs producing the number six. The Vedic astronomers revered the numbers 6 + 6 + 6 = 18 (as shown in the cubit), and the three dimensional cosmic cube of 6 x 6 x 6 = 216 –a number which appears throughout astronomy and cultural icons: The Moon's diameter is 2160 miles (6 x 360). The Precession of the Equinoxes takes 2160 years per zodiac sign. There are 21,600 nautical miles in the circumference of the globe. In Vedic-Hindu tradition there are 21,600 human breaths during 24 hours, and 2160 human heartbeats every 6 hours. Indeed, humans are the seed of the universe. We are the most articulated, intelligent, knowing, and *cosmo-synchronic* creatures –built in tune with the numbers, rhythms, and proportions of the universe.

The Measure of the Great Pyramid based on Earth and Moon

The Robin Heath diagram below is based upon ancient Egyptian traditions relating the pyramid to the size of the Earth and Moon. This is a powerful icon whose message uses the fundamental geometric forms of circle, square, and triangle to reveal the divine proportions of Pi π and Phi φ. These ancient proportions were brought to life again by the modern research of John Michell and Robin Heath.

The Great Pyramid of Giza

Robert M. Schoch and Robert Aquinas McNally, *Voyages of the Pyramid Builders* (2003) write that one of the great enigmas of antiquity is the presence of pyramids worldwide. To us, this suggests communication, as well as culture, and science. At present count there are about 100,000 known pyramids in the world.

Because the Giza shelf has long been above the floodplain, archaeologists have determined that the ground level has risen about 26 feet in 10,000 years, the Nile has changed its course multiple times, the Nile Delta has amassed huge portions of soil, post-Ice Age rains weathered the Sphinx while raising sea levels, and the Mediterranean coastline has shifted. Samples of the Great Pyramid found at the top of the structure are older than elsewhere, suggesting that this structure was rebuilt and restored several times. Restoration of pyramids is most vividly documented in the Central American pyramids, especially in Tikal.

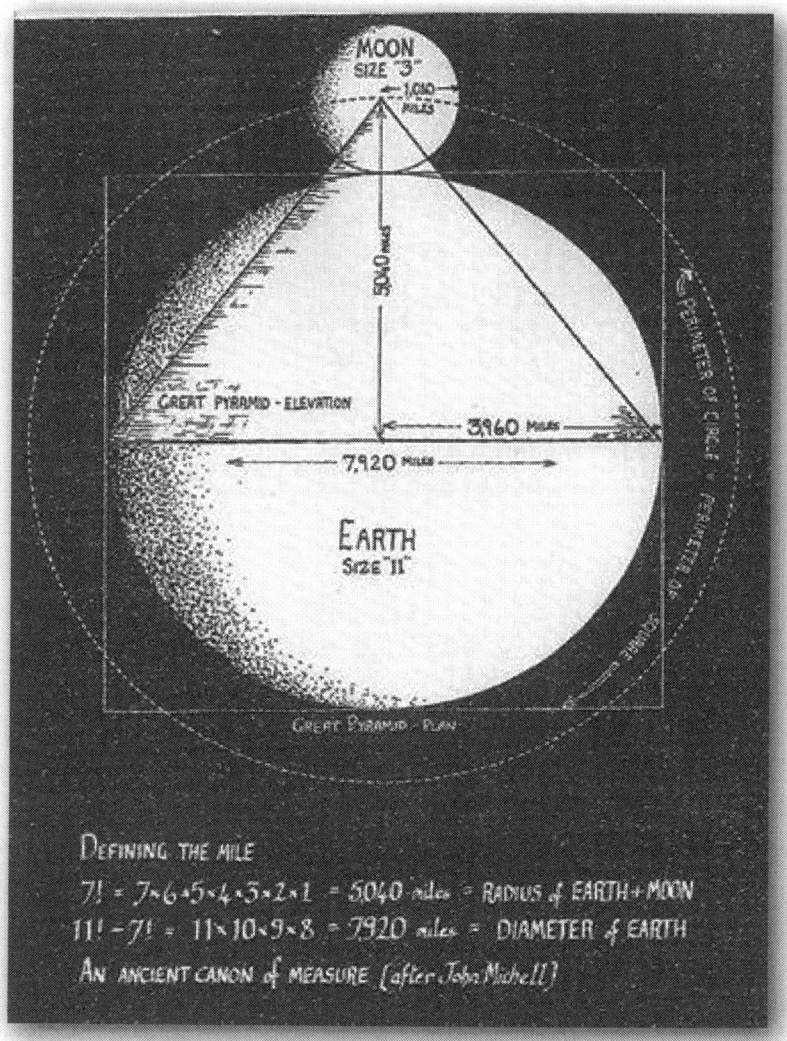

Many agree that Egypt was the source of Greek measurement standards. Having visited pyramids in Yucatan, Belize, and Guatemala it becomes apparent that pyramids are on-going projects which are often renovated, built-over, re-clad and re-aligned several times. Robert M. Schoch in *Pyramid Quest* says that the Giza pyramid is, "The end result of several rounds of construction, each successive phase elaborating on the ones before it…The temples at Karnak and Luxor were rebuilt and refurbished repeatedly."

Numbers and measurements

Using numbers and measurements it is possible to suggest that the Great Pyramid at Giza had been built at one time, renovated at another time, and once plundered of stone work; making a total of three distinct pyramid sizes namely: Antediluvian, Old Kingdom, and the current Contemporary Great Pyramid.

1. The original **Antediluvian Pyramid** (before the Flood) still exists as a core pyramid inside today's structure.
   Base: 440 cosmological cubits of 18 inches = <u>7920</u> inch base side ÷ 12 inches = 660 feet total. The 7920 inch side of the base represents the 7920 mile diameter of the Earth
   Height: 280 cosmological cubits of 18 inches = <u>5040</u> inch height ÷ 12 inches = 420 feet total. The 5040 inches represent the radius of the Sub-Lunar circle of life
   7920 ÷ 5040 = 1.57142857 x 2 = π Pi 3.142 (3.142857142→)
   5040 ÷ 7920 = 0.636363 x 2 = √1.618 Φ PHI 1.272727→ (1.272006289 actual)
2. The first renovation, after the flood, came in the time period of the **Old Kingdom** resulting in an exquisite super-structure with beautiful cladding to accommodate a new pyramid realignment of the north-south axis which had changed over this long course of time since before the Flood. These measurements are:
   A 440 Royal cubit x 21 inch = 9240 inch side base equaling 770 feet total
   A 280 Royal cubit x 21 inch = 5880 inch height equaling 490 foot height
   9240 ÷ 5880 = 1.57142857 x 2 = π Pi 3.142 (3.142857142→)

5880 ÷ 9240 = 0.636363 x 2 = √1.618 Φ PHI 1.272 (1.272006289 actual)

It should be noted that the Antediluvian Pyramid with a side of 660 feet, and the somewhat larger Old Kingdom Pyramid with a side of 770 feet both retained the identical relationship to Pi π and Phi Φ.

3. The **Current Modern Pyramid** has lost much of its Old Kingdom stone blocks used to realign the direction of the structure as well as the beautiful shell of polished limestone cladding to hide the structural changes. The greater part of this shell was disturbed by the Great Cairo Earthquake of 1301 AD and was used as a quarry to rebuild Cairo. The Great Pyramid also lost 7 or 8 courses of stone and its *pyramidion* capstone at the top: Current side of the plundered pyramid base is about 756 feet. The current height is about 455 feet.

The **Antediluvian Pyramid,** or pre-Flood pyramid was based upon the very ancient 18 inch Cosmic Cubit; such that <u>**440 Cosmic Cubits** of 18 inches</u> equaled 7920 inches which corresponded to the true diameter of the Earth as 7920 miles, such that Pi π x 7920 = 24,891 miles as the circumference of the Earth.

The **Old Kingdom**, the extended and realigned pyramid, built over the Antediluvian Core Pyramid was based upon <u>**440 Royal Cubits** of 21 inches</u> in length which equaled 9240 inches or 770 feet. Unfortunately, 9240 inches symbolizing 9240 miles is *not* the diameter of the Earth. So it appears that the Royal Cubit was *a direct consequence* of the restoration of the Great Pyramid at Giza.

The Great Pyramid represents the northern hemisphere in a scale of 1:43,200. Stecchini says this scale was chosen because there were 86,400 seconds in 24 hours (½ of 86,400 seconds is 43,200 seconds). Therefore, the perimeter of the base of the Great Pyramid was specifically designed to be one-half second of a degree of longitude at the equator (Thompson, Schoch & McNally).

The ancient cosmological worldview looked for order, synthesis, and synchronicity in the universe. Everything in the universe must be a microcosm related to the whole. The Egyptians were beholden to this system and perspective on life. They related the universe, Earth, Moon, Man, pyramid, geometry and numbers together in one whole. The Robin Heath diagram of ancient Egyptian cosmology is a wonderful expression of Hermetic order from the Golden Age.

Since the Pre-Flood Pyramid had lost its perfect alignment to the north-south axis; the Egyptians were certain that it had lost its astronomic alignment to sacred cosmic energy. They therefore measured and realigned a new larger pyramid above the olden core by slightly adjusting the new and larger jacket cladding to the current true north-south axis direction.

Cardinal Alignments to north-south-east-west move back and forth over a cycle of 41,000 years. This change in alignment is also demonstrated by the pyramids of the Sun and Moon, and the Avenue of the Dead at Teotihuacan, outside Mexico City. This entire complex is currently misaligned by 15.26° east of true north. Many superancient megalithic structures throughout the planet have become misaligned through time and also Continental Drift as the changes occur in the shape and spread of Pangaea.

The Great Pyramid at Giza needed to be extended and enlarged to allow the sides to be adjusted and reconfigured it to the current North Celestial Pole. The restoration and the overlay of cladding required a significant enlargement to gain room to seat heavy stones by creating a firm new outer surface layer. Petrie found a different orientation in the [Antediluvian] core relative to the casing stone [New Kingdom] from 25 centimeters up to about 6.33 feet (crystallinks.com 5/6/15). Petrie has already suggested that a redetermination of north was made in the renovation. But, was realignment of the pyramid so utterly critical? According to John De Salvo in *The Complete Pyramid Sourcebook* (2003), serious researchers who have conducted genuine experiments into *pyramidology* have found that alignment to the celestial north-pole is absolutely vital for any pyramid to function, absorb, and project cosmic and earth energies.

John DeSalvo (Appendix from *Operations at the Pyramids of Giza* by Col. R. Howard-Vyse - 1837) presents olden Arabic records of conversation with native Egyptians regarding the true history of the pyramids. Some of the testimony reveals that the structures were built prior to the Flood, and by a people so ancient that neither their names nor their origin were remembered. Many of the accounts do say that the pyramids were always connected with Thoth (also called Tehuti, Teoti, Hermes, Mercury, and possibly related to Enoch). The connection to Thoth may be the reason for the high regard of Hermetic information throughout all ages, suggesting a body of wisdom and knowledge of physics and science that expressed the true nature of the universe as a sacred relationship of God, nature, and man. Such was the science of the Golden Age; and it is still available to those who seek it.

The Sub-Lunar Circle of 31,680 Miles

The Robin Heath diagram shows the diameter of the Earth as 7920 miles. The sum of the four sides of the square touching the circle of the Earth (4 x 7920 = 31,680 miles) equals the circumference of the Sub-Lunar circle. This Sub-Lunar circle is an important concept in the ancient worldview. In the perspective of the Shaman, the Sub-Lunar circle is the Middle World in which we live among fish, land animals, and birds –between the Underworld and the Heavens. The Sub-Lunar Middle World on the crust of the Earth and below the orb of the Moon is where life takes place in the thermal atmosphere and the changing elements of water, heat, dry wind, and cold. These are the regions inhabited by clouds, lightning, the migratory passageways of birds, the crucible of mixing space, soma, and atmosphere with complex weather systems of swirling Highs and Lows, Coriolis effects, and massive energy systems. As every living thing has its own aura of life-energy around it; so too, the Sub-Lunar Circle is the halo of our living planet.

Because the perimeter of the Sub-Lunar circle is 31,680 miles, the builders of the Sarsen Stone Circle at Stonehenge made its circumference exactly 316.80 feet, as a fraction of the number 31,680. All around the world, many of the temple precincts are based upon fractions of the sacred Sub-Lunar circle.

The relationship of the diameter of the Earth to the Moon is 11: 3. The diameter of the Sub-Lunar circle is 14 (Earth diameter 11 + 1.5 half a Moon + 1.5 another half a Moon = 14). The circumference of the Sub-Lunar circle is 44 (4 sides of the square around the Earth x 11 = 44). Thus, the **relationship of the diameter of a circle to its circumference is Pi π** (44 ÷ 14 = 3.142857142). By multiplying the 7920 mile diameter of the Earth by 3.142857142, the result equals **24,891** miles. The inner circle of Blue-Stones at Stonehenge were originally 80 in number transported from the Preseli Hills in Wales, forming a circle of 248.91 feet in circumference. The current equatorial circumference of the Earth is 24,903 **(+12)** miles, and the modern meridian circumference is 24,883 (**-8**).

Symmetry of Earth, Moon, Man & Pyramid

It seems very natural that humankind learned to count numbers, cycles, speed, time, rotations, and revolutions through their observations of astronomy. What ancient people saw in the sky they also applied to measurements on Earth –whereby they developed a cosmic system that embraced both Heaven and Earth. Scientists of the Enlightenment like Greaves and Newton regarded the Great Pyramid as a standard of measurement, volume, weight, as well as a record of history and climate from ancient times. The pyramid itself was a canon more accurate than anything else because it was built to be commensurate with Earth, Moon, and Man.

Curiously, the number 7920 relates Earth, Man, and Pyramid; not only in inches, feet, and cubits; but also in furlongs, and miles. The number 7920 exhibits some amazing properties linking the number nine and the sequence: 4.5 – 9 – 18 – 36 – 72 – 144. This also holds true for the ethereal number eleven:

7920 miles is the diameter of the **Earth** which is related to the foot, cubit, furlong and the mile:

7920 ÷ 72 (**Man** is 6 **feet** or 72 **inches**)   7920 ÷ 7.2 = 1100
    = 110 men
7920 ÷ 36 = 220   7920 ÷ 11 = 720
7920 ÷ 18 = 440 (**cubits** of **Pyramid** side)   7920 ÷ 14.4 (7.2 + 7.2) = 550
7920 ÷ 9 = 880 (**yards** in **half a mile**)
7920 ÷ 4.5 = 1760 (**yards** in a **mile**) & 1760 **cubits** around the base of
    the **Pyramid** 440 x 4)

The number **7920** is also related to the sequence 1.5 – 3 – 6 – 12 – 24 shows:

7920 ÷ 24 = 330 (half a **furlong**)
7920 ÷ 12 = 660 (feet in a **furlong**) x 8 = 5280 feet in a **mile**.
7920 ÷ 6 = 1320 (4 x 1320 = 5280 feet in a **mile**)
7920 ÷ 3 = 2640 (feet in half a mile)
7920 ÷ 1.5 = 5280 (feet in a **mile**)

The Robin Heath Earth-Moon-Pyramid diagram configures the geometric forms of circle, square, and triangle. The radius of the Circle produces **six** arcs on its circumference. Square produces **four** sides and its sequence 4 – 8 – 16 – 32 – 64. Triangle produces the number **three** and 60°. Old English-Saxon land measurements bespeak a nautical culture which relied upon the sexagesimal system of astronomy to navigate and chart the seas and oceans:

1 chain = 66 feet = 792.0 inches = 4 rods, perches, or poles. There are 100 links in a chain. 1 link = .66 foot. 66 feet ÷ 4 = one rod of 16.5 feet x 2 = 33 feet.
1 furlong = 660 feet
1 mile = 8 furlongs x 660 feet = 5280 feet.
1 mile = 320 rods (perches or poles). 320 ÷ 4 = 80 x 66 = 5280 feet.
1 mile = 80 chains, or 8000 links.
1 acre = 43,560 square feet = 160 sq. rods.
1 square mile = 1 section = 640 acres.

It is apparent that the number 5280 is commensurate with Earth, Moon, Man, and Pyramid. It is rationally divisible by a great many numbers which highlight its utility. The diameter of Earth and Moon added together is 10,080 (7920 + 2160) multiplied by **3.142857143** = 31,680 miles. When 31,680 miles is divided by the six arcs of the circle, the result is **5,280, the number of feet in a mile**. Below are many of the divisors of 5280 that result in round numbers:

5280/2 = 2640	5280/10 = 528	5280/18 *****
5280/3 = 1760	5280/11 = 480	5280/19 *****
5280/4 = 1320	5280/12 = 440	5280/20 = 264
5280/5 = 1056	5280/13 *****	5280/22 = 240
5280/6 = 880	5280/14 *****	5280/24 = 220
5280/7 *****	5280/15 = 352	5280/30 = 176
5280/8 = 660	5280/16 = 330	5280/32 = 165
5280/9 *****	5280/17 *****	5280/48 = 110

The two most prominent number systems in the world are the eight-fold division of land and the six-fold division of the sky. 5280 is easily divisible by both the terrestrial and celestial number systems. Glastonbury Chapel was 52.80 feet long; while the later and larger Glastonbury Abbey retained the same numbers as 528.0 feet in length (John Michell). Copying cosmic numbers in architecture is demonstrated by the Freemason's Washington Memorial of 555.5 feet in height equaling 6666 inches. The famous 340 ton Er Grah, the Great Menhir at Carnac in Brittany on the Bay of Quiberon stood 66.6 feet tall. It served as the main astronomical sighting pillar for the Veneti, who were deep-ocean navigators that developed vessels like those of the Hanseatic League which came into existence some 1400 years later in history. Unfortunately, their advanced Atlantic science, culture, history, their race, and people were annihilated from the face of the earth by the arrogance of Rome in the person of Julius Caesar. Powerful people in history like Alexander, Julius Caesar, Charlemagne, Napoleon, and Hitler often plunge the world into abysmal darkness lasting through ages of time.

Seven and Eleven

The number seven divided by eleven is in the same relationship as the height and base of the Great Pyramid which gives us the Golden Ratio ($7 \div 11 = 0.636363 \times 2 = 1.272 = \sqrt{1.618}$ Φ). The number 7 is the product of the radius of the Earth + Moon ($5.5 + 1.5 = 7$). Again, this special relationship of 7 and 11 is not mysterious or magical. It is an astronomical number that is an agent of creation within the universe. The diagram of ancient relationships by Robin Heath confirms the ancient quest for order in the universe. Although we live in a universe of motion, tides, and frequencies; canonical numbers represent the median between the extreme swings of motion. While the members of the universe are subject to change in size, speed, and their cycles, they gravitate around their true divine median constant.

Consequences of this Analysis

The three different measurements for the Great Pyramid force us to acknowledge that there may be truth in the information that an unknown ancient people built the Antediluvian Pyramid. Also, that

Petrie's findings of a reorientation of the Old Kingdom Pyramid are absolutely correct. These facts force us to rethink history and our current worldview of science, man, and technology. We should acknowledge a debt of gratitude to Robin Heath for portraying these elements of ancient wisdom in a design equal to Leonardo Da Vinci's Vitruvian Man.

CHAPTER 8

MONAD & THE GOLDEN RATIO

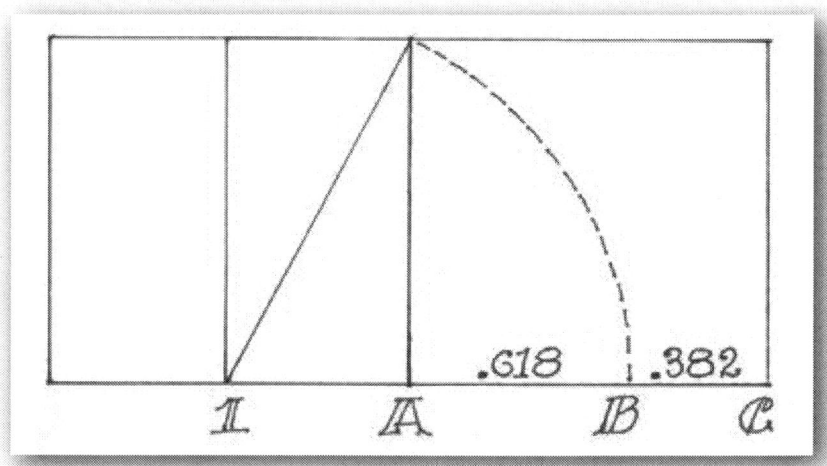

Figure 1.

The Golden Ratio may be constructed through the geometry of two boxes –where the diagonal formed upon half of box #1 is swung down to cut the base of the other box into a line divided into the Golden Mean Ratio such that: BC is to AB, as AB is to AC

AB is Phi .618 φ, while box 1 + AB = 1.618 PHI Φ (see **Figure 1**).

Another geometrical expression of the Golden Mean Ratio is seen among the segments of the interior triangles of the pentagram in **Figure 2** above.

In terms of mathematics, the Golden Mean Ration of Φ PHI is derived: (1 + square root of 5) ÷ 2 = 1.6180339887→. The Golden Mean Proportions of 0.6180339887→ and 1.6180339887→ are

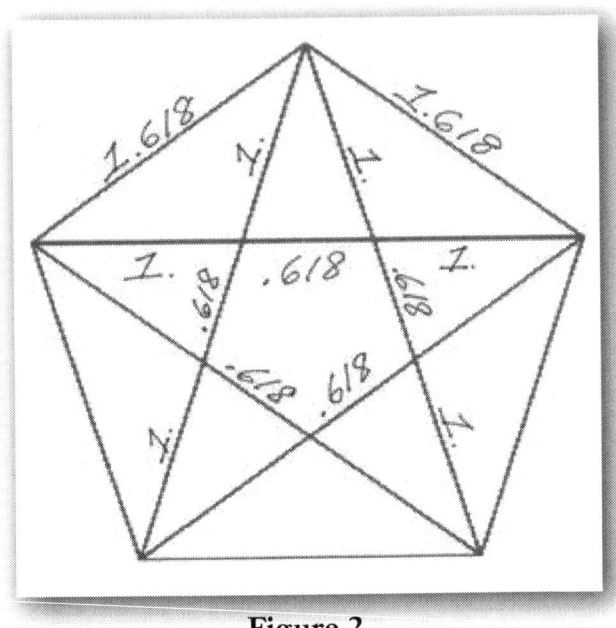

Figure 2.

irrational (not to be rationally expressed) and **incommensurable** numbers (cannot be measured) with never-ending fractions that proceed to infinity. This *never-ending* property was seen as 'eternal,' almost like a characteristic of God –so that the Golden Mean Ration took on a sacred aspect. Convention agrees to use the approximations: 1.618 for Φ, and 0.618 for φ for these un-measurable numbers. It will turn out that the Golden Mean is 'sacred' because in originates in the heavens. It is a multitasking tool of creation that builds, dismantles, and keeps the universe in motion.

Testimony & History of the Golden Mean Ratio

The philosopher Plato has followed ancient and Egyptian traditions by calling the Golden Mean Ratio **the source and structure of the cosmos and its physics.** The reason behind this sacred adulation of the Golden Mean is that it divides and cuts, but does not alter or destroy. Everything is in proportion to itself. What was cut can also be rejoined because nothing was wasted or thrown away. This allows the universe to change, move and grow –as well as shrink and contract.

Nicholas R. Mann in *Energy Secrets of Glastonbury Tor* writes, "Plato made the Golden Section **the mathematical key to the physics of the cosmos**. The Egyptians considered it to be the symbol of power that gave forth the endless series of numbers, measures, and proportions –the process of creation. It is the asymmetrical division of unity that leads to the diversity of creation and back to the symmetry of unity again. One to two, to three, to two to one." Mann cites William Preston (1772), "It is not only the heavens which declare the glory of God and the firmament which showeth his handiwork, but the humblest flower and the least shell which together with the mightiest objects in the heavens, are all made and act by means of a curve developed from the Golden Section."

Nicholas R. Mann follows Plato, and also concludes that the law and physics by which the Golden Section **grows the universe and ties it strongly together, as well as allowing motion and contraction is the following**:

> "The Golden Section describes an analogous progression of forms, numbers, and volumes where the original expands or contracts –so that the new is to the original as the original is to the whole: B is to A as A is to A plus B."

The noted mathematician and geometer, Pythagoras (570- 495 BC) of Croton, Italy, brought six silver flagons to the priests of the temples of Egypt to cajole them into sharing the secrets of their science with him. Pythagoras revealed that the Egyptians held that the Supreme Principal was the Holy Monad, the All and the One. The 'undefined' Dyad and the Triad sprang from the Monad. When

Pythagoras returned to Croton from his Grand Tour of the Middle East he assumed a persona of secrecy, mystery, and clandestine performances at night to large gatherings. Apparently he had learned a bit about stagecraft from the Chaldeans, Egyptians, and perhaps the people of Harran, and the followers of Zoroaster.

In *Lost Technologies of Ancient Egypt* (2010) Christopher Dunn has meticulously demonstrated that the ancient Egyptians used the Golden Mean, Golden Ratio, Golden Rectangle, and Golden Spiral in their art and architecture. Dunn uses his camera and computer generated graphs and Fibonacci spirals as an overlay to his photographs which examine the stone images of Ramses. His research epitomizes the simple classical beauty of nature based upon Golden Ratio Geometry as the foundation of all creation and art. Academia has consistently steered away from the connection of the Golden Ratio with art because this advances the notion of the underlying order in nature and man.

Humans seek order as a path to solving all problems. Clarification comes from cataloging and placing similar objects together to achieve an overview of what is to be kept; and what should be discarded as irrelevant to the solution. Numbers are one of the great systems toward establishing order. Mario Livio in *The Golden Ratio* writes, "Suddenly the Renaissance intellectuals saw a real opportunity to relate mathematics and rational logic to the universe around them…Concepts like the 'Divine Proportion' built, on one hand, a bridge between mathematics and the workings of the cosmos and, on the other, a relation among physics, theology, and metaphysics."

Mario Livio on the Golden Ratio
Consulting Mario Livio's book on *The Golden Ratio* (2002) we may learn the creativity of the Divine Proportion which seems to stand at the foundation of everything. In addition there are Golden Mean, Divine Proportion, Golden Spirals, Golden Triangles, and Golden

Angles. This section uses many selections from Marios Livio's book, *The Golden Ratio*:

Pythagoreans called the Egyptian Dyad, the 'undefined Dyad.' The Golden Mean (Phi φ) is also called 'undefined,' the never ending, never repeating, most irrational, incommensurable, endless expression, and unreachable point in infinity. The Golden Ratio is unique as a continued fraction that converges more slowly than *any other* continued fraction. It therefore assumes a supernatural character.

Leonardo Fibonacci of Pisa (1170-1250) wrote that Fibonacci numbers rapidly converge to the Golden Mean and then aspirate their ratios around Phi: 1, 1, 2, 3, 5, 8, 13, 21, 34, 55, 89, 144 where 89 ÷ 144 = 0.61805555→ *constant repeater*. Therefore the Fibonacci series may be regarded as an aspect of the Golden Ratio. The expression 1 ÷ 0.618 = 1.618122977346278 shows the unattainable nature of the Golden Ratio. Fibonacci numbers are related to Pythagorean triples in triangles such as 3-4-5, 5-12-13, and so on. Fibonacci's 'rabbit breeding problem' and all recursive generation problems in nature are governed by the Golden Mean. Mario Livio also cites problems in light refraction and genealogy tracing formulas. Fibonacci numbers have been found in East Indian manuscripts as early as the 6th century AD. Any odd number of rectangles with sides equal to successive Fibonacci numbers will fit perfectly into a square.

Le Corbusier (1887-1965), the renowned architect extrapolated the height of the Vitruvian man as six feet tall; as we have calculated. He interpreted the position of the navel as 0.618 of the height, and used this throughout his new architectural system of the 'Modulor.' In reality, the human navel is generally between 0.60 to 0.618 of the total height. Charles Henry wrote *Introduction a une esthetique scientifique* (a scientific aesthetic, 1885), but Mario Livio insists that the Golden Ratio does not provide a universal canon of beauty, even though our ordinary field of vision resembles the Golden Rectangle. However, as we have said above, Christopher Dunn in *Lost Technologies of Ancient Egypt* has analyzed statues of the Egyptian King Ramses which shows that they *were based* upon Fibonacci numbers, Golden Rectangles, and Golden Spirals –thus achieving a sacred 'golden art' form.

The Fine Structure Constant of the universe, 137.52°. The properties of the universe, atoms, and galaxies are determined by a few numbers known as constants of nature. These measure the strength of gravitational, electromagnetic, and two nuclear forces. The value of the constant is 1/137 and is called *the fine structure constant*. Where does this odd number come from? It comes from the creation of spirals by the Golden Angle which is 360° x 0.618 φ = 222.48° and its reciprocal of 137.52° (360° - 222.48° = 137.52°). This angle is the basis of the design of our Milky Way galaxy.

G. van Iterson showed in 1907 that if you packed successive points separated by 137.5° on tightly wound spirals that the eye would pick out one family of spiral patterns winding clockwise and one counterclockwise. This is demonstrated in the florets in the sunflower. Most commonly there are 34 spirals going one way and 55 going the other way. Other Fibonacci number spirals have been noted as large as 89, 144, and 233. Most field daisies have 13, 21, or 34 petals. If you dissect a rose you will discover the tightly packed petals separated by the Golden Angle at 137.5° which fills the spaces most efficiently. The leaves along a twig of a plant, or the stems along a branch tend to grow in a position that would optimize their exposure to Sun, rain, and air. As a vertical stem grows, it produces leaves at quite regular spacing –but not directly over one another, but in a screw-type generative spiral around a stem at the divergence Golden Angle of 137.5°. Leonardo da Vinci found that many of the spiral patterns in nature occur in cycles of five. Similar arrangements are found in the scales of a pinecone, a fir cone, and the seeds of a sunflower. This phenomenon is called *phyllotaxis*, or leaf-arrangement. Different plants use ½, 1/3, 2/5, 3/8 –all Fibonacci ratios (discovered by Kepler). Scales of the pineapple have spiral rows where each hexagonal scale is part of three different spirals –where 8 parallel rows slope gently from lower left to upper right, one of 13 parallel rows that slope more steeply from lower right to upper left, and one of 21 parallel rows that are very steep from lower left to upper right (5-8-13-21 are all Fibonacci numbers).

It seems absolutely astonishing that pineapples, pinecones, sunflowers, roses and all of nature are related in their design to the Milky Way Galaxy through the Golden Mean Ratio. Why, is this natural and universal constant not taught in early schooling –are people so afraid of the suggestion of a little bit of order in the universe? Perhaps the pineapple-shaped stone finials upon the homes and gates of the landed aristocracy were a secret sign that the owners of the property were conversant with ancient Hermetic knowledge.

Douady and Couder (1992-1996) experimented with a dish full of silicone oil in a magnetic field stronger at the dish's edge than in the center. Drops of magnetic fluid were dropped periodically at the center of the dish. The tiny magnets repelled each other and were pushed radically by the magnetic field gradient. Physical systems usually settle into states that minimize energy; and the magnetic fluid drops converged into a spiral on which the Golden Angle separated successive drops.

The shape of logarithmic spirals which grow wider as they move away from their source is based upon the Golden Spiral which creates the horns of rams, the curve of an elephant's tusk, sunflowers, climbing plants, seashells, the chambered nautilus, whirlpools, hurricanes, and giant spiral galaxies of the universe. The Golden Ratio confers being to the dodecahedron, since one cannot construct the dodecahedron without the Golden Ratio. Peregrine falcons follow the Golden Spiral as they dive toward their prey because it allows them to keep their head straight and still focus one eye continually upon their target.

There is also a study of Golden Music and 'the music of the spheres.' J.S. Bach even encrypted his name into his music. The violin sound-box contains twelve or more arcs of curvature centered upon the golden section. The octave on a piano keyboard consists of thirteen keys, eight white keys and five black. Mozart, Bartok, and Debussy may have used Golden Measures in their work.

In 1984 Dany Schectman discovered crystals of Manganese alloy that exhibit both long-range order and five-fold symmetry constructed from the Golden Ratio –basically a new form of matter. These are termed quasi-crystals which really share atoms and produce a system that is more stable with higher density and lower energy. Before this, physicists thought that solids could only come as highly ordered and fully periodic crystals or totally amorphous.

Thomas Aquinas (1225-1274) declared that the senses delight in things duly proportioned. Some 'Golden Numeralists' envisage a unified world of thought, spirit, and matter linked together by the mystery of numbers.

Let us look at the anatomy of a Golden Spiral, Fibonacci numbers, and geometry coming together to describe logarithmic or equiangular spirals. Geometrically, the Fibonacci series uses a grid-work of squares to generate spirals in nature by this formula of 1,1,2,3,5,8,13…and so on. Notice that the rectangle below is a golden rectangle of 8 x 13 squares:

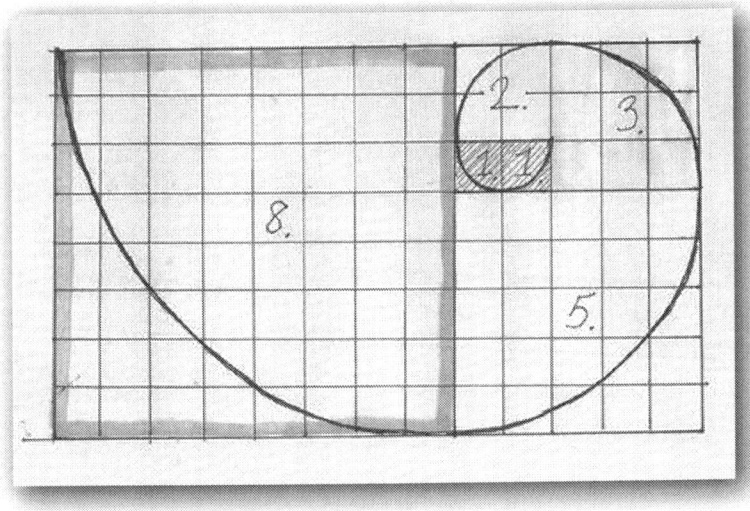

The Egyptian Concept of the Monad and the Golden Mean Ratio

The Egyptian measuring rule in the Turin museum is unlike any calibrated measuring device found in the world. It is divided into 28 sections; but these are of unequal length with no apparent system or unison. It is not possible to measure anything by an inconsistent ruler, and therefore this rule must represent an idea, a concept, or a canon. The number 28 suggests some relationship to the Moon cycle of 28 days.

Pythagoras spoke about the Monad as a 'first principle' of creation, hinting that the Monad was the universe which expanded by dividing itself into two portions. By this division, the mysterious 'undefined Dyad' was generated. Afterward, the Triad was formed. I have always imagined that the Turin rule (pictured below) illustrated the mystical creation of the Monad, Dyad, and Triad.

The scientific utility of numbers is beyond question. But, it must have come as a great shock to the ancients to discover that the ultimate building block of life was not a whole number but the Golden Mean Ratio, a sacred proportion that could ***not*** be expressed as a simple whole and rational number. It appears as if the Egyptians attempted to probe deeply into the fundamental nature of numbers by constructing a measuring stick like no other ever seen before.

Above, we see a portion of the right end of the Turin Rule which we suspect reveals the Egyptian concept of numbers and proportions beginning with the Monad on the far right, enclosed in the

Thomas Karl Dietrich

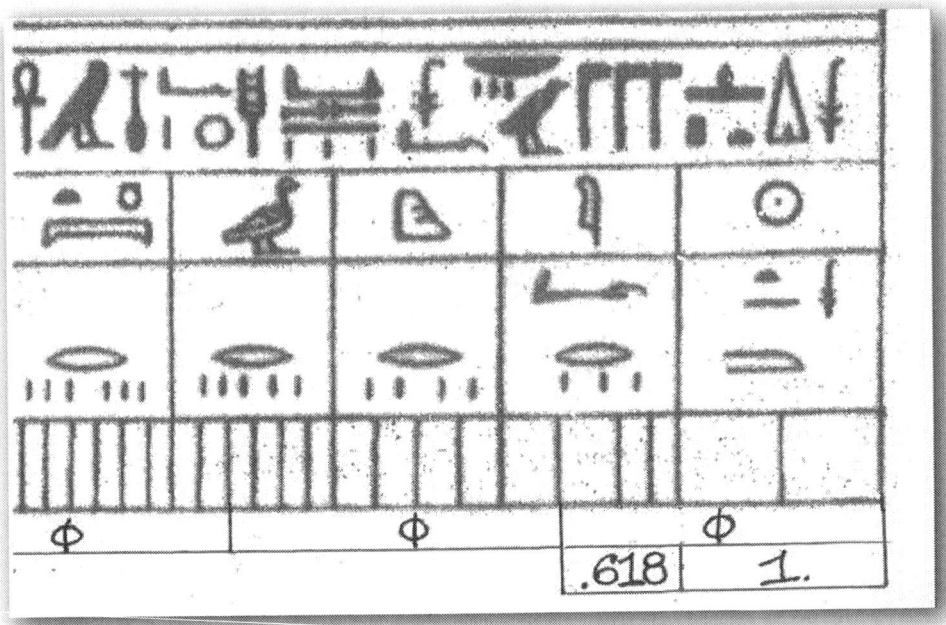

tall rectangle with the solar circle and dot. Below the rule we have drawn the symbol Φ, and below that the parts of the Golden Mean Proportion 0.618 and 1 to show how the ruler demonstrates Φ = 1.618.

The Monad unit is larger than the other sections of the rule. It is divided into two, like a cell. So we think that the Monad represents the cosmos, the One, and the All. In my mind the Monad also represents the 'undefined Dyad' because the Monad has been divided into two. The Monad has divided itself into halves or 1 + 1 = 2, demonstrating the source of numbers, the origin of the difference between cardinal and ordinal numbers, and the beginning of the Fibonacci series 1, 1, 2, 3, 5 –leading toward the Golden Mean proportion of φ 0.618.

Above the two boxes of the Monad is a forked or double stick possibly referring to the division of the Monad into two sections of the Dyad. To the left of the Monad-Dyad appears the Triad which shows three marks above its divisions. It may be noticed that the Triad is divided into three equal sections; *one of which is further sub-divided in half.* This appears to be the Egyptian representation of the Cardinal and the Ordinal concepts of numbers –as for example: The first cut of the Monad produces two; the two cuts of the Dyad produces three portions, the three cuts of the Triad produces four sections. The Egyptians reasoned that the cardinal (fundamental) numbers were created by the ordinal (ordering) numbers. Namely, that the first division or 'cut' on the ruler produces the numbers 1 + 1 = 2. The second cut produces the number 3. The third cut produces the number 4. The ordinal 4th cut produces the next number, the cardinal five; and so on down the line. Some also say that these divisions represent fractions.

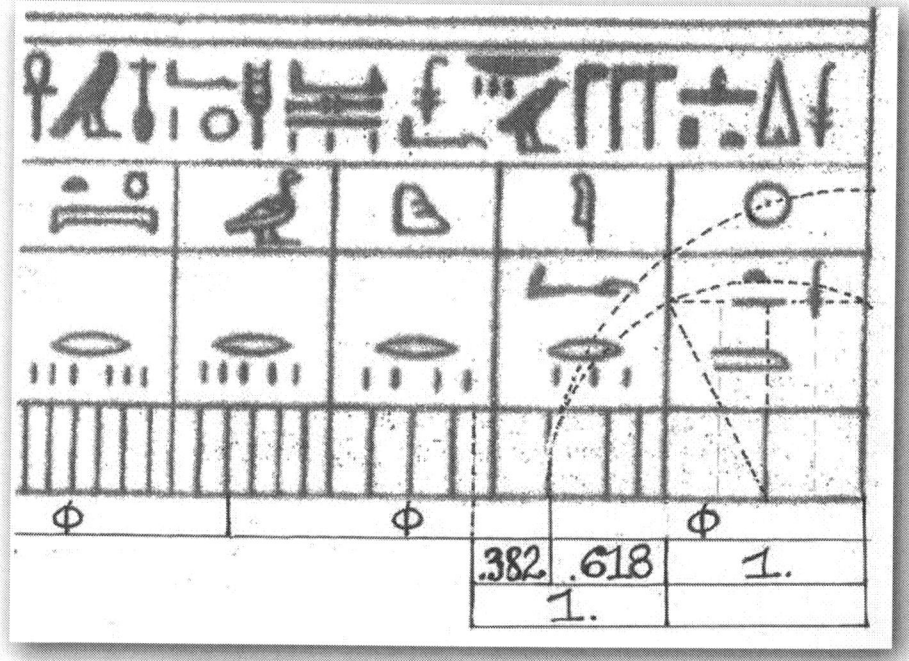

The image above shows how the Golden Mean Ratio φ 0.618 was derived from the Monad that split into two boxes and became the Dyad. If we harken back to the first image in this chapter; we were told that the Golden Mean Ratio could be geometrically derived from *two boxes, each of which were divided in half —where the diagonal of one-half of one box could be dropped down to cut the base of the adjoining box* into φ .618 and .382. In the case above, the Monad itself became the 'undefined Dyad' and the box-divided-into-half will produce the diagonal that cuts the Golden Ration of 0.618 upon the section to its left (the Triad). So far, no numbers are produced, only proportions.

If we look at our hands: two fingers are 1.5 inches wide, and four fingers equal a palm of 3 inches. Therefore, seven palms equal the Royal Cubit of 21 inches (3 x 7 = 21). Remember, the ancient older Cosmic Cubit is 18 inches of six palms (3 x 6 = 18).

It may be noticed that the Dyad boxes (within the Monad) are not square, nor is the base of the Monad indicated as a *square* by lines at the sides or top. So, we will have to <u>construct a square</u> upon the Monad-Dyad base by placing a compass set at the length of the base and swung upward to cut both vertical sides to equal the base —thus creating a true square. Please notice that the top line of the newly constructed square has been already marked by the Egyptians by a *dash* on the Turin rule. Now we may construct a diagonal from the center division of the Monad-Dyad base to the upper left-hand corner of our *artificially made-square* Monad-Dyad box. A compass placed upon this diagonal will drop down to cut the Triad base at 0.618 which, in conjunction with the Monad, forms PHI Φ 1.618 (1 Monad + 0.618).

Another dotted compass arc travels through the dot in the Sun circle by placing the point of the compass directly into the **most** right-hand corner of the base of the Monad (also cuts the base into Φ 1.618). The Turin rule is divided into sections of 28 Cardinal numbers and 29 sections of Ordinal numbers if we count the division of the Monad into two sections (1 + 1 = 2).

The Turin Rule expresses the following proportions:
14 Golden Mean Proportions of 1.618 PHI Φ
PHI Φ 1.618 = 2 fingers
28 fingers = a Royal Cubit

>   4 fingers = 1 Palm
>   6 Palms = 24 fingers = the old Cosmic Cubit
>   7 Palms = 28 fingers = the Royal Cubit

The Turin rule is an iconic masterpiece of the Egyptian cannon of the Monad, Dyad, and Triad; encompassing cardinal and ordinal numbers, Golden Mean Ratios, fingers, and palms –unifying Man, Pyramid, Earth, Moon, and cosmos through proportion and geometry. Of course, the 'G' in the Freemason's symbol stands for geometry. The change-over from the six to the seven palm system is highly significant showing a complete reversal from the 'solar six' to the 'lunar seven'. Vedic astronomy uses the number six as its basis, while Atlantic astronomy celebrates the number seven. For example, the seven saints of Ireland and Brittany and the seven daughters of Atlas; as well as the female societies (sympathetic to the Moon and seven) like the Amazons and Gorgons of the Eastern-Atlantic coastlands of Europe and Africa.

Seven and Eleven: Many ancient cultures loved the numbers 7 and 11 –and multiples and proportions thereof. The canonical value of Pie π is 44 ÷ 14 = 3.142857142. The radius of the Earth + Moon = 7, and their combined diameters = 14 (diameter of the Earth is 11 + 3 for the Moon). The numbers: 11 ÷ 7 = 1.57142857 x 2 = 3.142857142 π. There are fourteen Stations of the Cross in Christian churches. Most notable is the seven candle-stick holder of Hebrew culture.

Nature uses the Golden Mean Ratio abundantly in creation, growth, and development of all things from pine cones to mollusk shells to overlapping rose petals. The seeds of an apple are arranged in a five-pointed-star pattern, which generates the golden ratio. The mollusk shell of the nautilus is constructed on the basis of the Golden Mean. This nautilus shell is held by the Hindu goddess Shiva as a symbol of creation. The Golden Ratio is the simplest of the continued fractions, the incommensurable number that goes out to infinity –and the 'most irrational' of all irrationals. Yet, this most sacred proportion stands at the heart of an endless number of complex natural phenomena from sub-atomic matter to humans, and to the giant spiral galaxies of the universe.

Conclusions about the Golden Mean & Monad

The Golden Mean Ratio is a law of physics which has been accepted as an element of the universal language of science around the world. It is found in the cathedrals of Europe, the temples of Greece and Egypt, and the Taj Mahal of India.

The Golden Ratio is the medium that permits movement, change, and the conservation of energy. Thermodynamics says that 'energy cannot be created nor destroyed.' The Golden Mean cuts, joins, and disassembles –but it does not alter or destroy. The Golden Mean orders the physics and matter of the universe. It is the fundamental tool and building block of our world, nature, and the cosmos. Indeed it appears to join the entire universe together through bonds that are strong and yet equally retractable.

I would like to believe in a romanticized view of the Egyptians, that they were survivors of the Great Flood that occurred at the termination of the extremely dry Galactic Age of Capricorn. They came to a fertile and abundant country watered by the Nile complete with pyramids and Sphinx at the holy plateau of Giza. This ready-made place gave them the idea to resurrect Paradise and the Golden Age of truth, law, and justice through Ma'at; where everyone and everything was 'sacred' and had a place in a sacred land, guided by a sacred rulers who obeyed the cosmic physics and laws of God.

The Egyptians did everything differently from other people because they were given this amazing head-start to society, government, and civilization. They lived as a holy people, and seldom made wars. It is a documented fact that they permitted citizens of other countries to establish cities and embassies in their land. They opened the porticos of their temples to philosophers from all over the world who came to seek instruction from their priests and scientists. The Greek Renaissance began in 500 BC with Thales, Solon, and Pythagoras who were initiated at the temples of Egypt whose goal was to share what they had received so abundantly, and enlighten the world through a Golden Renaissance at their Temples of Heaven and Earth.

CHAPTER 9

TEMPLE & COSMIC RELIGION

The culture of the Golden Age respected every person as a sacred individual and partner in a sacred universe. All people were respected as children of the Creator, while the laws of hospitality and help prevailed throughout the world.

Ancient people were guided by a cosmological philosophy of astronomy and physics that showed them the dichotomy of chaos and order, and the necessity of motion and change to liberate energy confined in deteriorating systems. In their worldview, the Creator immersed himself into his own creation. Sacredness was seen everywhere and everything was worthy of adoration and respect. Here was a moral Age founded upon the physics and karma of the universe. We still adhere to expressions from the Golden Age such as: Do unto others as you would wish them do unto you…love God and neighbor as thyself.

Death itself was never to be feared because it was only a cycle within the larger physics of the All. The soul is intelligent energy – and energy cannot be created or destroyed. Ancestors participated in 'remanence' a form of existence beyond time and place which allowed them to be revered and consulted –nothing was lost because the fabric was woven out of the Creator and designed with the universal tools of geometry, numbers, and proportions. Close observation of the Sun, Moon, planets, and stars showed that these heavenly bodies activated energy-flows at portals in the landscape which produced beneficial power, health, mental acumen, and joy of life itself. Ancient people found that these fountain heads of energy were fed through caverns and faultlines in the natural geologic structure of the Earth. The people of the Golden Age ornamented and enhanced these holy sites with upright stone circles, avenues, henges, temples, precincts and pyramids. This constitutes our theme –energy, health, government, and religion at holy sites and the temple of God.

Our work will use the holy temple site as a focus around which to understand the ancient cosmological worldview of the Golden Age. All its philosophy, science, religion, and technology are best illuminated through this perspective. The holy temple is a treasury of mental and moral acumen transcending time and space where one may access the past, clearly see the present, and forecast the future. The Irish call these places *Caol ait* (pronounced 'Quail aught') which means 'thin places' where the veil between Heaven and Earth, spirit and matter is gossamer thin. Such locations are blessed and reassuring because they channel *Ma'at* –balance, truth, cosmic law, and inner peace. History records that holy sites have been passed down and accepted by different peoples with diverse deities and religions because they recognized a powerful energy common to humanity that allowed all races to communicate with their impression of God. Here was a place where they could step out of their mortality, history, and politics to experience their true humanity and commune with the divine.

Ancient man discovered earth-energy systems watching the activities of birds, animals, and insects resting and nesting over energy portals. These places likewise provided benefits to man in terms of health, cures, stimulation, clarity of thought, and illumination. Thus, standing stones and temples were built over and upon these beneficial spiritual fountains of energy which were naturally and sometimes artificially enhanced to align with the solstices and equinoxes to garner the best and most powerful aspect of cosmic energy from the heavens.

More sophisticated sites were laid out according to astronomical numbers and heavenly proportions. As more information was observed and gathered from astronomy and nature –more and more of an ordered system came to light. The physics of the universe expressed a sacred bond between Creator, nature, and man –thereby forming a sacred moral order and systems of cosmic law here upon the Earth. This was called the Golden Age.

The Alignment of Earth and Heaven

The Irish spoke of 'thin places' where Heaven and Earth meet separated by a gossamer thin veil. In the wisdom and intuition of the ancient Shaman; a sacred precinct is a point of access between three realities: the ancient Underworld of the past, the contemporary Middle World, and the Upper Spiritual World of Heaven. Here is a place of healing for body and soul, for singing, dancing, praying, and dedicated rituals to the Great Spirit, Creator, and Father of the Universe. We must try to align, synchronize, and make our world congruent with the past as well as Heaven in order to re-establish communication through prayer and ritual deriving the complete blessings and benefits of divine energy as a gift reserved for us from above.

All cultures have marked off a piece of land from common usage, and called it a 'temenos' (Greek); a sanctuary, holy precinct, or holy grove dedicated to the ministers of religion dedicated to the Creator Spirit. The temple and precinct are then aligned to the cardinal directions of north-south-east and west. By their very nature, the equinoxes always mark the east-west axis. The rising and setting sun on the summer solstice and the winter solstice must also be marked by wooden poles, stones or walls. Bisecting the rising and settings of the summer and winter solstice Sun will achieve a perfect north-south axis. The cosmically aligned temple now sits upon a portal of earth and cosmic energy uniting the Underworld (the past), the

Middle World (the present), and the Upper World (the future). This seven-fold connection through the four cardinal directions and the three levels of existence now cements the concepts of motion, time, and space within a total unity and alignment of all things below, in Heaven, and on Earth.

Maya Temple and Worldview

To be certain that we are truly expressing the global concept of the Temple of Heaven and Earth, let us travel to Central America to examine the worldview of the Maya. Karen Bassie-Sweet in *At the Edge of the World –Caves and Late Classic Maya World View* quotes Sir J. Eric Thompson who tells us that in Maya cosmology:

> The Earth was a square aligned to equinoxes and the solstices of the motions of the Sun. All the temples, homes, and fields were aligned in this manner to copy the orientation of the Earth. The sky was divided into 13 compartments in each of which certain gods resided. The corners of the Earth were placed where four Bacabs held up the sky. The mid-points of the sides were the positions of east-west-north-south. At the mid-points on the sides stood a sacred ceiba tree in front of a cave within a sacred mountain. Underneath the Earth was the Underworld of nine levels; 4 down from the west to the nadir (opposite the zenith) and 4 levels up again to the east. The Sun disappeared into the western cave for the night and reappeared at the eastern cave in the next morning.

Karen Bassie-Sweet says that this quadrilateral world was not only their building model, but that it represented their entire worldview of ancestors, spirits, astronomy, cycles of destruction and re-creation which were all incorporated into this mandala. Within these mountains lived their ancestors and guardian deities of lightning, rain, and wind. The ruling lineages believed that they originated from one of these caves marked by a new world tree which represented the latest new creation after cataclysm. The Maya considered the Earth to be a living, sacred entity. The surface of the Earth is frequently depicted as a turtle or a caiman. East was red, north was white, west was black, and south was associated with yellow. Offerings and ritual activity was always toward the cardinal midpoints of the quadrilateral world with its caves, trees, and mountains.

Bassie-Sweet writes that Heart of the Sky and Heart of the Earth created everything through words, "And then the earth rose because of them as they spoke, it was simply their word that brought it forth. For the forming of the earth they said 'Earth' and it arose suddenly, just like a cloud, like a mist, now forming, unfolding." Again the quadrilateral nature of the Earth is mentioned, and the stretching of the cord sounds very Egyptian-like:

> The fourfold siding, fourfold cornering,
> Measuring, fourfold staking,
> Halving the cord, stretching the cord
> In the sky, on the earth,
> the four sides, the four corners

In the four-square quadrilateral model east is true east, and west is true west; and the winter and summer solstices are 'symbolically' at the corners of the square. A true square mandala only works at the north or south *latitudes* identical to Stonehenge in England. The quadrilateral world is based upon the annular cycle of the Sun establishing order creating a safe place for humans to live.

The Maya mandala and attendant rituals are representative of all cosmic worldviews from the Golden Age. The *flat and square* Earth does not mean that anyone ever believed that the Earth was factually flat and square. The equinox Sun rises from our perspective in the middle of the east side of the square and sets in the middle of the west side of the square. The equinox rising is always east, and the equinox setting is always west. Drawing a line between east and west, and bisecting this line with ropes and pegs establishes a right angle in the center of the square which points to north and south. Therefore this temple-mandala is a schematic for the design of an astronomical observatory in any country of the world by adjusting the actual solstice points according to local latitude. Like all other ancient people, the Maya held traditions that the world had been destroyed through fire, drought, flood, and ice. The world was ever again re-created out of chaos and cataclysm by realigning the temple site to the new declinations of astronomy, namely the gradually changing motions and cycles of the Sun, Moon, Earth, and Milky Way.

In the Golden Age prior to the Great Flood, astronomy was the common language and understanding of all mankind. The main Hindu temple of *Candi Sewu* is a perfect example of a four-square building structure resembling the square Maya temple. This 8th century AD temple is composed of 249 rooms in Central Java and is the second largest Buddhist temple in Indonesia. It shares the ground pattern of the 13 squares of the South American Andean Cross.

Temple Church in London

The Crusaders of the Knights Templar built a round church (consecrated 1185 AD) in the heart of London for their English headquarters. The structure was based upon the Church of the Holy Sepulcher in Jerusalem. The London Temple Church served as the site of the Templar's ancient and secret initiation ceremonies; also as the seat of their international banking system, as well as the Royal Treasury under King John (1199-1216 AD). The Templars provided an opportunity for Christians to participate in worldwide finance, and for eastern money-lenders to establish connections in Europe. The Master of the Temple was regarded as the First Baron of the Realm in Parliament. In this capacity of First Baron, the famous

William Marshall, 1st Earl of Pembroke; soldier and statesman, negotiated the Magna Carta between king and the barons. Marshall was called 'the best knight that ever lived,', and is also famous for his building and conquests in Ireland. He and his two sons are buried in the London Temple Church.

The round Temple Church has a diameter of 55 feet which equals 172.8 feet in circumference (3.142857 x 55). The number 1728 symbolizes the cosmic cube of the universe (12 x 12 x 12 = 1728), a quintessential number in cosmology.

Mound Culture of Ohio

Along the Ohio and Mississippi River valleys and the Eastern United States there was a widespread astronomical culture whose people were of gigantic stature. Their time period was so ancient that upon excavating their skeletons; most of them turned to dust upon exposure to the air. These facts are copiously documented by early European settlers from many states, including President Abraham Lincoln who personally visited these amazing sites. Their many earthen structures were aligned to astronomical seasons and laid out in the cosmic-foot of 12 inches, and according to astronomical numbers from the sexagesimal system.

The Ohio Mound Culture recognized significant astronomical numbers that were used over and over again in their ground-plans such as: 30, 33, 120, 210, 212, 215, 420, 555, 555.5, 660, 666, 800, 1050, 1080, as cited by Fritz Zimmerman in his two recent books on the Ohio Mound Culture.

The number, 212 feet appears as the most common diameter of many of the Ohio henges producing a circumference of 666 feet (212 x 3.14159265359 *Modern Pi* = 666.0176 feet, or 666.2857142 feet in *Cosmic Pi*).

Yet another diameter of 210 feet was especially sacred because it produced a circle of exactly 660 feet <u>even</u> with the ancient derivation of Cosmic Pi as 44 ÷ 14 = 3.142857143 x 210 = 660.0.

Special Characteristics of a Holy Site
The material and craftsmanship at a holy site must be of the highest caliber because of the sacred nature of the location. At Machu Picchu rough-faced irregular stones are the material for the common houses; finer-shaped and fitted smooth-stones adorn the homes of the aristocracy and King who are the ambassadors of heaven; while the holy of holies and the temple is built with highly polished squared ashlars. The temple at Jerusalem, the pyramids at Giza, the Temple of Stonehenge, and Tiwanaku are all built with super-megalithic stones set to perfection with super-human capability. This over-building with super-stones, super-dimensions, super-precision and craftsmanship are a hallmark of the temple to express the highest level of human ability to honor the Divine Architect of the universe.

Just as the temple is an astronomical observatory, it fulfills numerous other functions as a place of study, exhilaration, and communion with God as may be seen at the men's and women's libraries next to the Sacred Wall in Jerusalem. Greek philosophers were permitted to study at the outer temple portico in Egypt, while occasionally some were permitted to enter into the higher wisdom of the Inner Temple. Nonetheless, many communities were served by modest natural energy sites where intuitive shaman could access the three worlds: Underworld, the present Middle World, and the future in the Heavens. It is reasonable to assume that shaman were early priests who counseled and safeguarded their communities; while later Priests, Druids, Rabbi, Prophets, Seers, and Philosophers cultivated the intuition and abilities of the shaman to transcend the realities of the three worlds.

Temple & Government
Every year the Doge of Venice and his fleet sailed out into the Adriatic in order to cast a golden ring into the water and renew his marriage with the sea-goddess that supplied wealth and prosperity to the city. In Ireland candidates for the High Kingship visited the

Stone of Destiny, the *Lia Fail*, upon the Hill of Tara which would cry out to confirm the rightful king. This signified that the goddess of the land would accept a union with this king. Tara was a matrix of energies where truth, right judgment, and law came down from heaven.

Most cultures have taken the simile of the *Temple as Earth and as Cosmos* to its ultimate conclusion that the Emperor-King is the ambassador of God. Within the precinct around the temple sits the Celestial Emperor who is the sacred agent of God, and presides over government on Earth. The King symbolized the Sun, while the Queen symbolized the Moon. The ministers and grand viziers were the embodiment of the planets and stars. The palace is surrounded by a river or moat and beautiful ornamental and medicinal gardens, often filled with animals and rare species. Norman Lockyer explains that most noted ancient sites display a context of stones, holy trees, holy wells and streams which worked in union with the ceremonies and celebrations at ancient sites. These temple cities and precincts held material treasures of gold and precious gems, libraries of science, history and traditions, trade secrets, and maps and charts of the Earth and sky.

Just as the human mind is a microcosm of the Cosmic Mind –so too, was the temple on Earth endowed with knowledge recorded in books, scrolls, and artwork, which was passed on in oral traditions by masters at the royal court. The Temple of Heaven and Earth was truly a special and sacred place –which emanated an aura which awed and impressed even to the most profane and lowly of citizens. This cosmic worldview of Heaven and Earth was religious, political, social, and scientific establishing the institution of the Divine Right of Kings to represent God, and to rule their countries with a paternal justice. Knowledge, power, and wealth were assembled here in the presence of God's divinely appointed representative on Earth. And around the temple was a city of artisans, farmers, butchers, bakers, and all those who supplied the material needs of the emperor, his ministers, advisors, scientists, philosophers, holy priests, and servers. So long as each and every one of these persons preformed their watchful duties to control and balance the state –an exceptional and divine harmony prevailed; and a true aristocracy of justice and law was formed. When any part exceeded or neglected its authority it was incumbent upon the others to remove injustice immediately.

Many people have been amazed by the concept of 'the Divine Right of Kings' when they encountered the idea in their history courses. It is really a very misunderstood concept suggesting royal excesses and improprieties. But in fact, these laws were a strict contract between ruler and his people –'I will be your king, and you will be my people.' This is a fiduciary contract with strict obligations on both sides to protect, feed, succor, and respect. Cosmic Cultures that have endured through long ages of time are the Atlantic, Japanese, Chinese, Egyptian, Maya, Aymara, and many Andean people.

Michell in *The Dimensions of Paradise* gives examples from the ancient Chinese *Great Law* (1050 BC):

> It is the constant duty of the government to carefully watch the phenomena of nature, which reflect the order and disorder in the world of government...When the course of nature runs properly, it is a sign that the government is good...Any disturbance in the Sun accuses the emperor. A disturbance around the Sun implicates the court and the ministers. Problems with the Moon point to the Queen and the concubines. Good weather that lasts too long shows that the emperor is too inactive. Days that continue to be cloudy show that the emperor lacks understanding...A good harvest proves that all is well, a bad harvest that the government is at fault.

According to the *I Ching* offenses against ritual, the appointment of unworthy persons, the dismissal of the worthy, and listening to slander cause outbreaks of fire and strokes of lightening. Excess and wastefulness in the administration bring about heart and abdominal disease, dust storms and earthquake.

Gardens, Water & Landscapes at the Sacred Sanctuary

The site of the Holy Temple was serviced by subterranean caverns, caves, and underground rivers that conveyed the beneficial energy which created the atmosphere of tranquility, inner peace, health, and inspiration. Another feature of a holy site was that it should be surrounded by medicinal gardens full of wondrous healing trees like the Garden of Eden and the Garden of the Hesperides which were said to contain fruits, shrubs, and herbs surrounded by water like a miniature Earth floating upon the cosmic ocean. The Tree of Life was said to have 12 kinds of fruits, yielding every month, and the leaves of the tree were for healing the nations. The garden paradise of flowers, fruits, nuts, and edibles growing in well-tended beds shaded by topiary and trimmed bushes supported feelings of well-being and the joy of life in an ordered and secure environment. Many of the overgrown pyramid complexes in Central America were found to be covered not by rough jungle vegetation, but by useful plants of great pharmacological value producing super-medications growing close to the energy center of the temples. Near the holy city of Cuzco, the Royal Horticultural Gardens of Tipon developed the modern potato and new varieties of high-altitude-tolerant potatoes, fruits, tubers, grains, and every manner of food stuff. Here too were high-technology terraces for the retention and recirculation of their limited and precious water resources. John Michell cites Dr. Raphael Patai's *Man and Temple* who writes about a subterranean network of irrigation canals that issue from underneath the Temple of Jerusalem and bring to each country its proper power to grow its particular assortments of fruits. At Glastonbury, England the surrounding landscape was shaped into gigantic zodiac figures.

Many great cities began as humble villages on islands near river mouths not far from the sea, in sheltered coves and bays surrounded by protective swamps, rich in wildlife, fish, berries, and edibles. We tend to forget that the greatest medium for human transportation were watercraft, boats, and ships with sails to serve the needs of growing economies, burgeoning trade and commerce. But there is a more important reason for the river locations of ancient cities – namely, the proximity of a powerful energy supply which is common to places where land and water meet. Again, it must be remembered that the temple came first; and that castles and kings, governments and cities followed to provide food, commerce, and to build ships for war and trade.

The energy flowing to the temple was often conducted by underground streams and aquifers. Many ancient temples were founded upon islands in a lake, bay, or sea. Other temples were located in or opposite to an ox-bow bend of a river. Earth-energy studies have concluded that peninsulas, ox bow bends in rivers, river islands, lakes, and oceans function as energy-accumulators and energy boundaries. Ancient people revered water as a magical and supernatural substance which could purify and sanctify people and objects. Water was brought from holy sites in ampules to bless people, homes, lands, and animals. The noted alchemist, Fulcanelli in *Le Mystere des Cathedrales* quotes a medieval alchemist saying, "The water which we use is a water containing all the virtues of heaven and earth; that is why it is *the general solvent of all nature*. It is this which opens the doors of our royal hermetic chamber...It is not like water from the clouds...it is a veritable magnet, which attracts to itself all the influences of the sky, the sun, the moon and the stars, in order to transmit them to earth." The author of the *Precptes du Pere Abraham* writes, "This primitive and celestial water...is the water in which the sun and moon bathe and that they dissolve of their own accord in this water, which is their first origin." This ancient esoteric language explains what we now know about the holy site: that it is a collector and portal of energetic-ether from the cosmic ocean, which modern science calls plasma, dark matter, and numerous other modern quasi-esoteric terms.

Fulcanelli further explains that the *Fountain of Life* or the *Fountain of Youth* may be found in the *Sacred Wells* associated with most Gothic churches in the Middle Ages. The water drawn from them was usually thought to have curative value, and was used in the treatment of many illnesses. The poem, the *Siege of Paris* by the Normans, reports various incidents attesting the marvelous properties and remedies of the water from the well of St. Germain-de-Pres…the well of St. Marcellus in Paris…the well of the Holy Virgin at Notre Dame at Lepine, and also the water of the well at Limoux had water to cure all diseases. Fulcanelli also elaborates upon the mystical nature of the Holy Virgin; who is called the *Vase containing the Spirit of Things*. He describes a painting showing this 'vase of spirit' which tradition held contained: one part wild honey; one part of terrestrial water; and finally a third part of celestial water.

In nature, wind and water are the most wonderful energy conductors that transport power, health, and inspiration to the energy portal of the temple. Bernard Roger reports in *The Bird of Truth* that the king's sons are sent to retrieve a flask of 'dancing water' which is magical and highly energetic. Most of the great sanctuaries like the Beijing Temple of Heaven, the Ming Tang temples in China, Angkor Wat in Cambodia, *Tenochtitlan* in Mexico City were surrounded by an artificial moat encompassing the sanctuary precinct. Many natural places like Machu Picchu in Peru, Bru na Boinne in Newgrange, Ireland, and Poverty Point in Louisiana are surrounded by a prominent bend in the river.

Nicholas R. Mann in *Energy Secrets of Glastonbury Tor* explains the Celtic name 'Avalon' referring to a mystical island with a cave in a high hill; and surrounded by water –such as Glastonbury appeared to be in ancient times. The island with the cavernous hill with springs and fountains was regarded as a place of union between Heaven and Earth where souls and their energy were recycled back into the other worlds of the universe. All these island sanctuaries possess a remarkable tree with special fruits. 'Avalon' in Welsh means 'apple.' Such islands are common in the traditions of ancient cultures such as the Islands of the Sun and Moon on Lake Titicaca, Peru, the Island of the Golden Apples of the Hesperides from the Greek traditions concerning the Atlantic Ocean, the island of *Tir na'Og* of the Irish, and the Chinese Ming Hill Temple on the Yangtze River.

In ancient art zigzag lines represent holy water offerings to the gods, lightning, and energetic water in the cosmic ocean. Both Chinese and British called subterranean energy lines, 'dragon-lines.' The Chinese New Year Dragons zigzagging in and out in parades symbolize the star-river of the Milky Way in the cosmic ocean. The zigzag bee-scout dances advertise the energy at new hive sites that they have investigated. Traditions of Dragon Hill by Glastonbury report numerous sightings of flying dragons along the Mary and Michael lay-line. Quetzalcoatl is the winged-dragon-serpent from the culture of the Americas. Water is an anomaly which reacts differently to change contrary to other elements because it expands during freezing (ice) and contracts upon heating (steam). It also has the facility to change rapidly through all the conditions of moist-hot-dry-cold. Because water has memory and can absorb and retain energy for a significant period of time; ancient people quickly discovered the health benefits of bathing in wells and ponds situated above energy gateways.

John Michell in *The Dimensions of Paradise* writes about the wells and water channels beneath the Temple at Jerusalem which energize the entire globe, and fruit trees gathered from the whole world by King Solomon. The energy font at the Atacama Pyramid in Tiwanaku, Bolivia is said to have stimulated the water that circulated throughout its structure poised upon a powerful energy portal. Such energized water stimulated crop nutrition and abundance. The heat of the Sun evaporates water from the oceans to form clouds and a life-giving atmosphere above the surface of our planet. This atmospheric ocean is churned by the jet stream flowing from west to east; and pushed by High and Low pressure spirals spinning clockwise and counterclockwise circulating energy throughout the system. In *The Land of Osiris*, Stephen Mehler discusses the holy virtues of water –a substance of harmony and balance, and the key to all life. Mehler says that water is divine. Water brings life to the Earth's crust in creating a circulatory system like the veins and arteries of the human body.

Holy Precincts & Astronomical Numbers

John Michell says that median circumference of the lintel of the Sarsen ring at Stonehenge is 316.8 feet. This same figure is also the circumference of the foundation pattern of sacred buildings at Glastonbury upon a circle of 316.8 feet. The perimeter of the domain called the Twelve Hides of Glastonbury is 31,680 feet. Michell cites the Roman author Pliny as writing that the measure around the whole universe is 3,168,000 miles. What is this 3168 number?

The atmospheric Halo around the Earth is also called 'the Sub-Lunar circle' between the Moon and the surface of the Earth:

The radius of the Earth (3,960 miles) added to the radius of the Moon (1080 miles) equals

5040 miles x 2 equals the diameter of the Sub-Lunar Circle multiplied by Pi π (3.142857 x 10,080 = **31,680**.000 miles)

The Book of Revelation by St. John the Divine says that each of the four sides of the New Jerusalem will be 12,000 furlongs in length (12,000 x 4 = 48,000 furlongs in perimeter x 660 feet in a furlong = **31,680**,000 feet ÷ 5280 feet in a mile = a square of 6,000 miles in perimeter, or 1500 miles per side. Again, the number **3168** and **31,680** appears.

An important point to remember in all this is that these very significant astronomical and cosmological numbers have been placed among religious texts in order to safe-guard and preserve them under the guardianship of priests, rabbi, and ministers of the sacred temple district. The New Jerusalem also had three gates on each of the four sides facing the cardinal directions, NSEW (3 gates x 4 sides are 12 portals of the zodiac). The height of the wall of the city was 144 *cubits* (144 x 18 inches = 2592 inches ÷ 12 inches = **216** feet {6 x 6 x 6} –the ancient canonical holy number of the sexagesimal system of astronomy).

John Michell reminds us that on the floor of the Temple was a huge native rock called the *Ebhen Shetyyah*, the Stone of Foundation – the Navel Omphalos of the Earth; the source of health, fertility, and inspiration to the world. John Michell in *The Dimensions of Paradise* cites Werner Wolf and Salverte who regarded the Temple of Solomon as an alchemical generator and storehouse of sacred energy because Josephus's *Antiquities of the Jews* described the inner chamber of the Holy of Holies as lined with golden-plated walls and containing numerous apparatus of brass –both known conductors of electrical energy. Others have noticed ancient accounts of sharp spikes with gilt tips on the roof of the temple and metallic tubes communicating with the caverns beneath the temple to guide electrical charges from Earth and Sky to commune together in a sacred marriage of Heaven and Earth. The Great Pyramid of Egypt at Giza and the Pyramid of the Sun at Tenochtitlan outside Mexico City have caves underneath their main structures. Most Gothic cathedrals in Europe have vaulted chambers and subterranean crypts below their main altars –in emulation of caves which were natural energy collectors. These crypts were often used as mausoleum to hold the bodies and sacred bones of saints and popes which ameliorated the holy energy at such a site; and therefore added sanctity to the rituals, prayers, and transubstantiations of material bread and wine into holy essences.

India, China & The Ming Tang –'Hall of Spiritual Illumination'

Laird Scranton in *China's Cosmological Prehistory* tells us that according to Paul Wheatley in *The Pivot of the Four Quarters* that most of the great and ancient cities of India, China, and Asia where planned as 'cosmic cities' aligned to the cardinal points of the compass and the seasonal motions of the Sun and Moon. Ancient Chinese culture was firmly entrenched in *feng shi* and the cosmological worldview of the connection between Heaven and Earth through emperor and government. They called their holy temple the *Ming Tang*, or the *Hall of Spiritual Illumination*.

Laird Scranton points out similarities of the Dogon ark or granary (which held the seeds of the eight cultivated grains), the Indian Stupa, and the Chinese Well-Field system within a perimeter of eight squares surrounding a central ninth square which contained a well. These fields created a checker-board pattern in the agricultural landscape. The act of plowing a field was equated with weaving cloth, as both these civilizing skills were carried out in the same method, which was said to mirror the very process of creation. Traditionally, each square measured eight cubits along one side (8 cubits x 18" = 144" ÷ 12" = 12 feet square). Each of the eight plots was cultivated by a family. The central square that contained the well belonged to the local lord or governing agency which assessed a tax on the other eight units ranging from 10% to 12.5%. Scranton says that the nine field plan was indeed the model for temples because of the well-defined astronomical grid upon which heavenly alignments could be recorded and shown by walls and stones. This traditional layout is seen in olden Chinese cities and palaces. We remember too that this square layout was the blueprint of the Maya which we discussed earlier, and the cultural pattern of temples in most cultures. This again supports the theory that astronomy made the temple, then the palace which in turn preceded the development of cities and the origins of the crafts and civilization.

Lockyer in *The Dawn of Astronomy* tells us that the temple of the Sun at Peking is orientated to the winter solstice, and is arranged according to the number nine (like the 9 field system). The altar is ascended by 27 steps. The circular roofed structure is 99 feet tall.

The south altar, consisting of triple circular terraces of the Temple of Heaven is 210 feet in diameter (like many of the mounds in the Ohio Valley: 210 x 3.142857 = 660 feet). On the pavement are nine circles of as many heavens, consisting of nine stones, then a circle of 18 stones, and then a circle of 27 stones. Yet, there are 28 constellations in the Chinese lunar zodiac.

Spiritual Temples of China

The article below by David W. Pankenier, Ph.D of Lehigh University, *Cosmic Capitals and Numinous Precincts in Early China* (Journal of Cosmology, 2010):

Classical texts tell us that following the establishment of the new Zhou dynasty (1046–256 BC) capital at Luoyang in mid-11th century BC, a precedent-setting assembly of all the vassals of the realm was convened in the sacred precinct called *Ming Tang*, 'Hall of Numinous Brightness', and the Grand Ancestral Temple of the Son of Heaven, wherein the Emperor sacrifices to his ancestors. The lineage of Xia called this place the Chamber of Generations.

The Northern Asterism dwells in its place (the Ming Tang) while all the myriad stars circle it, and the ten-thousand things are regulated by it. It is the source from which springs governance and instruction, and the origin of all change and transformation, manifesting unity. Therefore, it is said of the *Ming Tang* that its affairs are great and its meaning profound concerning the many aspects of Purity, Governance, Veneration, Light, and Learning. It is also referred to as the temple 'surrounded on four sides by water.'

Pankenier writes, "The Bright Hall is a microcosm in which both cosmos and state are completely realized. It is a ritual complex that combines rites to ancestors and cosmic deities; an administrative center where all officials are gathered and all policies enacted; and an educational institution in which all true teachings are presented. It is also the summation of the ritual structures of earlier dynasties.

As a chart of the cosmos, the source of order, and a summation of history, it becomes the perfect image of power."

The Ming Tang has political and religious significance. As well, the solar and lunar observations essential to calendric astronomy would also have been performed within these precincts. Given the archetypal role of proper orientation based on the guidance derived from the 'images' suspended in the heavens, it now seems clear that the 'Pure Temple,' namely the Great Square of Pegasus displayed so prominently in the night sky above –may actually have been the prototype of the *Ming Tang* on the ground.

In the *Records of Monthly Ordinances*, Cai Yong writes, "The *Mingtang* is that wherein the unification of all things by Heaven and Earth is manifest. The stellar image in Heaven through which the *Mingtang* communicates is called the Northern Asterism (Uma). Therefore, its twelve palaces here below are the twelve solar chronograms. The water surrounds it on the four sides, emblematic of the king's acting as the model for all under Heaven, his virtue reaching abroad to the Four Seas. Here we have it explicitly stated that the correspondence between *Mingtang* and Heaven is not merely one of cosmological analogy, but that, in fact, this sacred space is precisely the *axis mundi* through which the terrestrial sovereign communicates with his celestial counterpart at the Pole.

The yin and yang of the *Mingtang* are the means by which the kingly ruler responds to Heaven. The scheme of the *Mingtang* is that it is surrounded by water swirling leftward in imitation of Heaven. In the interior is the 'Great Hall' in imitation of the Purple Tenuity Palace –the circumpolar stars in *Uma* and *Draco*.

> To the south there is the *Mingtang*, in imitation of *taiwei*, Palace of Grand Tenuity –stars in Leo and Virgo
>
> Emerging from the west there is the Assembly of Emblems, in imitation of Five Ponds –the stars in Auriga.
>
> Emerging from it to the north there is the 'Somber Hall,' in imitation of the Square of Pegasus.

Emerging from it to the east there is the Green *yang*, in imitation of the Celestial Marketplace – stars in Ophiucus and Hercules.

The Supernal Lord Shangdi's four seasons govern its own palace. The kingly ruler carrying out Heaven's unification of all things attends to the affairs of the kingdom from the appropriate quarter.

The *Mingtang* was round above and square below, on the four sides there were twelve doors and nine rooms, without common walls. Outside the rooms, within the columns and beneath the silk atrium awnings were installed mechanical wheels and pale blue-green silk decorated with blue semi-precious stones which resembled the sky. On it were painted the Polar Asterism and lunar lodges, so that the temple resembled the canopy of Heaven. Each month as the Northern Dipper pointed to successive chronograms, it revolved to correspond to the way of Heaven. On top of the temple was added a Numinous Terrace, and below water was led in to form the Circular Moat, and along the water's edge stones were laid to form embankments, in this respect according with the ancient scheme.

The Qin Dynasty (221–206 BC) Cosmic Capital

Conscious imitation of the celestial patterns is perfectly consistent with the heavenward orientation of rulership in China from the outset, and in early imperial times gained physical expression, not only in the *Mingtang*, but in the imperial capital itself.

The audience halls to the south of the Wei River in the Menagerie...the E-pang palace, which was five-hundred paces from east to west and fifty rods from north to south . . . From all sides ran stepped passageways reaching directly from the Hall to the Southern Mountains. He built an elevated passageway from *E-pang* palace across the Wei to connect that hall to *Xianyang*, thereby symbolizing the *Gedao* "Stepped Passageway" of Cassiopeia which runs from near the Celestial Pole across the Milky Way to connect with lunar lodge *Yingshi*.

Note here the explicit communication between the opposite sides of the Milky Way being accomplished via the Stepped Passageway. Elsewhere in the same chapter:

> The *Sanfu huangtu* says: 'When the First Emperor of Qin unified all under heaven he made Xianyang his capital. Because he laid out a palace on North Hill, the *Zigong*, circumpolar Palace of Purple Tenuity resembled the Emperor's Palace. The Wei River ran through the capital, simulating the Milky Way.

In the First Emperor Qin's time, in late October to early November the brilliant silvery ribbon of the Milky Way arched across the sky from southwest to northeast, between the circumpolar palace of the heavens and lunar lodge Oxherd (β Cap), precisely like its terrestrial correlate, the Wei River. The Pure Temple (Great Square of Pegasus) was due south, perpendicular to the horizon and only at this moment capable of fulfilling its polar alignment function. Here we have the probable explanation for the Qin dynasty's choice of precisely this time to begin the New Year—the highly symbolic celebratory moment when Heaven above and the sub-celestial realm below were exactly congruent.

The Han Dynasty (206 BC–220 CE) Cosmic Capital

Stephen Hotaling suggests that the contours of the northern wall of the city reproduced the shape of the Northern Dipper, while the southern wall reproduced the shape of the Southern Dipper (lunar lodge #8, φ *Sgr*.) where the ecliptic intersects the Milky Way

> The south of the city wall was in the shape of the Southern Dipper, the north was in the shape of the Northern Dipper;

it is for this reason that until now people refer to the city wall of the Han capital as the 'Dipper wall'.

The east wall of the city, on the other hand, was aligned on true north, while the imperial palaces inside the city, such as the *Weiyang* 'Everlasting Palace,' were rectilinear and cardinally oriented.

Hotaling's drawing shows the stars Dubhe and Merak in the 'bowl' of Ursa Major pointing toward Polaris. However, Polaris was not the Pole Star in the early Han, and the Southern Dipper, whose outline is supposedly replicated in the south wall, should not lie due south directly *behind* the Northern Dipper. Instead it should lie well to the north of the southwesterly direction in which the 'handle' portion of Chang'an's north wall points in the reconstruction.

Hotaling's suggested configuration is one that would typically result from drawing the Dipper on a sheet of paper, then placing this chart face up on the ground in order to plan something according to the stellar pattern. However, proceeding in this fashion would invert the orientation of the Dipper, which is fine if the purpose is merely to draw a chart of the constellation. **To exactly replicate the stellar pattern on the ground, however, one has to place the drawing of the Dipper *face down*,** as if the circumpolar stars had floated down to the ground surface, or been projected through a template [This is the same problem as equating the Giza Pyramids with the belt stars of Orion]. This procedure correctly reproduces the precise configuration of the circumpolar sky on the ground, thereby preserving an *exact correspondence* between the imperial capital and the Supernal Lord's abode at the Pole.

Following the procedure described above: "looking up they took the images from Heaven", then floated them down unmediated to earth. They were not about mapping the sky, but about making a precise simulacrum of the Celestial Pole.

Given the precedent established by the First Emperor of Qin as documented above, who exploited the Wei River's course to make it flow through the capital of Xianyang, and given the fact of the Southern Dipper's actual location is in the "silvery river" of the Milky Way, this curious feature of the south wall of Chang'an also fits the pattern of heaven.

Cardinal alignment has yet to be systematically compiled and analyzed. A significant obstacle is that many site plans in the archaeological reports fail even to indicate the direction of magnetic north, much less axial alignments of structures in azimuth. *Mingtang* from the earliest period are notoriously difficult to identify from excavated foundations, but there are notable examples of precise north-south orientation, such as the Eastern Zhou (8th–7th century BC) royal city of Wangcheng (von Falkenhausen 2006, 172).

Qin tombs differ in two respects from Eastern Zhou-period tombs elsewhere in the Zhou culture sphere: they are overwhelmingly oriented east-west rather than north-south, and they feature flexed rather than extended burial. These idiosyncrasies have been taken as markers of an alien ethnic identity of the Qin people. And indeed it is impressive to observe how the predominant tomb orientation at central Shaanxi cemeteries suddenly shifted by 90 degrees at the transition from Western to Eastern Zhou, when the Qin took over the area from the royal Zhou.

Chinese Cosmology

Henderson in *The Development and Decline of Chinese Cosmology* (1984-2011) gives us much the same testimony regarding the ancient Ming Tang cosmological city and temple:

The city around the temple had to be cosmologically orientated to the four cardinal directions north-south-east-west. The city was a square (sometimes a rectangle) crossed by three roads running east-west, and three roads running north-south producing a royal and sacred city with 12 gates at the end of the roads. Medieval depictions of Jerusalem show it as a round city with two axial avenues crossing its middle; while the New Jerusalem written about in the Bible *Book of Revelation* (21:13) by St. John the Divine also had three gates on each of the four sides facing the cardinal directions like the ideal Ming Tang.

Sometimes the cosmic Ming Tang was crossed by two avenues east-west, and two avenues north-south creating a city of eight districts and a central holy place, equaling nine squares in all like the *well-field pattern* discussed above. In the olden traditions of China there were nine rivers, nine marshes, nine mountains, and nine branches of the Yellow River. Another, but rare form of the Ming Tang was the *quinary* model shaped like a Greek cross of five squares, creating a central holy square surrounded by four districts.

The base measurement of the Ming Tang temple must be 144 feet (12 x 12) on each side. The roof is round with a diameter of 216 feet (6 x 6 x 6). The Great Ancestral Temple of the Luminous Hall is 60 feet square on each side. There are 36 doors and 72 windows. The Chamber for Communicating with the Heavens is based on the number 81 (9 x 9).

Irish Round Towers as Temples

According to the ancient annals of Ireland seven round towers were purposely set alight by fires during sieges. Another seven towers were heavily damaged by thunderbolts of energy from the sky. The Towers of Antrim, Balla in Mayo, and Seir Kieran in Offaly had ballauns built into their structure. Ballaun (comes from French *bol* or bowl) are round indentations in large stones placed above energy spirals; and some are even found in the middle of streams. Many ballaun have multiple holes and occur in Ireland, France, Sweden, Gotland, and the Americas; especially in Peru and the Andes. Some of these generate water; accumulate water from rain, while others need to be filled with water and sometimes milk which is then energized from below. The energized water has spiritual and medicinal properties much sought after. Originally large rounded stones or pebbles were placed in each ballaun hole, and these portable stones, after they became energized, could be taken away to cure people in their homes. Several stones like the 'Deer Stone' in Glendalough are still in place in their ballaun.

Again, the signs for heaven and earth were circle and square; while an octagon symbolized the union of heaven and earth in a form halfway between a circle and a square. Two Irish Round (Heaven symbol) Towers actually sit directly upon square foundations topped with hexagonal foundations, topped with the circular base of the round tower. These towers are at Kilree and Aghaviller in Kilkenny. I have tested the two towers in Kilkenny and found strong currents of positive energy in the tower and equally strong negative emanations in the grounds in front of the tower. Adjacent positive and negative spirals appear at all holy places and signify a union between Heaven and Earth.

The round tower of Ferns in Wexford becomes round halfway up from a square tower beneath. The towers of Dungiven, Co. Derry and Tamlaght, Co. Derry rise from a square base. Rosserk, Co. Mayo has a carved image of a round tower on an octagonal base. Ferns, Co. Wexford is an engaged square tower that changes to a high round tower. St. Kevin's Glendalough II, Co. Wicklow is an engaged round tower upon rectangular church. Glendalough III is a square church tower supposed to have become a round tower above the roof line. Kinneigh, Co. Cork is a round tower springing from hexagonal lower tower.

Notable octagonal structures include: the Lateran Baptistery Rome (315 AD) and Church of the Nativity in Bethlehem (333 AD both built by Constantine), Church of Bosra, Syria (512 AD), San Vitale in Ravenna (526 AD), Muslim Dome of the Rock (mid to late 600's), Chapel at Aachen by Charlemagne (805 AD), Poplar Forest by Jefferson (1805).

Cosmological Worldview and Religion

Each person is a sacred individual in a sacred universe. Everyone is a microcosm of the macrocosm of the Cosmic Mind which has created the universe. As children of the macrocosm, we may ask the universe anything and receive the answer. This is the physics of prayer which many people still use today. The Ancient Cosmological Worldview is based upon these fundamentals that we are children loved by our creator. The Cosmos is energy in the form of a Universal Mind which electrifies, inspires, communicates with, and vivifies everything. Because we are all children of the Creator we should 'love God and neighbor as ourselves' –a saying from the Golden Age that has come down to us. Another saying from this wonderful time is 'On Earth as it is in Heaven,' and 'Do unto others as you wish them to do unto you.'

The physics of Golden Age science concerns a hierarchy of dispassionate counter-opposed cycles of moist-hot-dry-cold revolving over and over again. The universe constantly changes and in the person of Brahma lives a lifetime; and sleeps, recuperating for an equal period of time. The cosmos is composed of equal parts of Order and Chaos whose eternal conflict creates change and energy. Every person experiences equal portions of Order and Chaos –harm and joy. During the course of our lives we and our loved ones cross the path of the relentless physics of the universe. This is part of the order and chaos; and not part of anything personal. Learning this law helps us to understand without anger or jealousy. All of us are equally served.

Because we are the children of the Highest Intelligence, we are free to choose our course of action; and free to contemplate its outcome and our choice. Fate is the delusion of total Order which would grind the cosmos to a halt. The Universe is eternal –having no beginning, nor end. Therefore it has no goal or purpose for us or the universe, other than 'being' –which is sheer existence. If you must have a 'goal,' let it be 'love God and neighbor.' There is no battle between good and evil –no 'Armageddon.' There is no such thing as 'progress,' or that things are getting 'better.' All these ideas are the false propaganda of merchants, politicians, educators, and corrupt rulers of governments in this world.

There is no death because thermodynamic law of the conservation of energy says that energy can neither be created nor destroyed. The wonderful quality of energy is that it can be moved, transformed, changed, and transmuted; but never destroyed. The spark in the soul that incarnates life in matter enters our world from the matrix of the galaxy in the region on the border of Gemini and Taurus near the 'Hearth-stones of Creation' of Orion. At the conclusion of our time on Earth our souls are swallowed by the vortex between Scorpio and Sagittarius where modern science locates the 'Black Hole.'

Trans-Substantiation of Bread & Wine

It is an indisputable fact that the Roman and other Christian churches were founded upon pagan sites and that their high altars were placed over energy nodes used by ancient people. It is likely that Druids practiced trans-substantiation of ordinary water into energized water, a divine elixir of great power and blessings. The holy bread is fruit of the earth. The holy wine is the fruit of the Sun and the heavens. The Vatican Councils of the 1960's attempted to reform and modernize the liturgy as well as re-position the sacrificial altars of all Catholic churches –turning them around and moving them closer to the congregation with the priest facing the audience. This stupidity shifted the location of the vital ceremony of trans-substantiation of the bread and wine into the body and blood of our Savior away from the heart of the energy-portal. This portal traditionally existed below the main east-facing altar at the eastern gable-end of the church.

In addition, many priests have abandoned the pulpit, originally placed over an energy node to help project voice and encourage speaking the holy truth with sweet honeyed words. Ministers walk along the isles being chummy with the congregation which are truly not receiving the message, and are abandoning the church every week. Choirs were installed at special stations and places which assisted the sweet melodies of songs. During a trip to the Holy Land we were fortunate enough to visit most of the sites where Our Lord performed miracles. Each of these special places, bar one, was founded over an energy spiral.

The Roman Catholic Church made another grievous energy mistake in the 19th and 20th centuries by banning many of the frolicsome festivities at old fashioned "Patron Day" celebrations around olden churches, holy wells, and ancient sacred sites. In Ireland these were called "Patterns" of the local saint accompanied by jubilations, dancing, singing, sports, contests, and match-making around the ancient holy site. Because of the natural energy at these sites most people generally enjoyed the festivals and came away with a good feeling about the Church, their neighbors, and themselves. But because of some excesses between the opposite sexes, and over indulging in alcoholic spirits –the prudish Victorian priests put an end to these fun-filled occasions –thereby cutting off their nose to spite their face. The Catholic Church has been in decline ever since. Now the fun-starved public runs to unsuitable movies, absurd corporatized sports, and other forms of immoral entertainment. The Church used to be in charge of Time with their bells and clocks on church towers. Since the Middle Ages they were in control of education, schools, hospices, hospitals, alms, and social services. Gradually they have lost all these activities to governments controlled by corporations. Soon they will lose everything. And all this started with their abandonment of ancient sacred traditions concerning the very real and scientifically demonstrable Earth and cosmic energies.

LAWS PROTECTING HOLY SITES

Extreme difficulties exist in respect to the protection of Holy Sites because of their sanctity to different groups in the past; and their historical occupation by groups in the current time. If it can be agreed that a Holy Site has been recognized by different religions or cultures for over 2000 years –then it should be recognized as a World Holy Site accessible in respectful silence, decorum, and good manners to all humanity and protected by all humanity. It should be allowed to be open to those who pray and enjoy these powerful and inspiring places. In the event of wars and insurrections ambassadors may meet at such sites to attempt to expand a sacred peace to war-torn regions.

Protection of Holy Places Law 5727 (Adopted by the Knesset on 27 June 1967)

1. The Holy Places shall be protected from desecration and any other violation and from anything likely to violate the freedom of access of the members of the different religions to the places sacred to them or their feelings with regard to those places.
2. a. Whosoever desecrates or otherwise violates a Holy Place shall be liable to imprisonment for a term of seven years.
   b. Whosoever does anything likely to violate the freedom of access of the members of the different religions to the places sacred to them or their feelings with regard to those places shall be liable to imprisonment for a term of five years.
3. This Law shall add to, and not derogate from, any other law.
4. The Minister of Religious Affairs is charged with the implementation of this Law, and he may, after consultation with, or upon the proposal of, representatives of the religions concerned and with the consent of the Minister of Justice make regulations as to any matter relating to such implementation.
5. This Law shall come into force on the date of its adoption by the Knesset.

LEVI ESHKOL
Prime Minister

Cosmic inspiration at the Sacred Site
The Oracle of Delphi pronounced:

I can count the sands,
And I can measure the oceans.
I have ears for the deaf,
And I know what the dumb man is saying.
Lo, my sense is struck, with the smell of a turtle,
Boiling now in a cauldron with a lamb,
Brass is the cover above, and brass is the vessel beneath it.

The Glorious Hebrew prophet Isaiah, 55.8 proclaims:

"For my thoughts are not your thoughts, neither are your ways my ways, saith the Lord. For as the heavens are higher than the earth, so are my ways higher than your ways, and my thoughts than your thoughts."

The Christian prophet, St. John the Divine, writes in a sacred cave on the Island of Patmos:

The Revelation 1.10-7.17: "I was in the spirit on the Lord's day, and heard behind me a great voice, as of a trumpet saying, I am Alpha and Omega, the first and the last; and what thou seeth, write in a book…and round about the throne were four and twenty seats…and round about the throne were four beasts full of eyes before and behind…fell down before the lamb…and have washed their robes, and made them white in the blood of the lamb…shall lead them unto living fountains of waters: and God shall wipe away all tears from their eyes."

CHAPTER 10

COSMIC MIND

*The Hindu god Vishnu floating upon a coiled
serpent representing the Cosmic Ocean*

People of the Golden Age reasoned that there must be an 'oneness and unity' of complete connectedness throughout the universe for it to function and even exist. They compared the cosmos to the human body and the intelligent mind that controlled that body. These philosophers saw the universe as a giant Cosmic Mind, and that humans were microcosmic models of that Cosmic Mind. Humans could utilize this system to access information, gain answers, and receive cures and help. Because humans are dualistic creatures formed out of spirit and matter; our ancestors combined bodily material force and mental spiritual force to achieve incredible feats of transcendence through all realms of the universe.

Sleep, Dreams & Cogitations of the Mind

Joseph Campbell in *The Mythic Image* (1974) quotes: Shakespeare – *We are such stuff as dreams are made on, and our little life is rounded with a sleep.* A bushman of the Kalahari –*There is a dream dreaming us.* Chuang-tzu, the Chinese sage –*dreamt he was a butterfly, and upon waking wondered if he were a man dreaming, or might not now be a butterfly dreaming it was a man.* An Aztec Poem –*That we come to Earth to live is untrue: We come but to sleep, to dream.* Calderon in *La Vida es Sueno* –*Life is a dream.*

Campbell comments on the image shown above of the Hindu god, Vishnu, sleeping while floating [upon the cosmic ocean which is our Milky Way Galaxy]. The galaxy is portrayed as the coils of the serpent Ananta, whose name is 'Unending.' Below are the five senses, and their wife [or mother], *Draupadi*, the Mind. Growing out of the body of the sleeping Vishnu there is a lotus upon which the God of the Universe, Brahma, is seated high above all. To one side of Brahma is Shiva, the destroyer. On the other side of Brahma is Indra (Zeus-Jupiter) upon a four-tusked white elephant. I believe that Shiva is the element of 'resistance and destruction;' while Indra-Zeus represents the current cosmic age, and therefore represents 'creation.'

In our interpretation, this beautiful cosmic image of our human condition within the structure of the universe centers on the idea that the Cosmic Mind is symbolized by Vishnu with 'eyes closed' – not in sleep; but shutting out the senses, and turning his focus upon the intelligence in the mind. The Cosmic Mind is the creator of All. That is –creation is accomplished by the thoughts of the Creator. How else has anyone ever portrayed 'a thought' so simply and exquisitely? Often, when we think; we do close our eyes and say, "let me think now." Other cultures have used hieroglyphs to represent words or *logos* –to show that the cosmic mind creates, orders, and arranges form and matter through speech. Vishnu, however, is thinking the Creation –and communicating "thought and logos" from the Universe of Brahma –through the Milky Way Galaxy to our minds and senses. It is via this pathway that we share in the Cosmic Mind of the Universe. When we pray to God, we enact the principles of a microcosm (ourselves) communicating with the macrocosm (God), by asking God for help.

The image shows Shiva with two left arms, where one arm in repose suggests that Shiva is resting, while the other arm and hand is supporting Shiva's head in thought. Shiva's bed is the Cosmic Serpent of the Milky Way whose seven auxiliary heads form a halo-headdress around the cranium and mind of Shiva. The feathered headdress of the South and North Native Americans, and the medieval halos around the heads of saints and angels represent the connection of the human mind with the Mind and Energy of the Cosmos.

Dreams represent the formation of thoughts in the mind. And therefore, poets and philosophers have played upon the analogy of God materializing our existence in his thoughts; which some have called dreams. But truly, when we close our eyes –we shut off the bright world of the senses and our perceptions. We enter the illumination of the mind, and the realm of reason and logic. Deprived of the senses, the mind is filled with images, recollections of yesterday and projections of the future. This inner light is the candle of the soul, intimate companion of cosmic energy and the Cosmic Mind. Earlier, we have suggested that the words soul and spirit might be translated as 'intelligent energy.'

The Crystal Skull of the Maya culture is an icon of the Cosmic Mind. The skull is said to serve as a conduit to the Cosmic Mind and thereby the history, memory, and intelligence of the universe. I have heard (in a conversation in Sausalito, May 2013) of one instance of the owner of a massive crystal skull arranging a ceremony to 'en-soul' the skull; that is, to 'activate or tune' the crystal to the knowledge of the cosmos. In other conversations with crystal skull dealers and owners at a dowser's conference in Santa Cruz in 2013, I have heard reports of modern skulls 'visiting' ancient skulls which conversed overnight with the modern replicas. When the owners retrieved their modern skulls; they had to be hidden away for over a month until their constant excited jabbering stopped. In an interview by J. Douglas Kenyon (editor of *Atlantis Rising* & author of *Forbidden History*) –Peter Tompkins (*Secrets of the Great Pyramid* and *The Secret Life of Plants*) discusses the clairvoyant abilities of Geoffrey Hodgeson of New Zealand in the 1920's. Hodgeson had the clairvoyant gift of pinpointing the precise positions of the planets at any given time. Tompkins remarked that the ancients were able to achieve precise astronomical alignments without access to modern instruments because 'the information could be accessed out of themselves.'

Brahma –the Living Universe

Joseph Campbell writes that Brahma lives for 100 divine years which is equal to 311,040,000,000,000 human years. Brahma then rests for 100 divine years. Even though Brahma is the highest Creator god –he and all creation dissolve into the cosmic dreamer, Vishnu, who remains in a dreamless rest equal to Brahma's lifetime of 100 divine years of rest. After this period the lotus dream once again unfurls, and all begins anew. Moreover, in the distances of infinite space, innumerable lotus universes are everywhere unfurling, flowering, and fading, each with its Brahma, as on a boundless lotus lake. Nor in the infinitudes of time will there ever be an end –as in the past there was no beginning –of this flowering and fading of Brahma's worlds. Vishnu begins the terrible last work by pouring his infinite energy into the Sun. He himself becomes the Sun. With its fierce devouring rays, he draws into himself the eyesight of every animate being. The whole world dries up, and Vishnu becomes the wind, the cosmic life-breath, and pulls the enlivening air out of all creatures (Campbell p.143). Finally Vishnu becomes fire, then water; and all elements melt into an undifferentiated fluid out of which they once arose, and will rise again.

Native American Vision Quest

The 'Vision Quest' ritual of maturity and *coming of age* among the Native American Indians is derived from the concept of the Cosmic Mind. The journeying of the shaman to the other realities of the Underworld, Middle World, and the Upper World are a direct devolution from the Cosmic Mind presenting levels and pathways through a flowing and changing universe. On one of the journeys of discovery the shaman seeks his power-animal, a guardian-spirit like form from the animal kingdom. In the Golden Age people conversed with animals. In Greece, Egypt, the Americas, and around the world there are cartoons and images of animals walking upright exactly like Aesop's fables concerning animals behaving like humans. The shaman believes that everything has life, and even the stones can speak. Everything is an aspect of God who pervades all that he has created. Rather than being denounced as a primitive worldview –shamanism is one of the most universal, democratic, and scientific of philosophies. Everyone, even those in extreme poverty can seek and attain knowledge without universities, books, or the internet –by looking into themselves, and the three dimensions of reality, and asking the Cosmic Mind for help and information.

We are three persons in one body. We are born in the past in places and circumstances to a man and a woman from locations and backgrounds far afield. These, our parents tell us their philosophy, religion, and dreams which become our future existence and goals. Thus, we live in the rushing current of a raging river of change flowing from its source in the shadowy past toward its mouth in the nebulous future. Hopefully our parents have told us the truth, that the religion we have learned is unbiased and pure, and that our culture is moral and kind, yet perceptive of the dangers of hypocrisy and the threat of conquest from other lands of jealous and combative people.

The worldview of contemporary science relies upon the micronization and macronization of our senses on the premise that –if we can expand and amplify our hearing, seeing, and other senses, we will finally see everything! The shaman, however, believes that he must examine the three worlds of the subterranean, atmospheric, and cosmic realms to find cures and answers for those who live under the Moon and above the Underworld. This makes abundant good sense since we live between the cosmic and the subterranean domains which influence our lives strongly from above and below.

The Greek 'Cosmic' Philosophers

Alexander of Macedonia conquered the Near East, and promoted a combination of Greek and Oriental culture in the Library of Alexandria. Alexander sent his scouts throughout his newly acquired empire to collect manuscripts of ancient wisdom and science from other nations. But, on the other hand, Alexander ruthlessly burned and destroyed the temples, artwork, and documents of other nations. Please notice below that most of the early Greek philosophers were astronomers, and spoke in terms of a cosmic context.

Heraclitus (535-475 BC) was from the city of Ephesus in Turkey. He says, "Much learning does not teach understanding" and "There is more need to extinguish insolence than an outbreak of fire." The first of his three books was on the Universe. According to some he made his book more obscure in order that none but adepts should approach it. He criticizes his predecessors and contemporaries for their failure to see the unity in experience. He claims to announce an everlasting Word (Logos = word, reason, logic) according to which all things are one in essence. Opposites are necessary for life, but they are unified in a system of balanced exchanges. The world itself is governed by the law of the interchange of elements, symbolized by fire [Fire is the epitome of the cycle of metamorphosis through: water, fire, drought, and cold –over and over again]. Thus the world is not to be identified with any particular substance, but rather with an ongoing process governed by a law of change. Heraclitus is credited with seeking metaphysical foundations and moral applications within physics. Modern physicists also credit Heraclitus as the Father of the Law of the Conservation of Energy.

Anaxagoras (500-428 BC) of Clazomenae in Asia Minor upon the Gulf of Izmir spoke of *'Nous'*, mind and reason as the principle of all things. His fragments include, "For in everything there is a portion of everything...Nous is infinite...the individual mind stems from the cosmic mind." He reintroduced the ancient idea that the universe was Mind, the principle of all things which sets things in order. He also discussed molecules and atoms preparing the way for Aristotle and Democrates. He wrote, "All things were together; then came Mind and set them in order." After this statement he was nicknamed 'the Mind.' His relatives chided him for neglecting his great wealth –and he gave them all a share saying, "Here you look after it, if it bothers you so much." Another asked him, "Do you not have any concern for your native land?" Anaxagoras pointed up to the sky and replied, "I am greatly concerned with my fatherland." He was asked if the hills at Lampsacus would ever become sea, and answered, "Yes, it only needs time." Being asked to what end he had been born, he replied, "To study the Sun, Moon, and the heavens." He called the Sun a fiery mass, and that the Moon reflected the light of the Sun. Anaxagoras was the first to bring Ionian philosophy to Athens. Each year Apollo flew south to the city of Clazomenae for the winter on a chariot drawn by swans. Near this city is *Liman Tepe*, archaic burial sites, and 6th century BC olive presses. The city was the first to ask its farmers to lend it oil <u>*at interest*</u> to exchange it for much needed wheat for its citizens.

Empedocles (484-424 BC) was a native of Agrigentum in Sicily, and a pupil of Pythagoras. He was victorious in the Olympics in horse-racing. Empedocles was offered the kingship but refused because he preferred democracy and the frugal life. His doctrines were that there are four elements: fire, water, earth, and air which are united by love and separated by strife. Change never ceases, and the cycling elements go on through all eternity. Yet, at one time all things were united in one through Love. At another time all things are dispersed through strife. Empedocles said, "None of the gods has created the world; nor has any man –it has always been."

Creation through the Cosmic Mind

Minds communicate by thoughts expressed in words, or *logos*. St. John begins his gospel, "In the beginning was the Word *(Logos)*, and the Word was with God, and the Word was God." The prophet *Isaiah* (55:8-11) says, "My ways are not your ways, and my thoughts are not your thoughts, for as high as the Heavens are above the Earth; so are my ways higher than your ways, and my thoughts higher than your thoughts...for as the rain cometh down...and returns not thither, but waters the earth...So shall my word...go forth out of my mouth; it shall not return to me...but it shall accomplish that which I please, and it shall prosper in the thing whereto I sent it...For you shall go out with joy, and be led forth with peace: the mountains and the hills shall break forth before you into singing, and all the trees of the field shall clap their hands."

Karl Taube tells us in *Aztec and Maya Myths* that "Creation is the result of complementary opposition and conflict. Much like the dialogue between two individuals, the interaction and exchange between opposites constitute a creative act. Quetzalcoatl and Tezcatlipoca form Heaven and Earth in a creative duality of opposite forces. The earth and mountains rose from the primordial waters by the very speech and arguments of these two gods. Word and Mind are cosmological concepts that were common to all cultures during the Golden Age of humanity. Since we are all children of the Holy Cosmic Mind —then we are likewise sacred, equal, and deserving of respect. This is the essence of all law —love God and neighbor as thyself. Hunbatz Men reports that the Maya say, "You are me, and I am you." The Hindu philosophers pronounce, "Tatwam asi" —there go I.

The Laws of Mind
'Mental Change is Complete Change' is one of the conclusions of the *Kybalion —a study of the Hermetic Philosophy of Ancient Egypt and Greece* by Three Initiates (1908). The work says that while we cannot alter events; we can change our attitude about them by understanding the laws that govern them. Because the Universe is wholly mental, it follows that it may be ruled only by mentality. Attitude and personal Hermetic transmutation are accomplished by becoming part of the Principle, instead of opposing it. We are pawns obedient to the environment; the will and desires of others; our inherited tendencies; and numerous other influences. These are formidable obstacles to overcome. But, Mind may be transmuted from state to state, degree to degree, condition to condition, pole to pole, vibration to vibration. Many little things can change a big thing. 'Know thyself' and change thyself in thy Mind and become in tune with

the Mind of the Universe. Do not concern yourself with sweeping out the darkness; but only open the shutters to let in the light. One of the famous conclusions of the philosophy of mind is that nothing is bad for us –and everything can be turned to our advantage. We should not be driven by our desires, but respect everything that happens.

THE ALL is MIND; the Universe is Mental and Intelligent. The cosmos is not beyond our understanding. The individual is able to grasp the laws of the mental universe. Because we are made in the image of the creator, our mind is able to connect with the universal mind. If we are unsure of anything we may ask the cosmic mind for the answer. For as **Anaxagoras** has said, "For in everything there is a portion of everything...Nous is infinite...the individual mind stems from the cosmic mind." The Greeks say, "Man is the Measure of all Things." The human mind is based upon the physics and laws which operate the universe. To understand these physics is to gain mastery of one's own condition.

The Law of the Mirror of Heaven and Earth –the connection and correspondence
Thoth-Hermes-Mercury says, "As above –so it is below. As below –so it is above." This Universal Law allows us to reason from the known to the unknown –because the movements of the heavens have created nature and Earth. Newton expressed it well in saying the force that causes the apple to fall to the ground is the same force that holds the Moon in its orbit around the Earth. The Hubble telescope has shown that gravity is a true universal law that operates in deep space as shown by photos that spiral galaxies collide and buzz-saw through one another –releasing energy and debris into space moving in conformity to the laws of Newtonian gravity and physics. The universe of galaxies, suns and planets is one interconnected system under the same laws of gravity, physics, and energy.

The Law of Constant Motion & Change
Heraclitus of Ephesus proclaims, *"Panta Rei,* everything flows – nothing rests or remains the same." All things vibrate at a different rate and intensity. Today we describe this in terms of *electrical frequency*. Heraclitus said that the only thing that doesn't change is 'change.' He is noted for his remark that 'you cannot step into the same river twice,' because the river has changed, and you have changed. Spirit is at the highest pole of intensity; while matter is at the lowest pole of vibration. Spirit and matter span a spectrum of millions of different rates and modes of vibration. The *Quran* says (ii. 256), "They comprehend not aught of His Knowledge but of what He pleases. It was so destined by the command and wisdom of God the All-High that there should be nine spheres, twelve constellations of the zodiac; seven 'fathers' (planets), four 'mothers' (elements), and three kingdoms of nature (animal, vegetable, mineral). The universal Soul or Mind keeps all these spheres in constant motion."

The Law of the Poles of Duality
All that we experience are opposites: day and night, hot and cold, male and female. Everything is dual, polar, and opposite. Motion produces differences of degree, like hot and cold. The *Kybalion* says, "There is a rhythm in the ebb and flow of the tides of everything. **All things rise and fall. As far as the pendulum swings to the left, it will measure its swing to the right...** This law applies to both physical and mental planes... It is a principle of reaction which manifests itself in the creation and destruction of the worlds, in the rise and fall of nations; in the life history of all things; and finally in the mental states of man." Modern physics proclaims ancient laws such as, "For every action, there is an equal and opposite reaction." Everything in the universe moves in cycles. The great pendulum in the cathedral of the Zocalo in Mexico City swings back

and forth –while slowly advancing around in a circle, following the cycle of night and day. Sri Yukteswar explains in *The Yugas* that the Cycle of the Precession of the Vernal Equinoxes goes through a negative and depraved period of the Dark Ages culminating in the Kali Yuga; and afterward ascending to intellectual enlightenment and moral excellence once again in the Satya Yuga. The follower of Hermes understands the art of transmuting Evil into Good. The evil nightmares are dispelled by the light of day. Night follows day, what goes up must come down. One must pay for pleasure, one must accept pain. Stoicism accepts the laws of the physics of the universe.

The Law of Cause and Effect
The Kybalion says, "Every Cause has its Effect; every Effect has its Cause; everything happens according to the Law." Chance is but a name for a Law not recognized. The universe is a domain of law and order. 'Chance' is not the basis of the universe. Even the hairs on our head are numbered –as scripture tells us. There are chains of unseen preceding causes, all of which had a bearing upon the present. No event creates another event, but is merely a preceding link in the great orderly chain of events. There is continuity between all events precedent, consequent, and subsequent. There may be millions of causes behind the most trifling event.

Confucian and Taoist doctrines that originated from the *I Ching*, believe in the law of cause and effect operating not only in one generation, but through at least three generations, affecting their ancestors, themselves, and their descendants (the Underworld, the Middle-world, and the Upper-world, or the future from heaven). The Chinese believe in karmic retribution in that the effect of good deeds and evil acts remain generation after generation.

*Please note, I do not believe that this law is true to physics – because the universe is half chaos and half order; and if it were totally

regimented and ordered it could not change and would stop moving. Because we are both matter and spirit –we enjoy 'freedom of will' to choose between these two paths.

The Law of Gender
The Kybalion says, "Gender is in everything; everything has its Masculine and Feminine Principles; Gender manifests on all planes." No creation –physical, mental, or spiritual is possible without this principle. Every Male thing has the Female Element: every Female contains also the Male Principle. Jean Richer in *Sacred Geography of the Ancient Greeks* (p.40) writes, "The rite of transvestitism occurs in the initiations, and bisexuality is often associated with the process of immortalization." The ancient Egyptians allowed for male and female aspects of the elementary natures and primal gods. Male and female is expressed by positive and negative charges of energy, which is a canon of the Electrical Theory of the Universe. Gender appears in the Great Duality and Dichotomy of the universe, yin and yang. To this day in Ireland special healing prayers must be passed on from female to male to female to male, to be effective. Students who draw upon this duality of intuition and logic appear to others as charismatic and magnetic personalities. In astrology, the planets manifest gender by preceding the rising Sun. Therefore, Venus is masculine, hot, and warlike when rising before the Sun. When Venus rises after the Sun, she is gentle, moist, and kind.

In conclusion, many philosophers and scientists claim that we do not use the full potential of our mind. But, since our minds are microcosms of the entire potential of the universe; it stands to reason that we need only use a fraction of our minds to operate in the current ambient cycles of the cosmos. Shaman practices of venturing into the future and past regions of the universe to gain information and cures demonstrate the full capacities of our mind.

The Shaman Journey through the Cosmic Mind

In the renowned Golden Age it is said that humans knew the 'language of the birds', that fisherman could talk to fish in the sea, and that humans were in tune with animals and all of nature. The Shaman, Dowser, and Medicine Man were regarded as special persons who had the gift of 'knowing.' Psychologist Carl Jung named the Universal Mind 'the collective unconscious, or the super-conscious.' I was introduced to the concept of the Cosmic Mind at a Dowsing Conference in Santa Cruz, California. One gentleman there taught me to place my hand over an herbal medicine, and ask if it would contribute to my health? Only one medication out of 42 prompted a positive response from the swinging crystal pendulum. Later, I read in Dennis Wheatley's book that I could simply ask my pendulum the correct direction of the equinox or solstice for any place on Earth that I happened to be. This turned out to be a great convenience when investigating the alignments of ancient sites, and provides a great thrill when looking down a long avenue flanked by columns to find that it demarcates the exact position of the equinox for that site.

Our main authority on shamanism will be Michael Harner, *The Way of the Shaman* (1980, Harper & Row, New York); and *Cave and Cosmos*. (2013, North Atlantic Books, Berkeley, California). The art of shaman journeying to other realities is a most ancient form of investigating the Cosmic Mind. The earliest shaman experience comes from the same subterranean caves and channels that guide cosmic energy to the temples and pyramids built over the subterranean world. Brad Olsen writes that shaman believe that sickness is simply the loss of one's energy. In shamanic experience there are three worlds: the subterranean Underworld of the past, the Middle World of our present everyday experience, and the Upper World of Heaven, which is the future. The three worlds are stacked upon the Axis Mundi, or the World Tree, whose roots are in the Underworld, whose trunk is in the Middle World, and whose branches, leaves, and flowers penetrate the Upper World. The Axis Mundi is aligned to the four cardinal directions. Each of the three worlds may have various skins, levels, and dimensions. These layers are often spoken of as the nine levels of the Underworld, or the seven, or even thirteen planes of heaven.

Shamanism seems to lie at the root of ancient religion, philosophy, and tribal worldview. It appears as the intuitive aspect of human judgment, such as the 'knowing' of the dowser in finding water, lost articles, people; as well as diagnosing and effecting cures for the human body and soul. Sometimes these helpful activities are performed 'remotely' by the shaman or dowser to immediately aid persons far away. In my experience in Ireland, a neighbor was able to recite an ancient prayer that cured a cancerous growth in the brain of a lady in Cashel hospital to the utter amazement of the doctors who had told her husband that she would pass before morning.

Michael Harner remarks that the stories of journeying and flying to other worlds, meeting talking animals, historical and religious personalities, going over the rainbow, experiencing beautiful landscapes and gardens with fountains, Golden Cities, Golden Gates, Emerald Cities and crystal palaces –are reported by every culture around the globe. The similarity in myriads of accounts seems to confirm their veracity; but it is hard to differentiate if the person's accounts are original or if they were a mixture of fairy tales that were already heard within the context their culture. One may look at the icon of the Andean Cross from Raqchi, Peru composed of 13 squares within the axis of three worlds, their symbols and time-frame:

> Upper World – Condor – the Future
> Middle World – Puma – the Present
> Underworld – Snake – the Past

This context is surrounded by numerous cosmological rings and cycles which are supported by the dichotomy of day and night, Sun and Moon, male and female, Yin and Yang.

Shamanism awakens after a catastrophic breakdown of civilizations and in remote desolate regions to help native populations survive by offering help from the cosmos to institute basic moral, medical, scientific, astronomical, and religious systems. Shamanism is directly derived from astronomy and cosmology as presented in the worldview of the Golden Age Maya based upon the horizontal cardinal directions and the vertical axis of the three worlds of the world tree.

The Hopi Shaman say that animals, birds, insects, trees, plants, and stones appear in those forms as we see them, but share the same spark of life as we are given. The totem, or power animal, the *Nagual* guardian spirit belongs to the ancient, ancestral, and mythical past of the Golden Age when people conversed with the animals. These are the Worlds of Time which the astronomical cycles have created. The shaman can visit the future, and also communicate with ancestors of the past through frenzied drumming and dancing like Eastern Whirling Dervishes into states that open the door to change into eagles, owls, bears, and wolves, reindeer, and fish. Shamans fabricated masks of their power animals which were depicted on the totem poles of their tribes. The Catholic Church persecuted and denounced these individuals as witches, wizards, and sorcerers –like Giovanni Porta, the colleague of Galileo.

Michael Harner writes that shamanism is the most widespread methodological system of mind-body healing known to humanity. The shaman is the guardian of the psychic and ecological equilibrium of his group as an intermediary between the three worlds. The shaman believes in guardian spirits who give him an alter ego, a powerful alternative identity. Because some of the work that shamans preform requires amazing states of deep concentration most practitioners do not use mind-altering or psychoactive drugs. The studies of the shaman are a never-ending process of struggle and joy. The shaman is a philosopher forever trying to figure out the great puzzle of the universe through his journeys through the levels of the cosmos. He is an ancient scientist who stands in awe of nature and the Creation. Typically, shamans live their ordinary lives as clansmen within the tribe. They also experience the ecstasy of the supernatural world of transformations into other beings and translocation of their body to other places and time, much like the Guru of the Himalayas.

The shaman uses the drum and rattles as a vehicle to enter into the 'Shamanic State of Consciousness.' These instruments simulate a natural rhythm and a beat that are the 'horse, canoe, or vehicle' that transports them into the Upper or Lower Worlds. The Coast Salish of Washington State form a 'spirit boat' where a group of shaman, each with his magical cedar board stuck into the dirt floor, journey to recover a person's health and guardian spirit from the Underworld. The Tsimshian Gitksan actually returned all medical fees if the patient died in their care. Drumming produces changes in the central nervous system because the drum produces many sound frequencies, even though the drum beat itself is of a low frequency. Therefore more energy can be transmitted to the brain. It is the rattle that conveys higher frequency, but of low amplitude not to damage the ear receptors. The Tungus Shaman use bells and iron trinkets on their costumes. Dancing is a form of prayer and sacrifice of your personal energy to your ancestors and your ancient guardian and totem animals. The connection with this Past increases physical energy, mental alertness, self-confidence, and resistance to disease – as well as fighting lies and untruths.

Recognizing and saluting the canonical six directions of the astronomy of the universe the shaman shakes the rattle east, north, west, south; as well as up to the sky, and downward to the Underworld. They then whistle four times to summon the spirits. The shaman understands the physics of energy, and therefore avoids sending his own energy to help another person. He asks only for his own guardian spirit and the patient's guardian spirit's power to assist. Quartz crystals are regarded as 'solidified light' of the sky in order to see and be enlightened. Quartz crystals are a part of the shaman's 'medicine bundle,' and have been found in California burials dating from 8,000 years ago. In Australia quartz crystals were put into water for young shaman trainees to drink. Modern radios, computers, and timepieces use the remarkable electronic powers of crystals to function. Among the Australian Yualai, shamans practiced crystal-gazing to see visions of the past, the present, and the future. The Tsimshian of the Northwest coast of America sent the crystal to get an image of the sick person, and then redirected the crystal to heal that person. Many shaman carry a crystal as a guardian spirit and guide. Sometimes a crystal was given a hard blow to awaken its power and energy –a very dangerous practice in the case of these electrical storage devices.

In the mind of the shaman, pain and infection in the body is called an 'intrusion of harmful power'. Sometimes the shaman will attempt to 'mentally and emotionally' suck the harmful energy out of the person. This transference of dark energy may physically harm the shaman since; according to the laws of thermodynamics, energy cannot be created nor destroyed. Like the work of Edgar Casey, the shaman may enter the body of the patient to investigate the cause of the illness. Sometimes an entire group will form a power circle including the patient whose illness is absorbed bit by bit by the various members of the group. Harner says that this technique has an interesting resemblance to psychoanalysis, including the principle of *counter-transference*. Obviously, the Modern World has adopted all the best ideas from ancient culture. During the transfer the shaman will feel waves of sickness, or pain passing over him. This transfer reminds us of Christ's acceptance of the sins of mankind which were taken up at Calvary during the Crucifixion. The experienced shaman may just pass his hands or a feather over the patient to cleanse the negative energy. Harner quotes Albert Schweitzer who says that each of us have our own doctor within us. Many modern concepts have been directly borrowed from shamanism such as: holistic healing, visualization, altered state of consciousness, psychoanalysis, chemotherapy, hypnotherapy, meditation, positive attitude, stress-reduction, self-healing, and happiness techniques.

The shaman is a 'seeker,' a real philosopher, 'one who knows,' and a person who investigates the world to discover how things really work. Shamanism is an ancient form of intelligent leadership that begins in early maturity with a 'vision quest,' a journey of hardship, deprivation, and exhaustion to ultimately find oneself, and to get into contact with one's inner forces, energy, and their guardian tutelary spirits. The shaman travels from his mind into the Cosmic Mind to visit the 'magic cosmic mountain' and the perfect land of *Shambhala* at Mount Meru in the mythology of India and Tibet. Perhaps, the 'Hall of All Knowledge and Wisdom' may also only exist among the stars in the Upper World, or the caves of the Underworld. The most intellectually advanced cultures such as Egyptians, Vedic, and Maya strongly believed in the three realms of Underworld, Middle World, and the Upper World.

The repetitive drum-beating of shamanism hopes to induce a departure point to descend or to ascend to the different levels such as the holy Ceiba tree whose roots are in the ground, its trunk in the middle, while its branches, leaves and flowers seem to extend into the upper world. This is most dramatically true when the Ceiba tree lined up with the Milky Way establishing a true pathway to and from the sky. Other departure points are the European Christmas tree, the lodge-pole, May Pole, rainbow, Jacob's ladder, chimney, fire-sparks, smoke, smoke-hole, mountain top, rainbow, waterfall, pond, ray of light, flying carpet, mountain top, cave, cenote, rabbit-hole, and many, many other avenues. Folklore and children's fairy-tales also concern these departures and return portals like the rabbit-hole tunnel to another reality in *Alice through the Looking Glass* (originally called *Alice's Adventures Underground*). The Lapland Shaman, like Santa Claus, journey to other worlds on a reindeer sleigh bringing healing articles from foreign lands. The Maya use their smoking mirror and a drug-induced psychedelic state to apprehend and prognosticate the future.

The astrophysicist, Dr. Nikolai Kozyrev, left his special mirror telescope overnight focused on an empty region of the sky. What he found recorded on film was a sharp image of the Andromeda Galaxy where it actually is at the present time. We normally see the Andromeda Galaxy in the location in which it was two million years ago, because it takes that much time for light to travel to Earth. Other experiments were able to image the Andromeda Galaxy in past, present, and future positions. Therefore, the idea of different portals to time may only be portals to different perspectives.

Every action in life, health, and happiness can be reduced to a problem of energy availability. A person with high charisma has boundless energy. Eating pure, raw, and natural foods stimulates pure and powerful energy. Leading a moral life of honesty, truthfulness, and helpfulness transforms your body and mind into a temple of orderly energy and strength. Deception, harmful gossip, lying, stealing, and cheating enervate the body and soul; and allow negative influences to enter into the system. Michael Harner reports of true shamanic journeys involving dismemberment of the shaman's body and its re-memberment with gold, crystals, diamonds, and amethyst which are powerful concentrations of light and energy. The old, lifeless and useless body is given up; and the new vibrant and exciting body is embraced.

Australian Aboriginal
Brad Olsen tells us that the Aboriginal people of Australia are the oldest variety of Homo Sapiens. Creating a rhythm with two sticks and a hallow branch called a *didgeridoo*, the oldest musical instrument in the world, they would dance themselves into a deep trance-like state and invoke the energy of a sacred site located upon ley lines and dragon lines which they called 'song lines'. Aboriginals were hunted and culled like animals; but they are thankfully protected on large sanctuaries like Arnhem Land in the Northern Territory. Aboriginal art and artifacts date to 50,000 years ago, making them the oldest on Earth. In the City of the Moon, also called Burrangie,

there are Egyptian-like relics and tales of giant people who lived in the Golden Age of dreamtime. Aboriginals from 'dreamtime' could communicate telepathically; and therefore, most probably mastered all the arts connected with the belief of the oneness of all life and the cosmos –namely their participation in the knowledge of the Cosmic Mind.

Located in the middle of Australia is the massive orange slab called Ayers Rock, and 'Uluru' by the natives –meaning 'the all-knowing and everlasting,' the most sacred site in Australia. Many 'song lines' radiate toward the coasts from Uluru which has several sacred caves along its base, some of which contain images of snake-men and lizard-men.

Alchemy

Dr. W. Wynn Westcott, a member of multiple esoteric societies, such as Freemasons, Rosicrucian, and Order of the Golden Dawn quotes an Old French passage, "The Sun begins his special form of change in Leo, in his own house… next Scorpio follows and the work reaches completion in Sagittarius." Westcott says, "To perform Alchemical processes requires a simultaneous operation on the astral plane with that of the physical. Unless you are Adept enough to act by Will power. The origins of alchemy go back to the First Time, or Zep Tepi, Isis, the Companions of Horus, and the Followers of the Widow's Son (Horus son of Isis and the slain Osiris). *Al Chemis* comes from Khmi, 'black earth,' the name of Egypt. In Greek it is *Chmeia*, 'to cast together' and associated with Hermes Trismegistus, god of wisdom and Hermetic knowledge. The four male and four female 'chemical gods' of moist-hot-dry-cold were involved in 'khemia,' the transmutation of matter, a term used by Robert Boyle in the Secret College in 1661 AD which became 'chemistry.' In the *Fama Fraternitatis* the Rosicrucians professed that they could make gold out of lead but preferred the Higher Spiritual Alchemy to be more important to the coming Golden Age. (the above from: *Mysteries of the Great Cross of Hendaye –Alchemy and the End of Time* (1999), Weidner & Bridges).

It seems apparent that 'Alchemy' originates from, and is equivalent to 'Hermetic Wisdom.'

Ancient Chemistry or Alchemy is highly esoteric, and therefore has countless analogies like 'Hermetic Wisdom.' Its watchwords are: The Great Work, The Language of Birds, The Old Oak and The Fountain of Life, Chaos of the Wise, and the Beehive, the Widow's son. Alchemists mention many of the great personalities out of ancient mythology such as Atlas, the Hesperides, Jason and the Golden Fleece, and Solomon's seal and the key to all mysteries. In the modern world chemistry has taken over the production of many materials used in fabrication, as well as every sort of medication and panacea. All chemistry involves trade secrets. If one could produce gold out of lead, it is hardly imaginable that they would publish the formula.

The Last Magician

Lon Milo Duquette in *The Key to Solomon's Key* (2010) claims that magic is a 'psychological exercise' that redirects chaotic and destructive energies toward constructive goals. He asserts that *Solomonic Magic* expresses 'convenient personifications' of various potential powers and abilities in the form of 72 spirits and demons. All magic and newspaper astrology are degenerate forms of ancient wisdom, but should be investigated through 'reverse engineering' to arrive at original sources. Sir Isaac Newton has been erroneously labeled 'The Last Magician' because of his inquiring mind searching for answers among ancient disciplines. His introverted and anti-social character exposed him to criticism because he followed the directions of his racing mind.

Energy Vibrations

A crystal pendulum held over a chart developed by Antoine Bovis can measure the energy vibrations of objects held under the palm of your hand; while the objects are focused in your mind. The more frequency in vibrations, the more powerful the energy there is within an object.

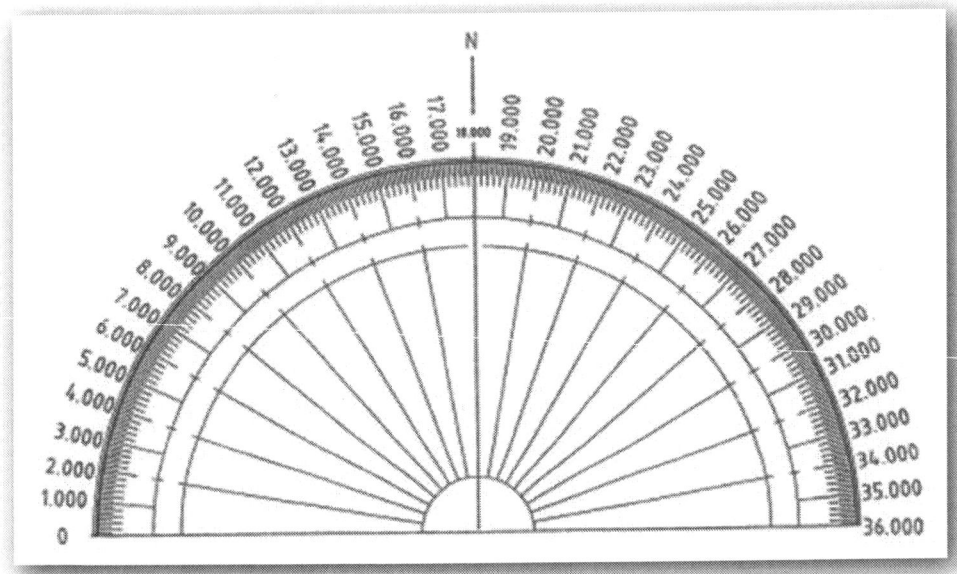

In the 1920's Antoine Bovis discovered that dead bodies of animals did not decay in the King's Chamber of the Great Pyramid at Giza. Such objects went through a process of dehydration. Bovis built a scale model of the pyramid and aligned it to true north. A dead cat also dehydrated underneath his model. In the 1940's unto the 1960's investigators in Czechoslovakia, like Karl Drbal confirmed Bovis' results with the pyramid. They also found that the pyramid kept food from decay, sharpened razors, quickly healed wounds, and helped plants to germinate and grow. Karl Drbal was interested in regeneration of energy, and maintained that the cavity of the Great Pyramid resonated with cosmic microwaves concentrated by the

Earth's magnetic field. Many scientists theorized that the King's Chamber may have been the focus of a powerful piezoelectric field; and indeed scientific magneto-meters registered high levels of geo-magnetic-field energy within the chamber.

The San Andreas Fault Line is a conduit for cosmic and earth energy. Channel 7 news in the Bay Area reported on May 29, 2013 that the Silicon Valley has the highest tuberculosis rates in the nation. Across the Golden Gate Bridge, the County of Marin has the highest cancer rates in the nation. It has often been said that the San Francisco Bay Area, especially Stanford University and Berkeley University have produced an astounding number of Nobel laureates, Olympic athletes, and electronic technology innovators. It may just be possible that athletes, inventors, and technical magicians have extraordinarily high thresholds of nervous energy which may be significantly tempered and balanced by the San Andreas –producing a most fruitful balance of hyper-activity and a strong sedative effect along the fault-line.

CHAPTER 11

DOWSING THE ENERGY GRID

The modern marvels of telephone, television, and telecommunication were achieved in the past using our own mind, body, and the power of an earth-energy site. Discovering energy locations is remarkably simple. Nature herself shows us energy portals where wild bee-hives are found; ant hills, and termite nests in trees. Energy places are easily recognized by extreme twisting and bending of trees and roots, mistletoe, and the strange growths called 'witch's broom.' Ancient people fenced off potential building sites and watched where sheep and cattle congregated, slept, and gave birth in order to locate the most salubrious place to build a house for themselves or a barn for their livestock. They followed the wild bees to their hives built in caves and rocky clefts, and places in the landscape where energy sprang forth to inspire the prophets, to facilitate remote-viewing, telecommunication, and give a golden voice and song to poets and musicians, promote strength, health, and truth in the counsel of their kings and leaders. Ancient people knew the signs of fruitful energy sites and they marked them with standing stones, megalithic art such as 'the Cheese Ring', or even curious symbols such as the *Sheila na Gig*, the counterpart to phallic imagery.

Humans are endowed with five senses which communicate information to the brain. The human body, animals, birds, insects, and bacteria also have many internal senses called 'interoception.' Previously, these internal senses were called 'intuition.' Senses are stimulated internally to alert and safeguard the body. Among them is the facility of 'electroreception' –the ability to detect electrical fields. This sense is found in several species of fish such as sharks and stingrays which have a specialized organ called the *Ampullae of Lorenzini*. Other mammals endowed with this sense include the monotreme orders, dolphins, and platypus. Another of the internal senses found in humans is 'magnetoreception,' the ability to perceive the Earth's magnetic field. This phenomenon has been observed in animal navigation and the migration of birds. It is common to birds, bees, cattle, dogs, foxes, worms, fruit-flies, mice, and bats. Even plants, through cell to cell communication, sense gravity, magnetic fields, light, temperature, humidity, mechanical pressure, and infections.

The human body is a highly-perceptive scientific instrument which has adapted to innumerable extreme conditions throughout the ages of changing climates and environments. It is important for our body mechanism to be able to assay information about gravity, electro-magnetism, and earth-energy. This triad of electricity, magnetism, and gravity may be abbreviated as EMG. Using the instrument of your body to find energy, underground water, petroleum, minerals, and cardinal directions has been called 'dowsing, divining, and witching.' Forked-Y-shaped hazel rods or willow branches, crystal pendulums, and thin copper wire –held in tension to amplify the receptors in the human hands, forearms, and body have all been used to sense and locate the energy vibrations of sought-for objects.

Locating healthy and energized springs of water is vital to temple and city. A forked stick from water-loving trees held in both hands with thumbs turned outwards will bend upward or downward above an underground source of water. Children automatically possess this primal art of dowsing which is part of the 'intuitive sense of knowing' in ancient and modern man. The highest level of this art is 'mental divining' where the practiced and adept person asks the cosmos to provide the answer to a question, or to heal someone far away. Divining and seeking is all part of human culture inherited from the Golden Age in such sayings as: 'Ask and you shall receive –the temple of God is within you –on Earth as it is in Heaven'. Many people still believe in the power of prayer, a remnant of the Golden Age.

The physics of life play out their drama on the surface of the Earth and the atmosphere below the orb of the Moon. The drama is a rich mixture of polarities of positive and negative energies swirling through space. Negative energy comes from beneath the surface of the spinning and revolving Earth, while Positive energy comes from the motion of the Sun and the universe. As we have repeatedly said, negative ground charges of energy seek channels along which they may flow freely such as: the borders of continental plates, fault lines, caves and caverns, subterranean rivers, and all such underground passageways. Barriers and boundaries such as *geological conductivity discontinuity* (caused by differing geologies & interfluves of several aquifer levels), and gravity anomalies become portals that allow these negative electromagnetic ground charges to escape and surge to the surface. It is directly upon these portals of earth-energy that megalithic people built their marvelous temples and structures. Standing stones, obelisks, stone circles, henges, earthen mounds, and pyramids are all efforts to control and channel positive energy from the sky to meld with the powerful negative earth forces in a safe and beneficial fashion. These places where energies from Earth and Heaven meet are called holy sites because of this sacred union which dispenses wondrous blessings, benefits and health to humans and the surrounding landscape.

The Earth's gravity anomalies are related to density distribution within the crust, mantel, and lithosphere. In ancient times gravity's relationship to mass was measured by timing swinging pendulums at different areas. Modern science measures changes in gravity using two satellites (GRACE project) which are on the same orbit with one leading the other by 137 miles (137 is the *fine structure constant* of the ancient Golden Mean proportion from the Golden Age). When the first satellite travels over a region of strong gravity it speeds up; while over an area of lower gravity it slows down minutely. This changes the distance between the two satellites and creates readings which calibrate gravity on Earth as never before. We might understand that strong gravity dominates electromagnetic forces, while weak gravity allows these forces to have greater play and effect.

Around the planet there are many areas of *geological conductivity discontinuity* along borders of different geological formations, and here too electromagnetic forces find their greatest realm of expression where two different geological landscapes meet –because neither one overwhelms the other. Unfortunately, there are too many confusing names for these energy gateways such as: blind springs, domes, spirals, portals, nodes, matrix, vortex, holy lines, dragon lines, lay lines, and sacred caves. I prefer the simple and all-encompassing term, 'energy portal.'

John A. Burke (*Seed of Knowledge, Stone of Plenty*, 2005) makes the illuminating statement that electricity and magnetism are twins because each of these forces generates the appearance of the other. Electricity creates magnetism; and magnetism brings forth electrical current. In reference to gravity and geological boundaries, it may be seen that electromagnetic forces display higher frequency and power when other forces are abated. Electromagnetic forces are heightened by the warmth and light of summertime, as well as 'Dawn Surge' at daybreak when the Earth's electromagnetic shield contracts to protect the Earth from excessive radiation. In rare instances there is a noonday rush of electromagnetic force as seen at the Lost World Pyramid at Tikal. Of course, astrological forces of the planets acting in unison within the solar system diminish or exalt the powers of the Sun and Moon, according to their aspects and relationships with one another. Cosmic energy from the universe is absorbed by the Milky Way galaxy which transfers this energy to the Sun, and ultimately to the Moon, planets and Earth.

High frequency electromagnetic forces are stimulating and beneficial to humans in moderate dosage. Protein is good; while poison is an overdose of protein. Namely, all things in excess are harmful, and all things used in balance and moderation are good for you. Bees, honey, and wax help our understanding of electromagnetic energy. Bees locate and swarm over portals of electromagnetic energy. Their honey was used in its fermented state to create mead, 'the drink of the gods.' Honey, bee pollen, and royal jelly are all super-foods which are highly nourishing, anti-bacterial, and promote weight-loss, strength and health. Wax is used to seal air-tight jugs to preserve food and many other articles. It would seem that honey and wax are holy and special because they are produced over an electromagnetic site where cosmic and earth energy stream forth.

The Cosmic Mind and all minds are scientific mechanisms that store and organize information. When data is better stored, there is more fluidly when retrieved and expertly used in thought and speech. The better used; the faster and more intelligent the composition, which in turn exalts the organism using the information, and allows creatures to operate in a higher zone of easy intellection.

Finally, we may appreciate that energy streams serve to connect greater sections of the Earth by ley lines (dragon lines) such as the Michael and Mary lines in Britain, and the Apollo line from Ireland to Mt. Carmel in the Holy Land. Ley lines were demarcated around Cuzco and Lake Titicaca. The spinning and orbiting Earth causes the dipolar energy of positive and negative charges to form spirals in the air, water, and underground. We should recognize the six-fold directional axis discovered by ancient people which is spinning upward, downward, north, south, east, and west. We shall discuss the teachings of three experts in the field of earth-energy: Guy Underwood (ancient underground water dowsing), Denis Wheatley (traditional water plus atmosphere dowsing), and John A. Burke (modern commercial & laboratory science).

Guy Underwood

In 1969, Master Traditional Dowser, Guy Underwood, wrote *The Pattern of the Past*, a seminal work about water and energy divining.

Country people have always known that wild and domesticated animals such as foxes, badger, cows, sheep, and dogs sought out safe places in the land for sleeping, birthing, and raising their young. The Greek-Phoenician Cadmus was enjoined by an oracle to follow a cow to a place where she would lie down; and there found the Greek city of Thebes. Old retired work horses look for a certain place in a field to stand and enjoy the day. It is natural that we should also seek out these special places to enjoy the benefits of health and energy that birds and foxes already enjoy. A large variety of trees will bend in the direction of underground energy springs. In China *feng-shui* proponents took note of where sheep and cattle consistently chose to lie-down in a field, as indicative of salubrious locations to build agreeable houses for human habitation.

In 1939 Reginald Allender Smith of the British Museum concluded that there might be some connection between the location of ancient monuments and the presence of underground water saying, "At the center of every prehistoric temple there would be found a spot from which a number of underground streams formed a radiating pattern." He called these spots 'Blind Springs,' and said that they existed at Stonehenge, Avebury, Stanton Drew, and all similar sites, as well as at every prehistoric barrow. Allender Smith continued to say, "The constant presence of underground water at the exact center of these circles and earthworks is a significant feature easily verified by others. If this is allowed to be intentional, then the selection of sites for consecration by the Druids and their predecessors no longer appears to be arbitrary, but dictated largely by geological conditions."

Six years earlier in 1933 French archaeologists wrote that the stone avenues at Carnac, Brittany and other stone structures in France were precisely aligned upon underground streams. But it is the *subterranean cavities* themselves which are the channels that conduct electro-magnetic charges, electrically-charged water, hot vapors, and gases directly to these sacred sites. Also, it is a fact that underground and surface streams exhibit a positive charge at their source, while the mouth of these streams is negative. Fish instinctively swim toward the positive pole, and this law is used in clearing fish ponds by inserting a weak positive electrical charge in one area.

The British Society of Dowsers later defined the 'Blind Spring or Dome' as, "A vertical shaft of ascending water that does not rise to the surface of the earth but disperses from a central point through several horizontal streams (usually an uneven number). These Domes/Blind Springs are found under many ancient sites and churches, but also to be found elsewhere throughout the countryside. There is an associated energy field that is unique to a water dome or blind spring."

Underwood was to discover that the location, size, and shape of all the details of stones and buildings upon prehistoric sites were dictated by a *Geodetic* system of energy spirals, lines and junctions in fault-lines, crevices, caverns, tubes, and other natural fissures under the ground. Underwood attests that the perception of these cosmic energies is based upon "Nous" or our participation in the cosmic mind. Knowledge of these geodetic phenomena and the astronomical numbers three and seven are clues to the location and reconstruction of lost and disrupted sites. There are three distinct types of geodetic force lines: water line (-), track line (+), and *aquastat* (+). The courses of these lines may be winding, zigzagged, looped, and folded. Water lines and aquastats often run together at important holy sites. Multiple water lines (up to twelve, but never 7 or 11) had a special significance.

Migrating birds and fish appear to use geodetic lines as part of their navigation maps. Horses, cattle, pigs, sheep, dogs, badgers, moles, hares, rabbits, tortoises, lizards, geese, owls, rooks, wild bees, ants, and gnats decidedly use this system of directional lines. Buffalo, caribou, elephants, deer, and kangaroo follow geodetic track-lines over hundreds of miles during their migrations. Ancient roads and paths have continually been founded upon track lines which follow along natural wandering courses. Mountain sheep have special scrapes and bays on the hills where they go to 'lamb.' Cattle frequently graze upon ancient mounds enjoying the healthy and nourishing energy coming from below. Old military men sleeping rough would try to find where a cow had laid down –a certain cure for their rheumatism. This malady is caused by sleeping directly over simple water-lines, while the other geodetic lines help to cure these aches and pains. During the Second World War about 15,000 people took refuge in Chislehurst Caves in Kent where many of the elderly citizens were cured of their rheumatism. Badger's sets and mole's fortresses are always over blind springs; where gnats hold their swarms and dances. The spire of Salisbury Cathedral is directly over a very large blind spring and the colonies of gnats swirling around the spire are so populous that they look like smoke coming from the tower. Ants and termites found their hills over water-lines, or where these cross one another; and their sink-shafts to their water supply are sometimes over 80 feet deep.

The geodetic lines of Earth-force do not generally influence the greater part of plant life. However certain trees and plants are strongly affected such as willow, apple, yew, cedar, elm, the May-Tree hawthorn, mistletoe, and crow garlic; all of which have been regarded sacred by the ancients. Many of the above varieties have been found in the wild growing over blind springs. Mistletoe has been regarded as an aphrodisiac, an all-heal, and a treatment for barren cattle. The yew tree is one of the oldest and longest lived trees in Britain, and usually found growing upon blind springs at ancient sites and churchyards. Its berries, dried foliage, and sap are accounted poisons. Willow is sacred to the Moon, produces salicylic acid which relieves rheumatism, and appears at the Holy Day of Willows during the Hebrew Feast of Tabernacles. Hazel is the forked twig used by water-diviners, and is likewise the magic wand and staff of the Druids. Apple trees were sacred to Venus and the Hesperides. Geodetic lines often form small loops which are so powerful that they can twist the entire trunk of a tree around. Often ash and other trees strongly lean toward blind springs.

Underwood reveals that ancient man used about thirty kinds of topographic markings to denote the variety of geodetic phenomena such as: ditches, lanes, raised paths and mounds, field divisions, terraces, stone rows and circles, lynchets, barrows, dolmens, rostra, stone seats, spirit holes, heel stones, slab fences, rocking Logan stones, pit dwellings, ponds, dew circles, and large stones which mark energy nodes. Incredibly, this system was used and recognized worldwide. All old walls, hedges, and roads are aligned on geodetic lines. Caesar states that the Druids adjudicated all boundary disputes. Other writers mention that the Druids were trained in geometry, geodesy, and measuring the Earth's surface. Underwood also mentions the importance of the stone gates of a city or temple which are always set over blind springs. He quotes *Proverbs* VIII that Wisdom (Logos) is to be found at the gates of ancient cities.

In his quest to understand earth-energy Guy Underwood examined the architecture of Medieval churches, and discovered that their ground plans directly corresponded to the natural geodetic lines upon which their foundations were placed. This meant that their ground-plan layouts were very irregular as at Southwark Cathedral which has a bend in the nave. At Chichester Cathedral there is hardly a line that is straight, two lines that are parallel, or any angle that is a right-angle. At Canterbury, the nave, choir, and retro-choir are all out of line, and the ground plan displays other marked irregularities. The Church of St. Savin in France has a curved axis. And that of Preuilly-sir-Claise in Touraine has several bends. These are not the only peculiarities to be observed in ecclesiastical architecture, because theoretically churches should point east, and yet few do so; as many are twenty, thirty, or more degrees out of true orientation. Some churches and cathedrals have steeples, Lady Chapels, side chapels, chantries, crypts or stoups, while others have none of these features. Many have a superfluity of doors, often now blocked, as well as apparently unnecessary differences in floor levels, necessitating flights of steps. Indeed, the very position of many churches is inexplicable. Though, there appear to be more convenient nearby sites; some churches are a mile or more from the villages they serve. Winchester Cathedral is built upon a swamp. Another point to be made is that the great size of some remote country churches is utterly disproportionate to past and present congregations.

Underwood's conclusions are that medieval builders and architects followed an almost identical system for location and layout as had been followed in respect to prehistoric temples and early Stone-Age monuments. Apparently, the builders were guided by a rule which they dared not to transgress, namely that they must follow the subterranean cavities and emanations of earth-energy from below in the structures above. As cited earlier, the directives of the early Church of Rome were that Christian missionaries were charged by Pope Gregory the Great to take over pagan sites and build churches directly upon them – keeping the location, and only destroying their pagan idols.

Underwood gives much of the credit for preserving these Stone-Age canons to the Druids, and partly to the Freemasons, and Knights of the Temple of Solomon who learned these traditions from King Hiram, the Phoenician. The Temple of Solomon was precisely orientated to the rising Sun in the east on the equinoxes; and perhaps attuned in some mysterious way to the Shekinah cycle –showing that the union of astronomy and earth-energy was the 'secret key' of the ancient builders. The knowledgeable Traveling Master Masons of the Medieval Ages were held in high regard, as consultants are today; and were exempt from taxes and to some extent the laws of the country. The more modern Freemasons, like George Washington took over the ancient *Native American* site of Jenkins Hill as the focal center of his Capitol Building. 'The Hill' as it is still called is sighted upon two ancient track lines which are naturally orientated –one to the summer solstice, and the other to the winter solstice. The Washington Memorial is 555.5 feet tall, which equals 6666 inches producing the sexagesimal foundation number (555.5 x 12 inches = 6666 inches).

Guy Underwood examined in great detail the geodetic lines underneath the hill figures like the Cerne Abbas Giant (a noted fertility site), the White Horse of Uffington, and also some of the famous medieval cathedrals such as Southwark, Salisbury, Winchester, Chichester, and Westminster.

Dowsing diagram of Salisbury Cathedral by Guy Underwood

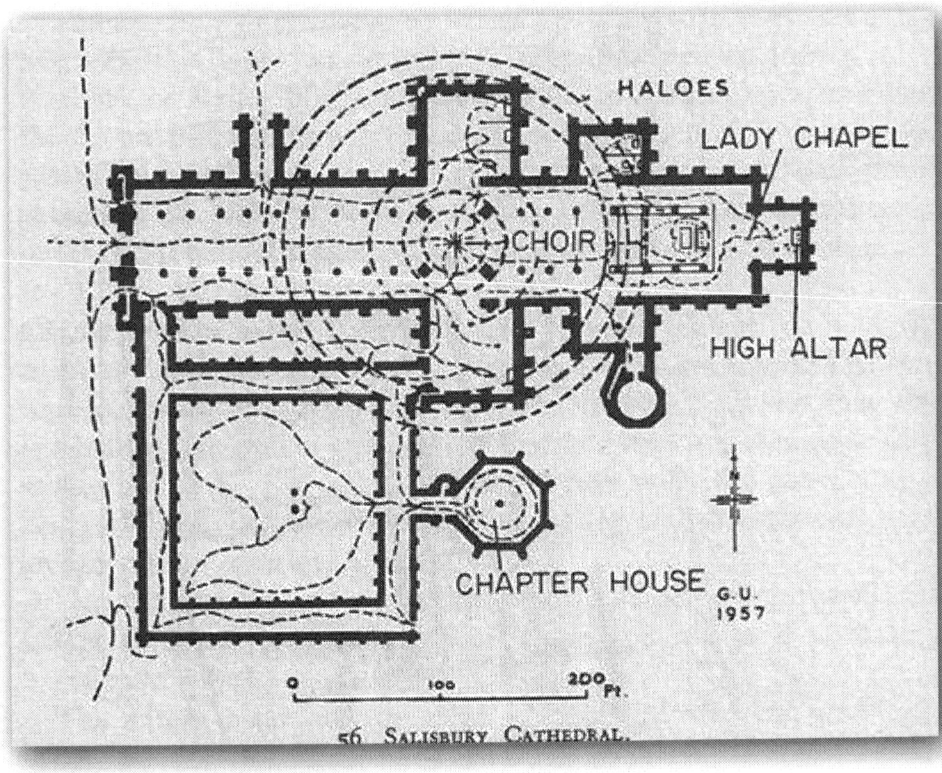

Concerning Stonehenge, Underwood says that a great many geodetic lines converge upon and emerge from the central site, "The number greatly exceeds that of any other site I have prospected." All in all, Guy Underwood has rediscovered an entire ancient science and system of architecture that fosters the participation in cosmic and earth-energy flows that promote good health, natural cures, tranquility, repentance, wisdom, truthful speaking, communication and divine inspiration. Guy Underwood should receive the highest commendation and applause for rediscovering so much of this ancient science. Again, there is nothing quite as profound as the amateur's love of his subject.

Master Dowser Denis Wheatley

Denis Wheatley and D.J. Conway in *The Essential Dowsing Guide* (2000), write that paintings in the Tassili Caves in south Algeria (c. 6000 BC) show human figures dowsing by holding forked sticks. Moses is described finding water with his wand or staff. Crystals attached to pendulums and wands, forked-sticks, and 'L-rods' have been used to discover water, gold, coal, and every useful type of mineral. Dowsers appear on a statue of Chinese Emperor Kwang Su (c.2200 BC) and Emperor Yu, (c.2000 BC) was likewise a noted dowser. Diviners are depicted in Egyptian carvings, while Cleopatra employed dowsers to discover gold. As early as 400 BC, and again in 325 AD and 392 AD, diviners in Rome were executed for attempting to discover state secrets. In 1326 AD Pope John issued a Bull against divining under which many midwives, healers, and dowsers were denounced as witches and burned by the Holy Roman Inquisition. Medieval books depict dowsers prospecting for minerals. General Patton employed dowsers to find water in the North African deserts. Famous names in dowsing are: Leonardo Da Vinci, Robert Boyle, Sir Isaac Newton, Johan Ritter, Thomas Edison, Albert Einstein, Sir J.J. Thompson, and Yuri Geller.

Nonetheless, successful dowsers for coal, water, and health were important, and were sheltered by the community. Since about the 1930's dowsers have been recognized by the Vatican, governments, municipalities, and Stanford Research International. Not recognizing the creative and intuitive abilities of the right brain is tantamount to walking around with one eye closed and one deaf ear. The surveyor's and carpenter's plumb bob has always served as a secret sign of the craft of 'knowers of arcane science.' H. Weaver conducted tests that demonstrate that dowsers and diviners respond to the vibrations of human auras and the electromagnetic fields of many kinds of objects.

Pendulums are made of a variety of objects and stones, though crystals are the most preferred because of their sensitivity to radio waves and electromagnetic phenomena. The suspending thread should be held between the thumb and forefinger because finger-tips are extremely sensitive. Hold your hand, fingers pointing downward, and the body in a relaxed but good posture. Readings are influenced by the Moon, barometric pressure, and one's personal state from time to time. Crystals should be cleaned with salt-water and placed in sunlight because they retain memory of past use and handling by other individuals. Fifteen minutes of practice should be allotted each day instructing the pendulum to circle clockwise, then counter-clockwise, then forward and back, and finally from side to side with either hand. You may then ask which movements represent the 'No' answer, and which movement represents the 'Yes' response. Upon further practice, one may attempt to find specific playing cards turned face-down upon a table; or finding an article that another person has hidden in a room or the garden. Dowsers have invented half-circle pie charts labeled with categories of questions. The pendulum is placed over the base diameter where the lines meet to be able to swing in the field of a specific category. Pendulums are held over the seven main chakras of the body moving clockwise to rebalance and recharge these 'light centers or wheels of light.' The centers are: base of the spine (red), midway between navel and pelvis (orange), the navel (yellow), center of the chest (green), base of the throat (blue), between the eyebrows (purple), and top of the head (lavender). Divining is an earnest and serious pursuit –not a game, and should be conducted with the utmost of humility and sincerity.

Denis Wheatley is a disciple of the legendary Guy Underwood, and inherited his research surveys and notes. Wheatley explains the art and intricacies of dowsing. The Earth is wrapped in a network of energy lines recognized and marked by ancient cultures in the Americas, Australia, Asia, and Africa. These include the St Michael-Apollo energy line which runs from Ireland to England, through France, Italy, Greece, and on to Mount Carmel in the Holy Land. In China these energy paths are called *Dragon Lines* and studied under the science of *Feng-shui* which sought to correct and equalize the flow of earth-energy through the landscape in a most balanced and beneficial way. It is imperative that nothing should block or hinder this flow of earth-energy. There are also 'Dark places' which inhibit the flow of energy and produce melancholy, psychological anguish, and other conditions.

In Britain the main energy lines were named after St. Michael Archangel (yang, male +) and Holy Mother Mary (yin, female -). In 1985 Hamish Miller and Paul Broadhurst tracked these two great geomantic rivers of energy over innumerable sacred places located on a diagonal line that runs through lower Britain, called the Michael and Mary line. Their researches along this line confirm that prehistoric monuments, stone circles, churches, and temples are directly founded upon earth-energy sites. In some places the energy flow is manifest above the ground and even high upon the standing stones.

Wheatley says that when objects are moved –they leave behind a three-dimensional etheric ghost of their past presence which can still be discovered. This applies to ancient stone circles such as Avebury where stones that have fallen or been removed can still be detected. Even a beam of light from a flashlight leaves behind a 'remanence trail' for a minute or so. People and animals also leave these trails behind and can be easily tracked. Trails seem to persist indefinitely so it is important to define a person and a specific time period for a trail that you wish to investigate. One should be very specific about what you wish to find in order to focus your perception of energies in the proper direction. First ask the crystal pendulum if there are coins buried in the field that you are investigating –if the answer is 'no' –do not waste any more time on that project.

The Water Planet

Ancient people regarded water as a sacred element because of its ability to shape-change and to store, conduct, and transmit energy and information. Our earthly-water was regarded as an aspect of the divine water of the Heavenly Ocean, the aether of the universe. In St. John (3,4:10-14) Jesus talks about Moses finding water in the wilderness, and John baptizing in Aenon, and the 'living water', saying; "Whosoever drinketh of the water that I shall give him shall never thirst…" I think that this 'living water' is the energized water found at holy sites where cosmic energy is mixed with earth energy. Thales (6th century BC) and the Asian sages regarded water as the basis of all creation. Water is involved in a continuous cycle evaporating from the oceans to become part of the atmosphere travelling on the wind currents, and falling as snow and rain onto the earth, descending by streams to the oceans in perpetual cycles, again and again. Along with earth, fire, and air; water was offered to the kings and gods in ritual. Most elements expand when heated, and contract when frozen –but water expands in freezing, and shrinks when heated. Water is still an elusive puzzle that has many magical properties; one of which is that it remembers energy, frequency, structure, and any elements with which it has come into contact. Water has memory of things placed into it; even after the substance has been removed. This memory allows water to become transformed into holy water by the energy at a holy site –so that it may convey health, and inspiration.

Dr. Mu Shik Jhon in *The Water Puzzle and the Hexagonal Key* (2004) writes that the amount of water that goes into any organism is the same amount that is expelled. Moisture in the air helps us breathe and keeps the membranes of our nose and throat from drying out. All civilizations have been founded in the proximity of rivers. In Russia water is being placed under pressure and magnetic fields to become a super-strong biomaterial that tolerates high cold and extreme heat. Unfortunately the amount of water on the planet is limited and does not change –even though the population is rising. This makes water high in demand and a great source of wealth. 70% of our planet is covered by water, and we are 70% 'water beings' who use water for saliva and throughout the entire process of digestion. The lubricant that allows our eyes to turn is mostly water. Our muscles are mostly water, as are the instructions of nerve impulses which are transmitted in water. Our blood resembles the chemistry of the ocean. Water is the source of our lives and is directly connected with our health. Turbulent natural water contains considerable oxygen and minerals, and is highly energized. When water freezes it releases a large amount of heat. When it vaporizes, it absorbs heat. Water has the highest surface tension of any liquid.

Both hydrogen and oxygen are gases at normal temperatures, but when they share electrons in covalent bonding water is produced. Water is usually found in five (pentagonal) or six (hexagonal) member units. In the six member hexagonal group water has an atomic weight of 108, and has a huge capacity (called *specific heat*) to store energy. Structured water in the six member hexagonal group is the ultimate safe energy carrier as well as the most efficient metabolic waste removal system for cells and organs. Hexagonal water increases vitality, slows the aging process, enhances the immune system, and prevents disease. Hexagonal units are able to penetrate cells more rapidly to assist in nutrient absorption, weight reduction, waste removal, and overall metabolic function. Structure-making ions like vitamin C and calcium in water assist in hexagonal structuring which can also be induced by electric and magnetic fields to realign the structure. This type of structured water benefits the growth, quality, and healthy taste of crops and meat.

On the other hand, pentagonal, or five-structured, water is brought on by stress, and is associated with cancer and diabetes. 90% of cancers are caused by harmful chemicals in the environment. Since water has memory, recycled and treated water from sewage plants, agricultural run-off and factories is <u>harmful</u> because of the doses of chlorine, bleaches, fluoride, and other chemical disinfectants that have been carried by the water.

After reading Dr. Jhon's book, I attempted to prove the memory factor of water by dropping a pure natural hexagonal crystal into our tap water which by itself registered 2500 on the Bovis scale. After about half an hour the crystal had reformed the water to register 13,000 on the Bovis scale. After that I added ice cubes to the water which then registered 55,000 on the Bovis scale after about two hours. The next morning long after the ice had melted the reading returned to 13,000 where it remained stable. Currently I am producing this energized water and drinking it in the hope that it may improve my health.

Healer Raymond Grace

Raymond Grace is a dowser and noted healer from the Appalachian Mountains of Virginia practicing Native American traditions and ideals of Vision Quests and Thought Forms. In his book, *The Future is Yours –Do Something About It*, he admits that everything has a specific frequency; and advocates 'the Power of Words and Thought.' He gives credit to several Native American teachers, and speaks about Cosmic Intelligence and Mind. From years of study over a broad spectrum of cultures, it is apparent that the idea of our unity with the universe and the Cosmic Mind is an ancient concept stemming from shaman and dowsers of the Golden Age. It is important to recognize this fact –otherwise these ancient and noble Golden Age principles appear as some kind of New-Age philosophy, at which it is easy to scoff and belittle.

Grace speaks about an experiment with energized water where a few drops were put into a swimming pool, and further energized with the aid of a homemade seven-foot diameter ball made out of copper in the form of a sacred-geometry icon called the Flower of Life. This icon is seen at Abydos in Egypt. Grace mentally placed this object in the pool with amazing results on the Bovis scale which registered off the chart. Water from this pool was instrumental in effecting cures for a large number of people.

John A. Burke, a Modern Energy Dowser

John A. Burke is the founder of Pro Seed Technologies which uses a 'carefully controlled shower of electrons' that mimics some of the physics at work at ancient holy energy sites. His artificial versions of electromagnetic energies promote faster growth, higher germination percentage, better stress tolerance, and higher crop yields. He writes that even today Maya farmers bring their seeds to the top of pyramids in Guatemala to be energized by Earth and cosmic power. Years of attempts by John to bring this technology to the world's seed companies failed because the financial profits which could be anticipated were *less* than those garnered by the current *genetically modified organisms*, GMO's.

Burke is a modern scientific energy dowser who uses electromagnetic instruments such as the proton precession magnetometers, fluxgate magnetometers, electrostatic voltmeters, and ground electrodes. He confirms the findings of the U.S. Geological Survey that time and again ancient stone and wooden structures reveal unusual concentrations of geo-magnetism, electrical ground currents, and electrical charge in the air. Burke lists the geological conditions at ancient structures found in Egypt, Europe, North America, Central America, and Peru. These are: gravity anomalies, magnetic anomalies, electric anomalies, geological conductivity discontinuity, seismic fault lines, and unique atmospheric anomalies such as periodic hot winds connected with certain places on the globe. Antoine Bovis, Siemens, DeSalvo, and hosts of others substantiate these gravitational and electromagnetic anomalies at holy sites. Sir William Siemens received a slight electrical shock at the top of the Great Pyramid as he took a sip from his wine bottle. He moistened a newspaper and wrapped it around the wine bottle creating an improvised Leyden jar. The bottle became increasingly charged with electricity, simply by holding it over his head. Then, when sparks began to emerge from the bottle the Arab guide accused him of witchcraft. Siemens touched him with the bottle and the shock knocked him to the ground. Joe Parr says that pyramids are sensitive to astronomical phenomena, the 11-year sunspot cycle, and Earth-Sun alignments to the constellation Orion which is opposite to the galactic center.

Burke tries to distance himself from 'magical incantations, ritual, and the belief in the gods of our forefathers' which ancient people invoked when they brought seeds to the holy places to be blessed. He says that the biochemical changes in the seeds can be replicated by artificial energies in today's modern laboratory. I would challenge this statement because there is an element of 'oneness with the cosmos' which is achieved by the native who offers the seed at the pyramid, and afterwards takes it home and plants it in his own land. Ritual is always the affirmation of the cosmic unity of Heaven and Earth. This affirmation is a belief in unity and love which cannot be replicated in the laboratory.

Burke discusses the Olmec farmers who had invested mind-boggling amounts of labor to build structures whose design concentrated natural earth and cosmic energies available at certain remarkable sites. The Olmec of San Lorenzo Plateau had moved enormous quantities of local basalt, and volcanic lava to build 200 small mounds, 20 man-made lakes lined with magnetic stones atop a 160 foot high flat-toped ridge around 1250 BC. They had also added 25-30 feet of stream gravel impregnated with iron pebbles which are electrically conductive. A magnetic compass needle device was excavated at this site. The ruins of La Venta lie on an island in the middle of a volcanic lake precisely atop one of the largest gravity anomalies in Mexico.

Burke says that we live our lives engaged in a daily electromagnetic-dance with our planet. The Earth is surrounded by its geomagnetic field which protects us from an overdose of radiation, or an over-powerful surge of cosmic energy. The geomagnetic field shrinks tightly as our planet spins each day toward the rising Sun and its powerful gusts of energy rich solar winds. The field then relaxes on the darkening side of the spinning Earth. Ancient man did not require the electromagnetic instruments of modern man because he still had the ability to sense and intuitively experience physical forces. The human body actually contains traces of magnetite (magnetic crystals) as do all animals that use the Earth's magnetic field to navigate when traveling to different places. Modern electromagnetic equipment confirms that all ancient sites were perfectly sited upon electromagnetic portals of energy, thereby attesting to the abilities of the ancient shaman and dowser. Burke personally witnessed the exhibition of these ancient skills by Dave Barron using 'L' shaped dowsing rods at Gungywamp Swamp in Connecticut.

Magnetism and electric force are inextricable twins. A moving electric current generates a magnetic field, and a charging magnetic field generates electric current in anything present that will conduct it. Power from coal, oil, or falling water moves a mass of copper wires past a huge magnet, and electric current is generated. This principle of physics is known as induction. Soil with metallic content or ground that is wet with water easily conducts telluric currents. But when drier soil with less metal content intersects the wet-metallic ground a *geological conductivity discontinuity* occurs. The ground current hitting this boundary has a tendency to reinforce or weaken the daily magnetic fluctuations by several hundred percent. These negative ground currents attract positive air molecules. All these electro-magnetic-gravity (EMG) effects are magnified on islands and peninsulas isolated by water, which thereby become electromagnetic accumulators.

Stone-Age Henges are ancient C-shaped ditches. Even a shallow three-foot deep ditch blocks the average electromagnetic ground current which then follows the path of least resistance around the 'C' and enters into the narrow opening to form a concentration of energy. This is similar to an ocean tidal pond –filling and emptying twice a day with the tides. The energy forces are more powerful during filling and emptying. The ordinary buildup of positive electrical charge in the Earth's atmosphere will find the shortest course to connect with negative electrical charge in the ground, especially an elevated surface such as the top of an artificial mound or pyramid.

The Atmosphere above the Earth

Ancient people called the atmosphere reaching from the crust of the Earth to the orb of the Moon the 'sub-lunar world.' Ancient philosophers divided the Earth from the Heavens, saying the earth is full of negative energy, while the heavens are full of positive energy. We see in the weather report that the atmosphere is full of positive High-Pressure atmospheric spirals spinning *clockwise*. There are also negative Low-Pressure atmospheric spirals spinning *counter-clockwise*. The sub-lunar world seems to be a place where the negative forces of the Earth meet the positive forces of Heaven.

Thunderstorms, Typhoons, and Hurricanes spin *counter-clockwise* and typically carry a negative electrical charge. Because of the prevalence of lightning strikes in the central states of America, mound and pyramid builders choose a flat-topped design often surmounted by wooden temples. This allowed for a balanced and safe energy cauldron to fructify their seeds, and turn their ritual offerings and prayers into direct communication with the divine. Yet, even these wooden temples were occasionally struck by lightning and burned to the ground. The builders chose an electrically active site to build upon like a *geological conductivity discontinuity* where the <u>gravitational forces are weakest</u> and the electromagnetic forces will dominate. Ionization of the atmosphere is when an atom or a molecule has a different number of electrons than protons. More electrons create a negative ion called *anion*. More protons create a positive ion called *cation*.

Burke lists several prominent energy sites in the Americas such as Bear Butte, Sedona, and mentions that the Sioux could not give up their Black Hills because it was their most beloved holy energy site. The famous flat-topped Lost World Pyramid at Tikal (600 BC) has been expanded six times. This pyramid concentrates negative ground current from below and links up with the positive airborne electrical field in the sky. Electrical charges in the air jumped significantly at sunrise when photos showed the atmosphere chocked with electrified light-balls. The main fertility god was Tlaloc, a rain and thunder god in charge of growth. Jaguars were fertility figures found by altars in caves where seeds were exposed as offerings to the gods; and then retrieved to be planted after having absorbed the cave's energy.

Chavin de Huantar (900 BC) in northern Peru at 10,300 feet altitude was a sacred oracular site where water was channeled through a complex system of elaborate stone passages underneath the site that helped expand the existing natural energy. Tiwanaku culture on Lake Titicaca at 13,000 feet above sea level produced raised-bed agricultural plots which tripled the produce compared to modern methods at that altitude. These beds became surrounded by water during the summer rainy season. Aerial views of the southern shore of the lake show endless stretches of ancient raised agricultural beds built in olden times when the water level was higher than now.

The village and the great temple compounds of Tiwanaku and Puma Punku were destroyed by earthquakes and tsunami from the lake. These wondrous complexes sit in a small valley flanked by seismically active fault lines. Tiwanaku is built of a type of basalt, a cousin of the highly magnetic diorite (like the famous bluestones of Stonehenge), which is locally called *andesite* and quarried 45 miles away at Copacabana and Huata across an arm of the lake. The fifty-six foot high Akapana pyramid is built of andesite and red sandstone fitted so exactly that a playing card cannot be inserted between the joints. Human skulls, lower jaws, and long bones were found under the foundations signifying a connection with ancestors, the past, and the Underworld. The pyramid was built in layers of clay and green copper pebbles from the lake as electric conductors.

Water in the pyramid flows through hermetically sealed drains of andesite and red sandstone which weave in and throughout the five levels of the Akapana pyramid as the water cascades downward. The electric-conducting blocks of stone are further connected with copper clamps, creating an electromagnetic circuit. The electromagnetically enhanced water was then conducted to the semi-subterranean courtyard of the Kalasya where the water ran around the inner edge of the walls. Flanking the courtyard are small stone rooms with sliding stone slabs over their small doorways where seeds or other articles were electromagnetically enhanced. At nearby Puma Punku, the Aymara people built a pyramid closer to the fault line upon an andesite outcrop. Here the stone channels still show that the cascading electrified-water was directly conducted to the raised agricultural beds. This highly active water enhanced the crops and also defended the growth during bitter cold nights at this high altitude. Really, this was an incredible achievement by extremely talented scientists and agriculturists.

Local Aymara Shaman make an annual springtime pilgrimage to the andesite hill above the village of Tiwanaku where they experience altered states of consciousness to predict future events including the likelihood of a prosperous growing season and harvest. At sunset by the far edge of the andesite where it meets a sandstone ridge, there is a granite outcrop and a spring (an obvious geological conductivity discontinuity) where the chief shaman often experience an epileptic-like convulsion prior to entering into a seer's trance.

Overlooking the lake at Copacabana there is a steep hill full of oval rock chambers with large flat roof slabs. These appear to be the forerunners of the later artificial pyramids used for seed enhancement at Tiwanaku. The Island of the Sun is an electromagnetic center crossed by a major seismic fault-line. This island is regarded as the birthplace of Andean culture; so much so that the Andean Noah and his ark full of animals landed here after the Great Flood. Earthquake lights have been seen at this famous site. Mysterious lights moving through the sky in the Hudson Valley in New York were also found to be clustered near negative magnetic anomalies.

In Britain, Silbury Hill is the largest man-made earthen-mound in Europe, the top of which was turned into a concentrator of electromagnetic energy. The stones at Avebury (c.2850 BC) are arranged in a perfect positive (male-upright); then negative (female-diamond shaped) sequence of very large stones all the way around its circle. Inside the major and minor circles, the south poles of all the stones point at the next stone in the circle in a clockwise direction, with two exceptions. The stones at the two intact causeway entrances have their magnetic poles aligned with those of the avenues, rather than the clockwise pattern of the circle. Back at the laboratory Burke found that the aligned magnets channeled airborne ions in one direction like an atomic collider or cyclotron. Again, it should be stated that ideas of positive-Heaven and negative-Earth go back to the physics of the Golden Age and the Chinese Yin Yang concepts. Windmill Hill on the Downs is full of numerous chalk hills which are perfect for generating natural electrical currents. Windmill Hill is called a causewayed enclosure which natural conducts electricity. Water is squeezed through the chalk and stripped of its electrons. Water molecules now have a net positive charge, and have left a negative charge behind in the chalk, which would in turn attract positively charged fields in the atmosphere. The entire area is a classic geological conductivity discontinuity of irregular aquifers made up of layers of different clays.

Among other sites founded upon unusual geological formations Burke mentions: Ohio's Serpent Mound (c.321 BC) which exhibits a large negative magnetic anomaly from a meteor strike which attracts positively charged particles from the sky. The Morbihan Peninsula by Carnac contains 11,000 stones aligned in rows. Locmariaquer peninsula is the most seismic region of France surrounded by 31 fault-lines. This region is littered with seismic, gravitational, and magnetic anomalies. At the Cahokia Mounds across the Mississippi from St. Louis there is a transition zone between lower and higher magnetism, where a conductivity discontinuity magnifies energy several fold.

Holy Food – Holy Temple – Holy Pyramid

There are two aphorisms that often come to mind: Baseball is a game of inches, and good health is really the most important thing that we have. Combining these thoughts we could say that life is a game of inches –and that any small advantage that we have over others is really a great advantage. Take for example the notion that the Temple in Jerusalem or the Holy Eucharist wafer of the Catholic Church provides holy food from the universe –food which conveys health, strength, and mental acumen. This would mean that followers of these religions would enjoy a significant advantage over everyone else. Those who received the holy food would be smarter, stronger, and fitter.

In *Seed of Knowledge, Stone of Plenty* John A. Burke and Kaj Halberg explain the pyramid structure and concept as based upon electromagnetic principles that use cosmic energy to create a healthier environment for citizens, as well as enhance foods to a higher level of health and power. The authors say that most of the pyramids were built upon a borderline (an *interfluve*) where multiple aquifer layers surface and create electrical currents. The Giza plateau itself enhances electromagnetic forces through its shape as a 'peninsula' founded upon the intersection of two major limestone layers: the Mokkatam and the Maadi. The Great Pyramid collected the natural electromagnetic forces from the limestone plateau and assembled and concentrated them within its own magnetized (magnesium-limestone) core which was insulated with an outside covering of non-magnetic Tura limestone. This construction directed all the usual negative ground charges toward the apex of the pyramid which was crowned with black granite or a dolomite-limestone cap called a 'pyramidion' (having a magnesium content above twenty-five percent). This pyramidion interacted powerfully with the positively charged *khamsin* winds producing ions and free nitrogen for the holy food and the human environment. Burke and Halberg say that the electric brush discharge would have caused the top of the pyramid to actively glow and ionize the nitrogen molecules in the air to become nitrates that plants can use. Burke suggests that during the rest of the year, during the absence of the khamsin winds, that the pyramids may have been producing negative oxygen ions like a modern ion generator in our living rooms. Proof of this 'brush discharge glow' has been seen many times on the dome of the limestone Church of St. Mary located near to the ancient site of the Shrine of the Phoenix.

We hope that this section has revealed an additional understanding of the physics of earth-energy; and that it may encourage readers to investigate the science and practice of dowsing.

CHAPTER 12

WONDERS OF THE WORLD

MACHU PICCHU – A MOST ANCIENT & HOLY MOUNTAIN

Three grades of stonework appear at Machu Picchu: one for common habitations, another for the Inca Monarch; and lastly, the finest highly polished ashlars for temples, astronomical observation windows and gnomes. The question of superior precision continues to arise again and again. Robert M. Schoch in *Pyramid Quest* discusses the fantasy theories attributing atomic, and death-star laser capabilities to the Great Pyramid. Yet, he finds these meritorious in the fact that they at least attempt to account for the astounding precision in the pyramid's construction and design –a matter which orthodox science fails to address.

The extraordinary care and precision in construction seems to suggest a higher religious motivation connected with all aspects of skywatching and astronomical investigation. One reason for such extraordinary measures could be that the temple was a mechanism for the purpose of capturing holy energy from the sky. Many cultures speak of soma, manna, and divine nectar coming from the heavens to feed and inspire humankind. Precision observation and alignment would be imperative to achieve communication with the divine and to receive the benefits of health, illumination, prophecy, and joy on this highest cosmic level.

Machu Picchu, A Civil Engineering Marvel by Kenneth Wright and Alfredo Zegarra, published by the American Society of Civil

Engineers tells us that Machu Picchu was founded upon a ridge between two mountains with sheer drop-offs on both sides to the Urubamba River which circles the site in ox-bow fashion 1640 feet below. The builders were confronted with 79 inches of rainfall, rock-slides, no level fields for growing any sort of crops, at a remote distance of 50 miles of steep passes and rugged mountain ranges from their capital at Cuzco. The ancient engineers had no draught animals, iron, or the wheel; but managed to move, fashion, and polish granite blocks up to 14 tons and 9 feet long. They were able to achieve a stone city of fountains, palaces, temples, popular housing, level ceremonial plazas, and agricultural terraces that survived intact and fully functioning aqueducts after an incredible period of 500 years. All this was achieved directly upon a wedge-shaped block, or *graben*, between two mountains and two high-angle reverse fault lines including lesser faults, crevices, caves, and shattered-rock located upon one of the most powerful active seismic areas in the world. Wright and Zegarra admit that the entire site is crossed by two major, and many minor geologic faultlines which have opened up numerous routes for water to flow through cracks and fissures.

The details of the construction and several deep excavations revealed even more astounding facts about overcoming the difficulties of the site, as well as uncovering evidence of pre-Inca walls and foundations upon which the Inca expanded. These features included an abandoned underground cave area, plus other subterranean caves, and 18 different masonry styles, types and patterns showing an incredible antiquity! Wright and Zegarra, and modern academics have a problem with the historical time-line trying to deal with the rapid, but brief rise of the Inca who exhibited such experience and knowledge of building and hydraulic engineering. They answer that the Inca watched and inherited their arts and science from the earlier Wari, Tiwanaku (Bolivia), and the Chimu Empire, as well as older Peruvian coastal cultures. [In this way they can keep the Inca in the 1450-1550 AD timeframe without admitting that the Inca were an episode within the advanced Tiwanaku culture that was tens of thousands of years old]. The authors write, "Machu Picchu is a pinnacle of the architectural and engineering works of the Inca civilization, which adopted public works technology from preceding civilizations and then carried that technology to new heights." The authors admit that, "Machu Picchu's drainage infrastructure and its special characteristics comprise the secret of its longevity. Archaeologists and scientists have long overlooked this fact, for without good drainage and foundation construction, not much would be left of the royal estate of Emperor Pachacuti." An estimated 60% of the Inca construction and site preparation lies unseen beneath the ground.

The daunting question must be asked, "Why, why, and why would anyone ever choose such an impossible location?" The authors failed to describe a more compelling context and relationship between Cuzco, the capital, and Machu Picchu; namely their connection through the Sacred Valley. Higher up the Urubamba River at the lowest end of the extremely fertile Sacred Valley (which sits across the mountain from Cuzco), lies one of the oldest continually inhabited cities in the Americas; namely Ollantaytambo, site of Temple Hill and the Six Monoliths. Ollantaytambo is a fortified city that guards the river route to Machu Picchu. The Sacred Valley and Machu Picchu bask in the benefit of the warm air coming upriver through the Urubamba River gorge from the Amazon jungle to warm the mild winter climate and promote abundant growth (without frost) as far up-river as the great agricultural terraces at Pisaq. The point is that Machu Picchu is a very significant element in the wonderful scheme of Cuzco, Sacred Valley, Tipon, and Ollantaytambo. Machu Picchu is the first important defense and fortress guarding the Inca Empire from attacks by the great ancient cities that existed long ago along the Amazon River basin.

But the question remains –why build upon such an unstable hill, when a strong fort like Ollantaytambo already guards the narrow river path? The only answer to this question is that this ancient *shattered* mountain of faults, caves, and water channels was a natural conductor of earth and cosmic energy. Machu Picchu is a natural formed pyramid of energy absorption and concentration.

Overlooking the valley to the east was the *Intimachay*, the Cave of the Sun, and a solar observatory where the sun's rays would penetrate the interior for a few days around the winter solstice. This cave was altered and embellished by the builders. Other ancient caves are to be found at the Temple of the Condor which has many levels and subterranean caves. Also, below the right wing of the Condor is a cave with niches, tall enough to stand in, and a man-made subterranean passage only accessible by crawling (currently closed off). There are many more caves in the surrounding area which were important to the Inca because they believed that they were the mountain entrances of the powerful and energetic gods.

The Inca, or their ancient predecessors, found and developed a perennial spring on the north slope of Machu Picchu Mountain. This supply was augmented by a cleverly designed tributary drainage basin over extensive faulting; and together both sources supported a resident population which varied from 300 to 1000 inhabitants from 1450 to 1550 AD according to the histories. Once these works and fountains were cleared of normal debris the entire system functioned as perfectly as on the first day –after being abandoned for 500 years. The authors explain in detail how elaborate the foundations, drainage systems, interlocking stone walls insured that it would last almost forever. The Inca had also incorporated several flood control systems that diverted excess water into large drainage systems before it would drench the temples, palaces, and homes. The authors also rediscovered the long-lost Inca trail to Vilcabamba in the Amazon rain forests. This trial had several fountains and a water tunnel inside the mountain, which also flowed freely again after minor clean up.

The agricultural terraces served to stabilize the fractured steep mountain by providing protection from excessive runoff and hillside erosion. These terraces were specifically constructed by deep foundation retaining walls, battered at an angle, backed and founded upon medium size stones which were topped by smaller size stones. This triple protection insured that wet soil expansion (like a sponge heavy with water) would not push the walls outward and destroy them. Then, the deep beds behind these retaining walls were carefully filled with a bottom layer of medium gravel (on top of the smaller rough foundation stones. Above this came a substantial depth of sand and fine gravel. Finally, above all this appeared a deep layer of quality loam soil. Wright and Zegarra say that the agricultural terraces high up on Machu Picchu did not produce enough to totally sustain the Inca and his extensive retinue, and some additional edibles, and delicacies were brought in. The Inca invented sustainability. There were special bathing rooms with drains, but no toilets, and human waste was consigned to the organic dung heap which upon curing and drying was spread out upon the terraces.

Wright and Zegarra grew to be amazed by the Inca hydraulic engineering because it exhibited an extremely 'high quality of care,' meaning that they built in reverence for the gods and time immemorial –to the highest possible standards of human ability. The authors write, "The standard of care that the Inca civil engineers and workmen demonstrated was high enough to preserve Machu Picchu for modern research and tourism." Not only that, but the Inca incorporated seismic safeguards, and principles that dealt with excessive water-flows and downpours, as well as water husbandry through droughts.

Curiously, water once used, was never reused or recycled for agriculture or any other purpose. All drains emptied into a large central drain (directly over a geologic fault) which communicated with other drains. In Catholicism, holy water, as well as water used during the washing of the priest's hands at mass, is not allowed to be disposed of in regular plumbing. Roman Catholic churches will usually have a special basin, a *sacrarium* where holy water was conveyed deep within the ground after its ceremonial use. One explanation might be that water was regarded as a conveyance of sacred energy and a conduit of information. Bathing, cooking, or rituals could not be performed with used water even though it may have been used in sacred rituals. This again brings up the 'memory retention' quality of water.

The Inca carried ancestor worship to an unheard of extreme in that their mummified progenitors retained the full measure of their estates in perpetuity. These forefathers were ritualistically fed on many festivals and paraded upon litters through the streets. They were prayed to, petitioned for help and advice, and worshipped as *huacas*, or idols. Native shaman often communicated with their ancestors from the past, asking for their help and advice. Therefore, it was quite natural to preserve and worship their ancient rulers. The Inca had a strong concept of a moral and social philosophy, believing that all citizens were children of the Creator; and therefore worthy of care and respect. In their time, the Inca excelled all other nations in producing surplus foods, blankets, and material goods –enough to sustain their population for several years of drought, famine, or any other need. This is an amazing fact considering that their Empire was larger than that of Alexander of Macedonia. It is also extraordinary that the American hemisphere developed 2/3's of the world's modern food supply. The Inca agricultural college at Tipon developed many hundreds of varieties of potatoes that could survive and prosper at various altitudes. Details of these wonders are to be found in Charles C. Mann's excellent but unappreciated book, *1491, New Revelations of the Americas before Columbus.*

The original Inca claimed to have come from three caves a few miles southwest of Cusco. This group was led by the first Inca monarch, Manco Capac. Other legends say that they originated on the Island of the Sun on Lake Titicaca from where they traveled to their caves of origin. They called their empire *Tawantinsuyu*, the Land of the Four Quarters. Their greatest builder was Sapa Inca, the Emperor Pachacuti, also called The Earth-shaker (an epithet that the Greeks applied to Poseidon). The Inca hierarchy was never more than 500 adult males and about 1,800 people of pure Inca blood. Below them, were the 'adopted Hahua Inca,' trusted neighboring people who filled important positions in the Empire. Below these were local ethnic lords of provincial nobility. Finally and lastly came the Hatun Runa, the heads of families as captains over groups of 10, 50, 100, 1,000, 5,000, and 100,000 families. These paid taxes in the form of labor, manufacturing clothing, and giving military service to the state. This insured that every citizen was fed, clothed, and cared for. The strict code of Inca laws was applied even more harshly to the nobility than the commoners.

Every race and nation from the Golden Age that perfected Temples of Heaven and Earth also adopted high moral and social standards that applied to king and peasant, because this great and illuminating science was based upon the unity of all things through the intelligent energy of the Cosmic Mind.

THE LEANING TOWER OF PISA

The Leaning Tower of Pisa looks like an unusual architectural accident in a country whose builders were renowned throughout the ancient and modern world. The large complex includes a walled fortress, the *Duomo* church, the Baptistery of San Giovanni, the monumental cemetery called the *Camposanto*, and the oratory set upon a site of powerful earth energy celebrated since ancient times.

Pisa was first settled by the Liguri, then the Etruscan-Tyrrhenians, whose sites were taken over by the Romans. Pisa was an ancient naval power, one of the four maritime republics along with Genoa, Venice, and Amalfi; and later a rival of Florence, Luca, and Genoa. The river Arno has silted-up the old harbor which is now 12 kilometers from the Tyrrhenian Sea. At least 16 ancient ships have been discovered in the mud, nine of which are being presently being recovered. More significantly, their cargo was found, including ropes, rigging, fishing equipment, anchors made from stone, wood, and iron, baskets and fishing pots.

The mysterious name *Piazza dei Miracoli* (the Field of Miracles) was created by the Italian writer and poet Gabriele d'Annunzio. The Cathedral or Duomo is the oldest building of the complex and it was dedicated to the Assumption of the Holy Virgin Mary 800 years before 'Assumption' was declared a dogma of the Catholic faith. It was founded in 1063 on the remains of the old Etruscan and Roman temples (*behindthetower.com* 6/6/14).

The tower was built between 1173 and the end of the 14th century. It took so long to build because it started to lean as soon as the third floor was completed and the works were blocked. A century later the works started again. The question must be asked –why would they continue to build it; why not just tear it down and start again? The tower sits upon a vortex which is contained in the apex of a triangle of confined *dead energy* marked by the two pathways on its north-western side. Natural and garden trees lean toward energy spirals in their vicinity and this tower is being pulled toward the large amount of *negative dark energy* in the triangle. This phenomenon may be caused by an ancient meteor strike creating a gravitational anomaly. No man-made solution can prevail over this geo-physical situation, and were the tower to be artificially righted it would snap in two in a very short time because of the pull of dark energy.

It is remarkable that the medieval builders carefully marked the black-energy lines with pathways coming away from the tower. The builders also marked energy-spiral locations with round limestone plugs which are located in the guttering surrounding the pathway around the large *Duomo* church –where these plugs appear to be located almost equally spaced upon an almost perfectly constructed circle walkway around the church. In some instances someone has also marked exceptionally *strong mini-spirals* with a small circular hole engraved upon the pathway stones. These circles are about two inches in diameter; and a crystal pendulum will spin madly like an airplane propeller at just an inch above the ground –an amazing sight!

MALTA'S TEMPLES

Malta is unique for the extreme age of its temples *in curious conjunction* with highly advanced unique construction techniques such as massive stone domes. Malta's geological history shows evidence of multiple floods and tsunami-like churned-up debris much like the evidence at Tiwanaku in Bolivia.

Existing roof corbelling at Hagar Qim, Mnajdra, and other structures curving inward above the walls demonstrate that the temples were domed and roofed in stone with a final oculus in the middle of their roof similar to the oculus in the Pantheon in Rome. The interior debris shows that these advanced cupola domes have fallen in over time. Carved images of stone-roofed temples are found upon temple walls. The thrust of the weight of the stone roof upon the interior walls was managed by rubble in-fill between them and the massive exterior walls of giant stones. This system supported corbelled stones to form a basilica-like cupola over each main chamber. The ground-plans of these temples are very sophisticated just like Renaissance cathedrals with multiple side altars and apses for special devotions. This is remarkable because the temples of Malta are the oldest in the world as affirmed by carbon 14 tests –yet their complex geometry and design places them among the *most advanced* of all megalithic buildings every constructed.

In *Underworld* (p.356) Graham Hancock quotes the work of Anton Mifsud who says, "The accumulation of human remains at the Hypogeum in Hal Saflieni were not related to primary ritual burial, but were brought down into the Hypogeum labyrinth through the action of flood water in a matrix of red earth and soil." Hancock also quotes Renfrew as saying that, "The bones it contained were indeed in such an extreme state of disarrangement that any form of regular internment was out of the question." Hancock then cites the excavation reports which describe disarticulated, non-anatomically disposed remains in an entirely 'unstratified deposit' made of the red earth one finds in our fields. Mifsud argues that only one agency is capable of forming such a conglomerate of animal and human bones, and assorted other materials, all muddled up together and evenly spread throughout –namely a powerful flood. Mifsud then cites the natural limestone caves of Ghar Dalam which contains six distinct layers of flood deposits over a period of 200,000 years. The nearby Tarxien temple complex was covered by a one meter layer of sterile silt. The description of these flood deposits is *precisely similar* to the description of the flood deposits found at Tiwanaku on Lake Titicaca, Bolivia. These descriptions from Tiwanaku were filed away on purpose for the obvious reason that they substantiate the idea of cycles of human devolution, decline, and destruction. The Hypogeum in Malta and Tiwanaku in Bolivia were overwhelmed by a tsunami flood as evidenced in the excavations of a tangled-mess of human bones, domestic animals, household pots and implements in both these sites. Malta also exhibits examples of elongated skulls exactly like those found in South America.

There has been a determined reluctance in the past to admit that the temples of Malta are aligned to numerous astronomical phenomena. In Klaus Albrecht's *Malta's Temples, Alignments and Religious Motives* (2007) and his film *Light and Stone, Malta's Temples at Winter Solstice*, there is absolute documented confirmation of solar and stellar alignments. Albrecht also has superimposed an outline of one of the many 'fat lady' images upon one of the temple ground plans which results in a very close fit. This analogy also allows the solstice light-ray to impregnate the 'fat lady image' in a sacred symbolic light-show of the cosmos energizing and fructifying our planet, Mother-Earth. Klaus Albrecht has patiently subjected most of the incredible temples to scrupulous personal review, documenting equinoctial and solstical alignments. Though the temples of Malta are among the oldest on the planet, yet they are precisely constructed upon intersecting circles, *vesica pisces*, and pentagons (supposedly unknown in those distant times).

The southern temple at Mnajdra still shows much of the lower structure of the dome with clever wedging at the joints. The space between the rounded five chambers and the outer circle of the temple is again filled with stone while the footing of the outer wall is placed upon flat-lying stones to prevent outward slippage. Even today there is an extraordinary frequency of domes on churches in Malta testifying to the people's ancient culture and skill in building these complicated structures. The combination of astronomical alignments, geometric ground plans, domes, and megalithic engineering of the highest caliber makes these temples among the most amazing wonders of the world.

One of the great charms of Malta are the many statues of the so called 'fat ladies' of antiquity. This is a very gross and ignorant misnomer because the round and corpulent fat-lady is of course our Mother Earth, the ancient goddess Ge or Gaia, consort to Uranus, the god of the heavens. Uranus and Ge ruled the Age of Scorpio. They produced the all-powerful Great Titians of the subsequent Age of Sagittarius, builders and surveyors of the Golden Age. Klaus Albrecht shows how 'the Round Earth Mother' design actually fits into the ground plan of the unusual temples of Malta. The Matrix of Round Earth Mother is precisely aligned to the morning rays of the Summer Solstice to receive the seed and energy of the universe from our galaxy, and through the Sun in order to create and refresh life on our planet.

ENERGY IN THE HOLY LAND

In 2013 we were very fortunate to participate in a pilgrimage from St. Mary's parish in Lucan, Ireland which involved a variety of especially nice people from all over the island. Since my teenage years, I have been blessed with a special gift of perceiving what is commonly called earth energy. The tour included a great variety of the holy places mentioned in the New and Old Testament.

<u>All of the following sites</u> tested positive for strong emanations of earth-energy except one:

Baptismal site of Bethany on the Jordan, Petra Treasury, Jerash (Roman town with solar and cardinal alignments), Capernaum, Tabgha (multiplication of the loaves & fishes), Church of the Primacy of St. Peter (Mensa Christi), Mount of Beatitudes (Sermon on the Mount), Mount Tabor (Church of Transfiguration), Cana (First Miracle of water into wine), Nazareth (Mary's Well), Church of the Annunciation, Home of the Holy Family, St. Joseph's Workshop (There was no energy by the altar –but ample energy at the bathing pool), Church of the Ascension, Pater Noster & Dominus Flevit, Garden of Gethsemane, Bethlehem Church of the Nativity, Church of St. Ann and Pool of Bethesda, Church of Flagellation, Holy Sepulcher (There was no energy at the thin yellow marble slab where Christ was said to have been laid near the entrance), Tomb of King David on Mt. Zion, the Upper Room and the Dormition Abbey, Ein Karem and the Church of the Visitation, and finally the Church of St. John.

ANCIENT GIANTS OF THE OHIO VALLEY MOUND CULTURE

Recently an archaeologist came out with the statement that there are vestiges of tens of thousands of stone circles upon the American Great Plains. Reports concerning a scientifically advanced history and antiquity of North America have always been quashed by contemporary academics and carefully controlled and edited by the Smithsonian Institute to preserve the simple fable that Europeans came to an almost virgin 'new continent' laid out for them, and sparsely populated by a handful of Asiatic immigrants who had crossed a northern land or ice-bridge.

It is quite certain that many people have heard of the ancient Serpent Mound in Ohio. It is also quite certain that very few people know that the Allegewi-Hopewell culture credited with this site is also responsible for no less than 17,000 burial mounds, henges, strong fortresses, and sophisticated astronomical holy sites in America. The President of the United States, Abraham Lincoln, actually came in contact with some of these ancient works, and is quoted as saying, "The eyes of that species of extinct giants, whose bones fill the mounds of America, have gazed upon the Niagara, as ours do now."

In the Allegewi-Hopewell culture of Ohio, Black Elk speaks, "Wanka Tanka placed the stars in such a manner so that what is in the heavens is on Earth, what is on Earth is in the heavens in the same way. When we pray in this manner, what is done in the skies is done on Earth in the same way. Together, all creation participates in the ceremonies every year." Near the Mississippi river at Cahokia (City of the Sun) lies Monk's Mound, a tall flat-topped earthen structure with a base of 16 acres –larger than the Great Pyramid at Giza. Because of its many astronomical alignments, this site became the birthplace of American archaeoastronomy.

In *The Nephilim Chronicles –A Travel Guide to the Ancient Ruins in the Ohio Valley* (2010) and also *The Nephilim Chronicles –Fallen Angels in the Ohio Valley* (2010), Fritz Zimmerman discusses the astronomical alignments of many of these works which tracked the solstices, equinoxes, cardinal directions, the agricultural quarter-days (May 1st & Nov. 1st), as well as the 18.618 year cycle of the most northerly and southerly declinations of Moon. Indeed, the astronomy of the Allegewi-Hopewell was as well-developed as any astronomy upon the face of the globe. Having been educated in America, this is an astounding revelation of Golden Age science and culture that existed all over the world –but someone forgot to mention it in the classes I took.

In general the dating of these sites must be suspect because most of the skeletal and woven cloth remains turned to dust when exposed to the air. The average remains were giants from seven to twelve feet tall with a median height of eight feet. At many of these excavations people were able to put the entire giant cranium over their own head like a helmet. Giants have been found in Tibet, Pohnpei at Nan Madol where highly magnetized large crystals are present in the basalt rocks. Many other places on the globe have traditions about giants, namely England, Ireland, Morocco, Germany, Malta, Baalbek, China, and Tibet. Names of giants such as Atlas, Antaeus, Hercules, Nimrod are associated with the Golden Age before the Great Flood.

At the North Fork Works near Chillicothe the massive skeleton of a man was encased in a veritable copper armor including a copper cap with jaw moldings and copper-covered wooden antlers protruding on each side of his helmet. Copper plates also covered the chest, stomach and arms. Around his neck was a necklace of bear's teeth set with pearls. The mouth of the warrior was stuffed with pearls of immense size. He was accompanied by a woman buried alongside. At Seip Mound and Earthworks in the Paint Creek Valley a Pan-pipe instrument was found. Four bodies were shrouded in a colorful fabric completely covered with holed-pearls. Such a costume is reminiscent of the *star-mantel* of the Maya kings. Unfortunately this fabric soon crumbled in the warm air, but was luckily photographed and sketched as well.

Zimmerman cites the significant numbers that were used over and over again: 3, 8, 30, 33, 120, 210, 212, 215, 240, 250, 420, 555, 555.5, 660, 666, 800, 1050, 1080, 1740, and 1746. The number, 212 feet appears as a common diameter of the Ohio henges producing a circumference of 666 feet, an important sexagesimal number (212 x 3.142857 = 666.285 feet). Another common diameter is 210 feet producing a circumference of 660 feet (210 x 3.142857143 = 660.000 feet).

Some esoteric scholars say that 666 is said to represent the male Sun, while 1080 represents the Earth- Mother. However, 1080 is the radius of the Moon! The combination of Sun and Moon would be 666 + 1080 = 1746. Curiously, a line of henges on the White River were arranged in distances of 555.5 feet (3.142857142 x 555.5 = 1745.857142 or 1746, the sacred marriage of male and female, yin yang, Heaven and Earth. Sometimes the gateway to these henges is nearly 33 feet wide (32.86335345 squared = 1080, the Moon radius).

One testimony says, "The most skillful engineer of the day would find it difficult, without the aid of instruments, to lay down an accurate square of the great dimensions of those above represented, measuring as they do more than four-fifths of a mile in circumference (*Ancient Monuments of the Mississippi Valley, 1848 Frankfort Works*)." Most of the holy sites are combinations of perfect circles, squares, and octagons. One such square contains an incredible area of 27 acres.

The Great Serpent Mound aligned to the summer solstice sunset. Each of the curves in the snake's body is aligned to the maximums and minimums of the Moon's risings and settings. There are examples of vitrified stone evident at Spruce Hill, Bourneville Village. Unfortunately, many of the artifacts from Mound City were sold to museums in England.

A 12 foot tall giant would probably have a two-foot-long foot, and their standard measurement would be a two-foot long rule. There actually is a *Twenty-Four Inch Gauge* –a working tool of the operative stone mason. Yet, the 12 inch cosmic-astronomical foot appears to be the commonplace measurement in the Ohio Mound cultures. Zimmerman shows that measurements of 210, 555, 660, and 666 feet were used at the Park Complex as distances between the main circle and the mounds aligned toward the summer solstice sunset. The Ohio culture has demonstrated amazing skills in large scale survey and layout. They certainly knew the *canonical* value of Pi described by John Michell as 44 ÷ 14 (or 22 ÷ 7) = 3.142857142 and were able to deal with the concept of square root.

Amazingly, the Newark Henge with a 1250 foot diameter equals that of the Great Henge in Avebury England which also has a 1250 foot diameter (1250 − 666 = 584 days synodic period of Venus). Many of the new American cities were founded upon the ancient Allegewi sites such as Washington D.C., South Charleston, Ashland, Cincinnati, Kalamazoo, Grand Rapids, Aurora, Marion, New Castle, Vincennes, Chillicothe, Frankfort, Portsmouth, and many others. The Native Americans encountered by the European pioneers claimed that they had no knowledge of these Ohio Valley giants being their forbearers and ancestors.

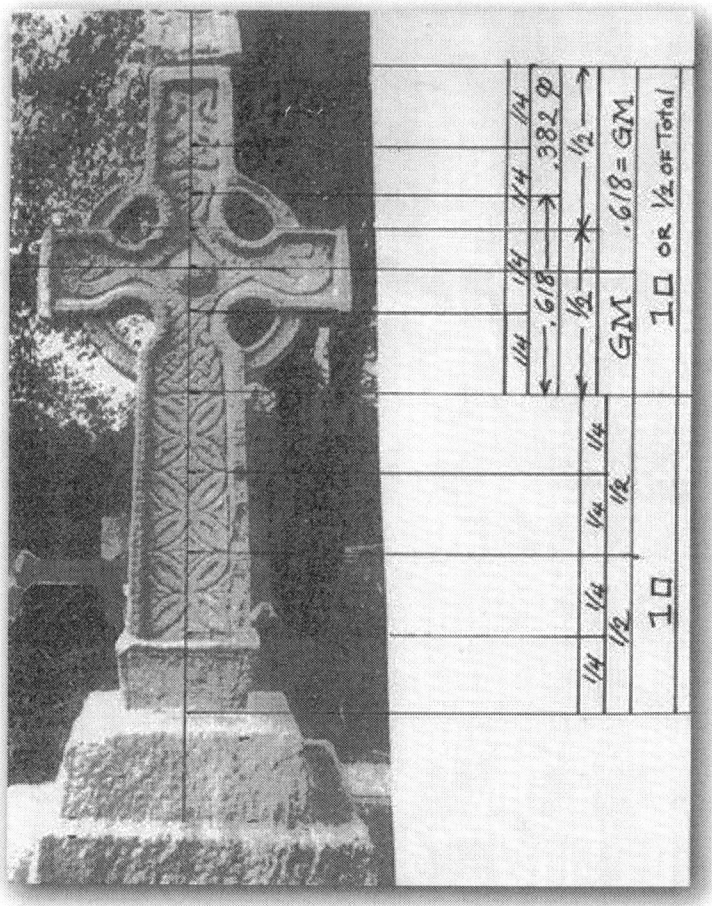

BEE CULTURE & ANCIENT IRISH HIGH CROSSES OF WESTERN OSSORY

The Killamery High Cross is one of the ancient cosmological crosses of Western Ossory, Ireland. This Cross portrays the equinoxes as intertwined double serpents whose bodies cross over one another. This crossover suggests the Sun's passage above and below the equator during the spring and the autumn equinoxes. The pyramid at Chichen Itza in the Yucatan also shows a shadow-play of serpents descending the staircase during the equinoxes. Killamery has three four-petal flowers of the twelve-fold division of the zodiac. The cosmic monster of Mayan tradition appears at the very top of the cross. The Golden Mean (.618 φ) of the top square is the centerline of the cross arm and the central boss. The major Golden Mean (1 + 0.618 Φ) goes through the mystical knot above the boss and below the cosmic monster. Equinox snakes, magic knot, and woven pattern are all positioned within the astronomical circle.

Academics continue to claim that the Golden Mean proportion and Pi were developed in the cultures of the Middle East; and were unknown in Ireland. Yet, Atlas of Fez & Morocco has been consistently revered as the world's greatest astronomer and geographer. His Ancient Prime Meridian off the coast of Africa through the Canary Islands (the Hesperides) was used throughout antiquity, by the Renaissance and modern cartographers until nearly the 18th century of our era.

THE AHENNY COSMOLOGICAL CROSS

The name Ahenny comes from *Ath Eine* (Anna) –the Fort of the Moon. It is perhaps *the* most ancient of the Ossory Cosmological Crosses, which bear no Christian or Old Testament figures.

The Ahenny Cross is not laid upon 0.618 = the Golden Mean; but the approximation that 5 of 8 squares = 0.625. The Golden Ratio is 98.88% of 0.625. This 5/8 trick was used by common craftsmen as

a quick approximation of the Golden Ratio because it was easy to lay out any length into eight boxes where five boxes were close to the mark, namely 98.88% of the Golden Mean.

The proportions of this cross are by no means as elegant as the later High Crosses because it attempts to utilize the base, cross, and beehive cap for the entire Golden Ratio, making the monument too tall and clumsy in relation to the later examples of High Crosses. The mountain range upon which the High Crosses are located is called the Slievenamon. The exact Irish version of this name renders, *The Mountain of the Fair Women*, or a variant which could be interpreted as *The Mountain of the White (Fair) Lady*. Throughout Ireland and England, the White Lady is an epithet of the Moon. Above Ahenny and the Slate Quarries there is a very ancient astronomical observation site called Knockroe which is aligned to the winter solstice like Newgrange.

The clumsiness of this early attempt to create an icon of the advent of the Age of the Messiah rests in the fact of having to incorporate a cosmic cross in between the very ancient base and the capstone which originally surmounted this base. The measurements of this base are absolutely incredible!

Cosmological Numbers of the Ahenny base-stone
The base of the Ahenny Cross tappers from top to bottom. It is therefore proper to measure both the top of the base and the bottom to determine a correct average volume:

> Top of base is: 44" long x 36" wide x 22" tall = 34,848 sq. inches
> Bottom of base is: 48" long x 42" wide x 22" tall = 44,352 sq. inches.
> The average between the two is 39,600 sq. inches (34,848 + 44,352 = **79,200** ÷ 2 = 39,600 sq.in.

The number 39,600 is a factor of the **radius of the Earth, 3,960 miles.**

The number 79,200 is a factor of the **diameter of the Earth 7,920 miles.**

The height of the base, cross, and Omphalos Cap is 96 (± ½ inch) = 8 feet

Each of the eight sections that the artist has created is 12 inches tall. The Cross can also be divided into four main sections of 24 inches each, like the Mason's Gauge.

Therefore, the cross-arm and central boss of the circle is 60 inches tall. 60 inches is a canonical number in the sexagesimal system which the artist chose to represent the center of the cosmos.

SACRED BEE CULTURE

It is suggested that in very ancient times there was no cross at Ahenny, but only the base and the bee-hive Omphalos to mark the site of holy energy, enlightenment and strength –which bees had originally discovered and used for their own benefit.

Guy Underwood, the noted energy dowser, writes that wild bee-hives in nature are found over significant energy portals. This is one of the sacred aspects of the nature of bees; that they are fully in tune with beneficial energy portals; to which they trust their home, their honey factory, and their total survival. This is the meaning of the Omphalos around the world; namely that people have anciently followed the bee to these remarkable places of power which humans adopted as temples, oracles, and holy sites. Karen Bassie-Sweet in *At the Edge of the World, Caves and Late Classical Maya Worldview* (1996) writes that the Maya glyph for fertility is a cave with a beehive inside. The worldwide use of the beehive form is found from the New England rock chambers to the beehive Monk's cells in Ireland, the rounded tumulus chamber at Newgrange, the rounded stone-roofed temples of Malta and the Mediterranean, and the *thalos* tomb of Atreus in Mycenae.

Anciently the Oracle of Delphi was the prophetic seat of Ge (wife of Uranus), the Earth Mother and Great Mother –anciently styled the 'Queen Bee.' The ancient nymphs of divination at Mt. Parnassus above Delphi were called *Melissa* (bees). These nymphs were endowed with song and prophetic power when they dined on honey from the mountain. They became the nurses and teachers of Apollo. After the time of Ge, the second temple was said to have been built by bees. The Pythian priestess of the Oracle of Delphi was called as the 'Delphic Bee.' Pausanias tells of an ancient oracle of Trophonius in Boeotia which was lost and could not be found. The delegation to find the oracle saw a swarm of bees and followed them to a cave in the earth where they rediscovered the oracle. There were nymphs of the 'bee-haunted cave' on Ithaca. Wild bees that lived in clefts of rocks and caves were associated with the *transmigration* of the souls of the dead. Porphyry (233-304 AD) tells us that the exaltation of the Moon is the celestial house of the zodiac sign Taurus from which new souls re-enter the Earth.

Hilda M. Ransome in *The Sacred Bee in Ancient Times and Folklore* describes the ancient bee culture of the Golden Age. In Greek tradition, long before Dionysius introduced wine to the gods, the Olympians enjoyed honey from the bees as their divine beverage, conveying health and energy. Bees were prized for their sweet honey which has innumerable medical benefits. It is a known antibacterial widely used in compound with other drugs and food. It was widely used in rituals and offerings to the gods among many ancient nations; and said to promote sweetness, truth, and facility in speech. Honey was also used as the divine drink for the ritual of 'opening the mouth of the deceased' to give him sustenance. Honey was used to pour into wounds that would not heal, as a preservative and an aid to mummification. Alexander is said to have been swathed in bee's wax and covered in a pure bath of honey, as was the case for prominent rulers in those times. It is recorded that honey was poured as a consecration over the newly laid foundations of temples; such as the Temple of the Moon-god, named Sin at Harran. Bee's wax was used for holy candles, air-tight preservation of perishables, and the disappearing-wax method used in pouring bronze and metals into molds for statues, swords, and implements.

Honey was fermented into mead as 'the nectar of the gods,' and later to provide an intoxicating beverage for humankind. The hexagonal form of the cells in the hive also promotes energy, just like the hexagonal structure of natural flowing water and frozen water as snow. The hard-working, highly efficient, and organized bee culture has always been a model of order and virtue to mankind. The musical song of bees typifies the strong vibration of life. Their dancing demonstrates knowledge of time, distance, and the motions of the Sun and Moon. Ancient kings, queens, priests and priestesses dressed as bees and wore beehive tiaras and miters; especially the Golden Bee of Minoan culture. The 'Melissae' bee priestesses were known as 'Deborah' in Hebrew culture.

Ransome continues to say that there are many instances where bees became like soldiers to protect their owners and saints. Honey-cake was traditionally given to newly married couples. The mass of the people used honey to mix with their porridge, and basted their meat and fish in honey. Bees were protected by countless laws in many countries. There were innumerable and complex statutes concerning the ownership and rights to claim honey and wax on one's own lands and swarms that settled upon them. The Brehon Law contained an entire section on 'Bee-Judgments.' Even the bee-keeper had to pay a small portion of honey to the neighbors where the bees collected their nectar. Tithes were also assessed on honey and wax. The mead-brewer and butler were accounted privileged persons under the law, protected during the brewing period of mead. The Highland Scots made a drink of hazelnut-milk and honey. Curious weights and measures obtained such as 12 full hen-eggshells equaled a pint. Bee's wax candles were used for the measurement of time, and were the only type of candle used in the church. In 1580 AD Queen Elizabeth passed laws prohibiting the adulteration of wax and honey which had become a major profitable export. All makers of wax-cake had to mark them with their initials, while all corrupt wares were confiscated.

The Aztec and Maya were beekeepers who also concocted an intoxicating mead sometimes adding agave to make honey-wine. Their bees were of the *Melipona fulvipes* or *Trigona cupira* variety, which do not sting. They fabricated cylindrical hives of ornate earthenware which they hung suspended by cords in the verandas of their homes. It has been suggested that the 'Bee God' was connected with the planet Venus. Miller and Taube in *The Gods and Symbols of Ancient Mexico and the Maya* find it odd that the important office of the 'Skyholder Pauahtun' should be given to a god who is often portrayed as a drunken and lecherous old man.

Ransome continues to say that bees are in touch with the next world, that they abhor cursing and bad rough language; and will only work for intelligent and good owners. Everything in the folklore and culture of bees connects them with the 'sacred nature of the cosmos'. They are never said to 'perish or waste away' like animals; but they are said to 'die' as one would refer to a human being. Honey has always been regarded as a cure-all because bees browse on so many varieties of blossoms that honey furnishes a wide variety of cures. Hares also forage on many herbs, and therefore country doctors often recommended a hare-stew. Again, honey is a sacred product, and its consumption was said to provide an insight into the future. The website *mirrorofisis* says that the Melissae sometimes used toxic honey, gathered from oleander, rhododendron, and the heath family which was highly psychoactive.

Cretan Zeus belongs to the Age of Cronus-Saturn, also called the Golden Age when the honey-tongued poets Hesiod, Vergil, Ovid, and Horace have told us that honey dripped from the oaks and that milk pails overflowed in abundance. This Cretan Zeus was brought up in a cave (where bees often have their hives over holy spirals) and was fed with *melikraton* –a mixture of milk and honey. This mixture was standard nourishment for children, and an offering to the *Spirits of the Dead* in the Underworld. Melikraton and the Land of Milk and Honey are a part of the traditions of the Land of the Gods, Isles of the Blessed, Land of Promise, Heavenly Jerusalem, and the Phrygian Mithras. *Melisseus*, King of Crete, is said to have been the discoverer of honey and beekeeping.

AVEBURY, A SOPHSTICATED ASTRONOMICAL SITE

The authors of *The Sun and the Serpent* say that Avebury was the Omphalos of Britain, positioned half-way along the St Michael's Line. Here was a meeting place between Heaven and Earth. It was the cosmic center from which the world was nourished. These authors noticed a different kind of energy following streams and portals of the Earth; interacting with the prominent male current which followed the hilltops and heights of the Michael Line. All of the 31 long barrows in the neighborhood are orientated to the extreme movements of the Sun and Moon.

This 'Mother-Circle of Britain' is the largest earthwork and stone-circle in Europe. It is about one thousand feet across, and almost absolutely circular to within a few inches. Its ditch is as deep as 33 feet in some places. The rough stones weigh up to 60 tons and are arranged in sequence of alternating energy as phallus (male, +) and *on-edge-diamond* shapes (female, -). A mile away stands the man-made conical hill of Silbury, and the West Kennet Long Barrow, the largest of its kind in Britain. Originally, Avebury was enhanced by 600 huge stones which were vandalized and destroyed through the ages, and now only 76 remain. In 1719 the Rev. William Stukeley illustrated the original structure as 'a monstrous serpent spread across the countryside.'

Avebury Henge was originally surrounded by a ditch and white chalk bank 18 feet high. *Avebury: Sun, Moon, and Earth* (2008) by Maria Wheatley and Busty Taylor has some interesting things to say about one of the largest stone circle henges in the world. Maria is the daughter of the noted dowser, Dennis Wheatley. But, visiting Avebury is fraught with disappointment as the place is much desecrated by wanton attacks on the site over several hundred years. Access is from a parking field with no real connection or introduction to the site. There is a pub, a farmstead, and the main street of a village at the center of Avebury; and a public road actually traverses the holy ground. Gigantic stones were exploded by bonfires to be used as gravel and road fill; or just to get them out of the way. The complex extends to Windmill Hill to the North, and West Kennett Avenue toward the Sanctuary and Overton Hill Barrows, including Silbury Hill (the largest earthen cone pyramid in the world), and the West Kennett Long Burrow to the South. All of this is interconnected and woven through by the Mary and Michael energy lines. Lack of adequate scope like a broad visual entrance harms this complex which could be the premier site in all of archaeology and ancient heritage. The first thing to be done would be to plant yew trees to represent all the 548 missing stones. The 60 ton, giant Devil's Chair stone commands a spectacular view of the rising midwinter solstice and rebirth of the Sun. The pitch-black night sky with Moon, planets, supernovas, meteors, and the river of the Milky Way is very visible.

In Ireland and Britain the high henge architecture permitted light to wondrously illuminate the stone circle at the precise moments of solar alignments. A henge with a perfectly leveled top with posts served as a wonderful back-sight for all the alignments of the heavens upon the hills or seas of the horizon. *Bru na Boinne* in Newgrange, Ireland has its light box which casts a beam of light during the winter solstice into the cavernous mound and its trifold cave, illuminating its spiral markings. Brad Olsen has connected Newgrange with Malta where 'light boxes' seem to have originated. Outside the tumulus Martin Brennan discovered that outlying stones' shadows would target rock carvings upon the *edging stones* that surround the mound. Wheatley and Taylor have used Paul Devereux's findings to affirm the presence of bands of magnetic hot-spots on the Devil's Chair (in the neighborhood of the head and neck of the sitter). Devereux suggests that the priests entered deep meditation through fasting and hallucinogenic mushrooms.

In 1801 Thomas Maurice said that the huge Obelisk Stone at the center of the southern of the two circles within Avebury was a sundial for the time of year. In *The Secrets of the Avebury Stones* (1999) Dr. Terrence Meaden also calculated that the shadow of the Obelisk would fall upon a stone to mark a particular festival making the surrounding ring into a sundial of the seasons. The Celtic Druids followed the ancient form of marking the Quarter days and the Cross Quarter Days: 1st November (Samhain or Halloween), 1st February (Imbolc), 1st May (Beltane), and 1st August (Lughnasadh or Lammas). These points are roughly between the solstices and the equinoxes. Meaden says that all these eight holidays are clearly marked by shadows falling from the central Obelisk upon stones in the surrounding circle. For example, during the summer solstice sunrise the Obelisk shadow would fall upon stone #120, and that evening the sunset would fall upon stone #112.

Wheatley and Taylor suggest that the Avebury Henge builders elevated the ground of the inner northern and southern circles, creating a sloping effect to maximize the length of the shadows at sunrise and sunset. William Stukeley recognized that the northern circle was associated with the Sun, while the southern circle was closely associated with the movements of the Moon. Aubrey Burl suggested that the Cove stones at the center of the southern circle were aligned to the Moon's northernmost moonrise.

THE HAUNTED MOSS BEACH DISTILLERY

Along the beautiful coastline between Half Moon Bay and Linda Mar sits a California Historical Point of Interest called the Moss Beach Distillery, a notorious haunt of liquor smuggling during

Prohibition because of its usually calm and well sheltered sand beach below guardian cliffs. The locale has been featured on several television documentaries including *A & E's They See Dead People*, because of the ghostly appearances of the *Blue Lady*. Back in 1926 the property was taken over and called 'Frank's Roadhouse' operating as a restaurant and a 'protected speakeasy.' The place was never raided because it was a celebrity venue of movie stars like Fatty Arbuckle, writer Dashiell Hammett, and prominent politicians. A young, good-looking female employee of this roadhouse seems to have become involved with the piano player. One night the estranged husband of the girl picked a fight with the piano player and a raucous fight ensued in the bar, then outside and below on the beach. The next morning the beautiful young woman was found stabbed to death on the strand in her long blue evening dress.

The ghost of the 'Blue Lady' has been repeatedly seen in a very definite and clear image from the 1930's to 1970's. After the 70's appearances have tapper off, but there have been many paranormal sights like glasses flying through the air, boxes stacked against the inside door of the blind storage room, chairs levitating and flipping over, lights turning on and off by themselves during very calm weather periods, suspended lamps swinging of their own accord, patrons sensing the strong aura of some presence in the main dining room. The Blue Lady has been the subject of books, conferences, and documentaries with psychics and mediums coming from around the world to interact with this local celebrity.

My wife and I frequently dine at the Distillery and on 5/11/2016 used a common crystal pendulum to dowse the most haunted areas of the restaurant property. My wife Nuala does not really like to play with these 'witching toys' because of her strict Irish upbringing – even though she is a *natural*. Once upon a time we were in Sedona in a *minerals* shop where I was looking at some crystal pendulums hanging from a light wooden bar supported by two thin poles at each end. When Nuala approached and while she was standing beside me, the pendulums started dancing wildly about trying to attract her attention, as if saying, 'buy me, buy me.'

I needed Nuala's help as confirmation, and one of the places involved was the ladies' restroom. Every place that was significant showed powerful energy emanations, indeed the entire site was blasting energy everywhere shown by the speed of revolutions of the pendulum which was flat-out horizontal, whirring like the propeller of a P-51 Mustang fighter-bomber. I have not felt such exhilaration since I was at Glastonbury. Under the restaurant-bar and outdoor area was an enormous negative (counter-clockwise vortex) spiral; while adjoining to the south was a positive (clockwise matrix) spiral. The lay of the land showed a prominent cleft in the cliff running down to the beach, a sharp promontory to the left facing the ocean, and a left side defile to this jut into the Pacific. I would say that here was a typical geological conductivity discontinuity where several different geologies meet.

Concerning the presence of ghost, I can only repeat what others have said about 'remanence' of beings and material in a powerful electromagnetic place over time. Again, we may consider *astronomical concordance with earth energy* in producing such paranormal events. The exact date is difficult to find, some saying around Christmas Eve 1927. Actually, one version reports that there were five separate ghosts which haunt this area. I find it very revealing that there are numerous instances of chairs and many other things levitating, for we have surmised that 'levitation' has consistently been a possibility at an energy site –given the proper astronomical conditions.

CONCLUSION TO THE TEMPLE OF HEAVEN & EARTH

The idea that we live in a sacred universe stems from the Golden Age –a time when man could achieve anything –not through magic or machines; but through belief in the interconnectedness of all things through the Cosmic Mind. Every question produced its answer, every location was accessible in a flash of light, and people recognized divinity in their fellows and nature in their environment.

Ancient people were guided by astronomy and physics that showed them the duality in the cycles of nature through the revolution of night and day, the dichotomy of order and chaos, conflict and love. Motion and change liberated energy from entrapment in one place to be used again in another. The supreme Creator immersed himself in his own creation. Sacredness was seen throughout everywhere and everything required adoration and respect in all its parts and fabric. Here was a moral principle founded in physics and expressed: 'Do unto others as you would wish them to do unto you…love God and neighbor as thyself.'

Death itself was never to be feared because it was only a cycle within the larger physics of the All. Ancestors participated in 'remanence' a form of existence beyond time and place which allowed them to be revered as well as consulted –nothing was lost because the fabric was woven out of the Creator and designed with the tools of geometry, numbers, and proportions shown in the cycles in the sky and taught through the study of astronomy. Close observation of the Sun, Moon, planets, and stars showed that they activated the energy flows at certain portals in the landscape which transmitted earth and cosmic energies to fountain heads of beneficial power that contributed to health, mental acumen, and joy of life itself. Ancient people found that these holy energy portals were fed through caverns and faultlines in the natural geologic structure of the Earth. The people of the Golden Age ornamented and enhanced these holy sites with upright stone circles, avenues, temples, henges, precincts and pyramids.

Many have speculated upon the powerful secret of the Templars that permitted them to travel unhindered throughout the world, and control banking institutions that liberated money and credit from all state and local control. The *Poor Knights of the Temple of Solomon* were the *cosmopolitans* and citizens of the New World Order at their time. One of the keys to this mystery is the Knights association with the architects and contractors, notably the Freemasons –the original and genuine travelling builders who enjoyed free access to cross borders into other lands, as well as a status that placed them above many laws and restrictions in foreign lands. But, researchers have also failed to find historical documents connecting Masonry with the Knights Templar prior to 1737 in a speech at the Grand Lodge of France by A.M. Ramsey. From this line of speculation it is very obvious that the Knights managed to take over and adopt all the rights and privileges of the travelling masons. And why could they, and why would they be able to do that? Because the nine French Knights under Hughes de Payens, who took up residence in the bowels of the Temple of Solomon in 1118 AD (with the sanction of the Patriarch of Jerusalem and King Baldwin II of Palestine) had learned the 'energy secrets' of the Temple Mount –a science more precious than rare gems and gold. The Knights became Masons whose independent status suited their intentions of controlling the globe. The Mason builder's wonderful and powerful 'trade secrets' were respected throughout antiquity by all kings, emperors, and religious leaders. The Knights Templar were able to enjoy the subterfuge of being the directors of the ancient Order of Freemasons until October 13, 1307 when they became fugitives under the law. Even the most ancient laws of Ireland gave respect to the stone mason only second in rank to the king. Of course these masons were also carpenters, designers, master builders, and architects all in one. The secret is that the Ancient Order of Masons came first; then the Knights Templar.

Bibliography

The American Dowser (Quarterly Digest). Danville, Vermont. www.dowsers.org 1961-2014

The Art of the Picts –sculpture and metal work in early Medieval Scotland by George & Isabel Henderson. 2004, Thames & Hudson, New York, NY

The Atlas of Holy Places & Sacred Sites by Colin Wilson. 1996, DK Publishing Inc. New York, NY

Atlantis Rising Magazine. Published bi-monthly by J. Douglas Kenyon. Livingston, Montana 59047

Albrecht, Klaus. *Malta's Temples, Alignments and Religious Motives.* 2007. Sven Nather Verlag, Potsdam, (2001)

Anderson, Richard J. *The Heart of the Vortex*, 2005-07. Sedonawind.com, Arizona, USA

Atkinson, William Walker. *The Kabalion*, 1908. Yogi Publication Society. USA

Bassie-Sweet, Karen. *At the Edge of the World –Caves and the Late Classical Maya World View.* University of Oklahoma Press, Norman Publishing Division. 1996

Basic Dowsing School. The American Society of Dowsers *founded 1961.* Danville Vermount

Book of Fenagh by St. Caillin. Translated by D.H. Kelly. Annotated by W.M. Hennessy. Printed by Alexander Thom. Dublin, 1875 (reproduced by the Ordinance Survey 1939)

Bauval, Robert & Ahmed Osman. *Breaking the Mirror of Heaven, the Conspiracy to Suppress the Voice of Ancient Egypt.* 2012. Bear & Company, Rochester, Vermont.

Bauval, Robert & Chiara Hohenzollern & Sandro Zicari, *The Vatican Heresy.* 2014. Bear & Company, Rochester, Vermont.

Brennan, Martin, *The Stones of Time –Calendars, Sundials, and Stone Chambers of Ancient Ireland.* 1994. Inner Traditions, Rochester, Vermont, U.S.A.

Brophy, Thomas G. *The Origin Map.* 2002. Writers Club Press, Lincoln, Nebraska

Bryce, Derek. *Symbolism of the Celtic Cross.* (1989) 1995. Samuel Weiser Inc., York Beach, Maine.

Bord, Janet. *Cures and Curses –Ritual and Cult at Holy Wells.* 2006. Heart of Albion Press, Loughborough, England.

Burke, John & Kaj Halberg. *Seed of Knowledge, Stone of Plenty.* Council Oak Books, San Francisco, California 2005

Campbell, Joseph. *The Mythic Image.* 1974. Princeton University Press, Princeton, New Jersey.

Celestial Charts –Antique Maps of the Heavens. 1988. Carole Stott. Crescent Books, New York.

Clifton, Gloria. *Royal Observatory Greenwich.* 2010. Belmont Press, UK

Collins, Andrew. *Beneath the Pyramids.* 2009. 4th Dimension Press, Virginia Beach, Virginia

Condos, Theony. *Star Myths of the Greeks and Romans.* 1997. Phanes Press, Grand Rapids, Michigan, USA

Conway, D.J. *A Little Book of Pendulum Magic.* 2001. The Crossing Press, Freedom, California

Copacabana de los Incas –Documentos Auto-linguisticos e isografiados del Aymaru-Aymara. J. Viscarra F. La Paz, 1901 (from original documents beginning 1623 AD)

Cremo, Michael A. & Richard L. Thompson. *The Hidden History of the Human Race,*1999-2008. Bhaktivedanta Book Publishing, Los Angeles, California, USA

Cremo, Michael A. *The Forbidden Archeologist,*2010. Bhaktivedanta Book Publishing, Los Angeles, California, USA

Critchlow, Keith. *Islamic Patterns.*1976, 1999. Inner Traditions, Rochester, Vermont

Davidson, Wilma. *Dowsing for Answers.* 2007. Green Magic, Somerset, England

DeSalvo, John. *The Complete Pyramid Sourcebook.* 2003. 1st Books Library. Printed in USA

Diehl, Richard A. *The Olmecs, America's First Civilization.* 2004. Thames & Hudson Ltd, London

Diodorus Siculus, *Library of History.* Trans. C.H. Oldfather. Loeb Classical Library. Harvard University Press. 1935. Cambridge, Massachusetts

Diogenes Laertius, *Lives of the Eminent Philosophers.* 1965. Trans: R.D. Hicks. Harvard University Press. Massachusetts

Dunn, Christopher. *The Giza Power Plant.* 1998. Bear & Co. Rochester, Vermont

Dunn, Christopher. *Lost Technologies of Ancient Egypt.* 2010. Bear & Co. Rochester, Vermont

DuQuette, Lon Milo. *The Key to Solomon's Key.* 2010. Consortium of Collective Consciousness, San Francisco, California

Elst, Koenraad, *Update on the Aryan Invasion Debate.* 1999. Aditya Prakashan, New Delhi, India

Farrell, Joseph P, *Financial Vipers of Venice.* 2010. Feral House, Port Townsend, WA

Farrell, Joseph P., *The Third Way –European Union, Corporate Fascism.* 2015, Adventures Unlimited Press, Kempton, Illinois

Firestone, Richard, and Allen West, and Simon Warwick-Smith. *The Cycle of Cosmic Catastrophies.* 2006. Bear & Company, Rochester, Vermont

Flanagan, G. Pat. *Pyramid Power.* 1973 (1974). Pyramid Publishers, Glendale, CA

Frazer, James G. *The Golden Bough, the Roots of Religion and Folklore.* 1890 (1981). Avenel Books, New York

Fulcanelli, *Le Mystere des Cathedrales –Esoteric Interpretation of the Hermetic Symbols of The Great Work.* (1922), 1964, 2000 edition. Brotherhood of Life, Inc. Las Vegas, Nevada

Grace, Raymond. *The Future is Yours, Do something About It.* 2003. Hampton Roads Publishing, Charlottesville, VA

Grant, John. *Corrupted Science –Fraud, ideology, and Politics in Science.* 2007. Facts, Figures & Fun, Surrey, England

Graves, Robert. *The White Goddess.* 1948, 2013. Farrar, Straus & Giroux, New York, NY

Hancock, Graham and Robert Bauval. *The Master Game, Unmasking the Secret Rulers of the World.* 2011. The Disinformation Co. Ltd, New York, NY

Harner, Michael. *The Way of the Shaman: A Guide to Power and Healing.* 1980. Harper and Row, New York.

Harner, Michael. *Cave and Cosmos.* 2013. North Atlantic Books, Berkeley, California.

Healy, John; D.D., Bishop of Clonfert in his *Ireland's Ancient Schools and Scholars.* Ireland. M.H. Gill & Sons. 1890 (1902)

Heath, Richard. *Matrix of Creation, Sacred Geometry in the Realm of the Planets.* 2002 & 2004. Inner Traditions, Rochester, Vermont

Heath, Richard. *Sacred Number, and the Origins of Civilization –the unfolding of History through the Mystery of Number.* 2007. Inner Traditions, Rochester, Vermont

Heath, Richard. *Precessional Time and the Evolution of Consciousness, how Stories Create the World.* 2011. Inner Traditions, Rochester, Vermont.

Heath, Robin, *Sun, Moon, & Earth.* Wooden Books. Wales. 1999

Heath, Robin and John Michell, *The Lost Science of Measuring the Earth*. Adventures Unlimited Press. Kempton, Illinois. 2006

Henderson, John B. *The Development & Decline of Chinese Cosmology*. 1984-2011. Windstone Press Ltd., Taipei, Taiwan

Erik Hornung. *The Ancient Egyptian Books of the Afterlife*, 1999, translated by David Lorton. Cornell University Press, Ithaca and London

Hoyle, Fred. *On Stonehenge*. 1977. Freeman & Co. San Francisco, California

Huang, Alfred. *The Complete I Ching –The Definitive Translation*. 1998. Inner Traditions, Rochester Vermont

Iamblichus. *Life of Pythagoras*. Translated by Thomas Taylor (1818), 1986 reprint Inner Traditions, Rochester, Vermont

Jhon, Dr. Mu Shik. *The Water Puzzle and the Hexagonal Key*. 2004, Upliftimg Press, USA

Johnson, Anthony, *Solving Stonehenge, the New Key to an Ancient Enigma*. 2008. Thames and Hudson. London.

Karim, Dr. Ibrahim F, *Back to a Future for Mankind –BioGeometry* (2010), BioGeometry Consulting Ltd. Egypt [Questionable source –but contains Egyptian-Moslem perspective]

Kenyon, J. Douglas, editor. *Forbidden History –prehistoric technologies, origins of civilization* [an Anthology of prominent writers]. 2005. Bear & Co. Rochester, Vermont

Knight, Christopher & Alan Butler. *Solomon's Power Brokers*. 2007. Watkins Publishing, London

Knight, Christopher & Alan Butler. *Before the Pyramids*. 2009-2011. Watkins Publishing, London.

Knight, Christopher & Robert Lomas. *Uriel's Machine*. 1999. Fair Winds Press, Gloucester, Massachusetts

Kreisberg, Glenn. *Lost Knowledge of the Ancients –A Graham Hancock Reader*. 2010. Bear & Company, Rochester, Vermont

Lalor, Brian. *The Irish Round Tower* presents a catalogue of existing Irish towers noting a wide variety of anomalies and differences

LaViolette, Paul A. *Earth under Fire –Humanity's Survival of the Ice Age*. 1997, 2005. Bear & Company. Rochester, Vermont

LaViolette, Paul A. *Genesis of the Cosmos*. 1995, 2004. Bear & Company. Rochester, Vermont.

Livio, Mario. *The Golden Ratio*. 2002. Broadway Books-Random House, New York, New York,

Lockyer, J. Norman. *The Dawn of Astronomy*. 1894, 2006. Dover Publications, Mineola, New York

Lockyer, Norman. *Stonehenge and Other British Stone Monuments Astronomically Considered* 1906. Reprinted by Bibliobazaar 2008, Charleston, SC, USA

Lynn, Chris. *Navan Fort* [Emain Macha], *Archaeology and Myth*. 2003. Wordwell Ltd, Wicklow, Ireland

Maher, James. *Romantic Slievenamon*. 1955. Kickham Street, Mullinahone, Co. Tipperary, Ireland

Mann, Nicholas R. *Energy Secrets of Glastonbury Tor.* 2004. Green Magic, Sutton Mallet, Somerset, England

Mann, Nicholas R., *The Sacred Geometry of Washington, D.C.* 2006. Green Magic. Sutton Mallet, England

Mann, Nicholas R. & Maya Magee Sutton, *The Practice of Celtic Wisdom –Druid Magic.* 2000 (2014). Llewellyn Publications, Woodbury, MN

Malkowski, Edward F., *Ancient Egypt 39,000 BC, the History, Technology, and Philosophy of Civilization X.* 2010. Bear & Company, Rochester, Canada

Martineau, John, *A Little Book of Coincidence –Pattern in the Solar System.* 2001 Wooden Books, Wales

Meehan, Gary, *Sacred Ireland,* 2002. Gothic Image, Glastonbury, England

Meyer, Stephen C. *Darwin's Doubts.* 2013. Harper One, Harper Collins, New York, NY

Mehler, Stephen, *The Land of Osiris.* Adventures Unlimited, Kempton, Illinois. 2001

Men, Hunbatz, *The 8 Calendars of the Maya.* 1983. Bear & Co. Rochester, Vermont.

Michell, John, *The New View Over Atlantis.* 1969-1983. Thames and Hudson. London.

Michell, John, *The Dimensions of Paradise.* 1971, 1988, 2008. Garnstone Press, England

Michell, John, *A Little History of Astro-Archaeology*. 1977. Thames & Hudson, New York.

Michell, John, *New Light on the Ancient Mystery of Glastonbury*. 1990 Gothic Image, Glastonbury, England.

Michell, John, *Twelve-Tribe Nations*. 1991. Inner Traditions, Rochester, Vermont

Michell, John with Allan Brown, *How the World is Made, the Story of Creation according to Sacred Geometry*. 2009. Inner Traditions, Rochester, Vermont

Milla Villena, Carlos. *Genesis de la Cultura Andina*. (1983) continually updated 2008. Amaru Wayra. Lima, Peru

Montefiore, Simon Sebag, *Jerusalem, the Biography*. 2011. Vintage Books-Random House, New York

Morana, M. *The Hypogeum, A Jewel of Ancient Malta*. No date. M.J. Publications

Nyland, Dr. A. *Complete Books of Enoch*. 2010. Smith & Sterling, Mermaid Beach, Qld, 4218 Australia

Olsen, Brad. *Sacred Places around the World*. 2004. Consortium of Collective Consciousness, San Francisco, California

Olsen, Brad. *Sacred Places Europe*. 2007. Consortium of Collective Consciousness, San Francisco, California

Olsen, Brad. *Sacred Places North America*. 2008. Consortium of Collective Consciousness, San Francisco, California

Pace, Anthony. *The Tarxien Temples.* 2006, 2010. Heritage Books, Malta

Pankenier, David W. Ph.D of Lehigh University, *Cosmic Capitals and Numinous Precincts in Early China* appeared in Journal of Cosmology, 2010, Vol 9, 2030-2040

Pauly-Wissowa Real-Encylopedie des Klassischen Altertumwissenschaft. Stuttgart, 1912

Quinn, Bob. *The Atlantean Irish –Ireland's Oriental and Maritime Heritage.* 2005. The Lilliput Press, Dublin, Ireland

Ransome, Hilda M. 1937, 2004. *The Sacred Bee in Ancient Times and Folklore.* Dover Publications. Mineola, New York

Richards, H.J. *Pilgrim to the Holy Land.* 1982-2011 updated. McRimmons, Essex, England.

Richer, Jean. *Sacred Geography of the Ancient Greeks.* Trans. Christine Rhone. State University of New York Press. Albany New York. 1994

Redding, Moses W. *The Remarkable Ancient Quarry under Jerusalem.* Kessinger Publishing. No date. Kessinger.net

Roger, Bernard. *The Initiatory Path in Fairy Tales –the Alchemical Secrets of Mother Goose.* 2013, 2015. Inner Traditions, Rochester, Vermont

Seneca, Lucius Annaeus (c.4 BC). *Naturales Quaestiones*, I & II. Loeb Classical Library. Harvard University Press. 1971 [concerning astronomy]

Schele, Linda & David Freidel, *Maya Cosmos*, 1993. William Morrow & Co. New York

Schoch, Robert M. & R.A. McNally. *Pyramid Quest*. 2005. Tarcher/Penguin Group, New York

Schoch, Robert M. *Forgotten Civilization, The Role of Solar Outbursts in our Past and Future*. Inner Traditions, Rochester, Vermont. 2012

Schrag, Paul & Haze, Xaviant, *The Suppressed History of America*. Bear & Co., Rochester, Vermont. 2011

Scranton, Laird. *China's Cosmological Prehistory*. Inner Traditions, Rochester, Vermont. 2014

Seeley, Thomas D. *Honeybee Democracy*. 2010, Princeton University Press, Princeton and Oxford, Oxfordshire, UK

Selbie, Joseph & David Steinmetz. *The Yugas*. Crystal Clarity Publishers, Nevada City, Califronia. 2010

Sora, Steven, *Secret Societies of America's Elite*. 2003. Destiny Books, Rochester, Vermont

Squire, Charles. *The Mythology of the British Islands –Celtic Myth, Legend, Poetry, and Romance*. 1905. Blackie & Son. London/Forgotten Books reprint.

Stonehenge. English Heritage Guidebooks. London. 2005

Thom, Alexander. *Megalithic Sites in Britain*. 1967. Clarendon Press, Oxford, England

Twyman, Tracy R. *Solomon's Treasure, the Magic and Mystery of America's Money.* 2005, Dragon Key Press, Portland, Oregon

Thompkins, Peter. *Secrets of the Great Pyramid*

Underwood, Guy. *The Pattern of the Past.* 1969. Pitman Publishing, London

Vassallo, Bernard. *Prehistoric Malta, Europe and North Africa.* 2007. Allied Publications Ltd, Valletta, Malta

Waters, Frank. *Book of the Hopi, The First Revelation of the Hopi's Historical and Religious Worldview.* 1963. Viking-Penguin Inc. New York, N.Y.

Westbrook, Charles. *The Kabalyon Key.* 2004-09. Cathedrall Press, Greenville, North Carolina, USA

Wheatley, Maria and Busty Taylor. *Avebury, Sun, Moon, and Earth.* 2008. Wessex Books, Wiltshire, England

Wilkins, W.J. *Hindu Mythology, Vedic and Puranic.* 1882. Thacker, Spink & Co., Calcutta, India

Witkowski, Igor. *The Axis of the World, the Search for the Oldest American Civilization.* 2008. Adventures Unlimited Press, Kempton, Illinois, USA

Wright, Kenneth R. & Alfredo Valencia Zegarra. *Machu Picchu, A Civil Engineering Marvel.* 2000. American Society of Civil Engineers, Reston, Virginia

Yates, Dame Frances. *Giordano Bruno and the Hermetic Tradition.* 1964. The University of Chicago Press, Chicago and London

Yates, Dame Frances. *The Rosicrucian Enlightenment.* 1972. Routledge & Kegan Paul, London and New York

Yates, Dame Frances. *The Art of Memory.* The University of Chicago Press. Chicago. 1966

Zimmerman, Fritz. *The Nephilim Chronicles –a Travel Guide to the Ancient Ruins in the Ohio Valley.* 2010. Privately published

Zimmerman, Fritz. *The Nephilim Chronicles –Fallen Angels in the Ohio Valley.* 2010. Privately published

ABOUT THE AUTHOR

Thomas Karl Dietrich is a professional stone-image carver, and student of philosophy, astronomy, and classics. He is a graduate of the Jesuit University of San Francisco, and has spent a lifetime reading ancient history, mythology and science. He has lived in Ireland for 13 years and travelled with his wife, Nuala investigating ancient sites for the presence of earth-energy throughout Europe and the Mediterranean to Corsica, Sardinia, Tenerife, Malta, Rhodes, Crete, Greece, Turkey, Egypt, the Red Sea, Israel, Jordan, and the American Southwest, Mexico, Yucatan, Belize, Guatemala, and South America, Ecuador, Bolivia and Peru.

Dietrich has researched and written the following books:

THE EARTHOLDER (1983) showed that Irish genealogy, one of the oldest continuous histories in the world, had been altered and abridged by the early Roman Church in league with the Irish High King, and later restructured by Anglo-Saxon and Norman invaders.

THE ORIGIN OF CULTURE AND CIVILIZATION (2005) demonstrated that the Greek *Generations of the Gods* is a scientific record based upon the relationship of cosmic myth and the rotation of the Milky Way Galaxy around the zodiac. Secondly, it presented the notion that cartography was a closely guarded secret of monarchs and emperors –that maps with advanced projections had been made for the entire planet in deepest antiquity and had been safeguarded in the royal treasuries of kings.

CULTURE OF ASTRONOMY (2011) illuminates the marvelous multi-synchronic astronomical systems of the Maya and Vedic traditions. The Maya calendar combines cycles in nature, man, Sun, Moon, and planets, creating accuracy equal to the atomic clock. A close study of these amazing systems and the ancient Stone-Age observatories reveals a remarkable synchronicity and ordering of the cosmos.

TEMPLE OF HEAVEN & EARTH (2016) is a summation of the worldview, philosophy, and science of the Golden Age. This is a study of traditions, life and death in a truly sacred universe of 'intelligent energy' –a scientific way of describing the 'spiritual universe.'

Thomas Karl Dietrich was born near the site of the Sacred Jupiter-Oak of the Germans near the walled and turreted city of *Frideslar*. This giant tree was felled by St. Boniface in 723 AD announcing the advent of Christianity to the pagan Franks and Germans. The city became a royal palace of Charlemagne, and served as a seat of synods and ecclesiastical convocations. In 1066 AD royal ownership was transferred to the Archbishop of Mainz who constructed a Cathedral in the town. According to church records Dietrich's ancestors came as agents of the first Archbishop. Dietrichs have been writers, teachers, millers, apothecaries, innkeepers, sheriffs, mayors, judges, and secret custodians of the Cathedral treasures, as well as Governor of Hessen during the American occupation. This heritage is ingrained in the writer whose views are steeped in antiquity, history, and traditions of American, European, and Irish cultures.

Thomas is responsible for many extraordinary discoveries which may be viewed on the internet website: cosmomyth.com

Contact: atlas@cosmomyth.com Stonework: www.donohoememorials.com

© 2016 Thomas Karl Dietrich. All rights reserved

Made in the USA
Charleston, SC
25 November 2016